WHEN CLARA
WAS TWELVE

Other novels by Terence Clarke:
My Father in the Night
The King of Rumah Nadai
A Kiss for Señor Guevara
The Notorious Dream of Jesús Lázaro
The Splendid City

Short story collections by Terence Clarke:
The Day Nothing Happened
Little Bridget and the Flames of Hell
New York

Non-fiction by Terence Clarke:
Fathers, Sons, and Seizures
The Sea Lion and the Sculptor: The Tale of a Vagabond Bohemian Artist
An Arena of Truth: Conflict in Black and White

WHEN CLARA WAS TWELVE

A NOVEL

TERENCE CLARKE

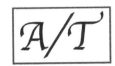

ISBN (print edition): 978-1-7329195-2-5
ISBN (ebook edition): 978-1-7329195-3-2

Published by A/T Publishers, San Francisco, California, USA.

To contact the author or publisher, please visit https://terenceclarke.org.
Requests for author appearances, educational and library pricing, and licensing regarding A/T Publishing titles are welcome.

Photo of Terence Clarke by Nancy Dionne (http://www.nancydionne.com)

For Beatrice Bowles

Parting is such sweet sorrow.

TO PARIS EUROPE FRANCE

1

In her dream, Clara was immersed in smoke. As she grasped her throat, she feared that this was the end of the world.

She got a breath, but then was asphyxiated again. She shouted out for her mother Lauren, dreaming of her thrashing at the flames that scoured her face. The smoke could not be avoided. It got into Clara's hair and clogged her throat, causing her to choke. Her mother disappeared altogether, swirling into pieces of ragged cloth, jewelry, and fire.

"Clara!"

She awoke as her father Martin swept her from her bed and hurried with her in his arms toward the bedroom door. Her cheeks gleamed with tears. "Daddy! Where—"

"Down, sweetheart. Down! Don't breathe the smoke!"

She threw her arms about his neck and held on as he descended the steps. Her cheek brushed against the rough stubble of his beard. She heard her mother screaming in the back of the house, and smoke, electrified with flames, swirled from the living room entry.

"Get out to the street." Martin dropped Clara to the ground at the bottom of the front steps, and ran back into the house. The rainwater on the front walk iced Clara's bare feet. She ran to the sidewalk. The house was now completely overtaken by fire.

The Christmas tree in the living room window formed a ravaging triangle of flame. The ornaments, twisting about in the heat-driven air, were themselves on fire. Worst of all for Clara, the carved wooden angel that had topped the tree and given it such saintly beauty had disappeared. It had been a gift itself a few Christmases before, from a distant relative named Jack Roman, who lived in France and whom Clara had never met. Now there was just a bristling uprising of flames. The angel was perishing in hell.

Clara was certain her parents were trapped. The house itself seemed to rise before her on the fire that exploded from the windows.

When the firemen finally arrived, Clara shouted at them. Her parents were inside. "Save them! Please!"

Her stomach felt that it would fall through her gut. Suddenly a long overcoat was thrown about her, and Mr. Nash from across the street took her by the shoulders. "Come on, sweetheart. Come on."

Mrs. Nash wrapped a blanket around Clara as well. The woman's pink slippers, soiled slightly with age, looked like lumps of Pepto Bismol.

"They'll be all right," Mr. Nash said.

Clara pushed him away. "Mother!"

"Clara!"

Lauren emerged from the flames, running up the brick pathway by the side of the house. She was dressed in her robe and carried the plant—a broad-leafed ivy—that her own mother had given her as a child. Martin came along behind her. He was blackened with soot but unhurt. He carried the wooden box in which, Clara knew, he kept all his checkbooks and papers. She had never been able to figure out why they were so important. Her father was like the bank. He seemed always to be surrounded by paper.

Lauren knelt and took Clara into her arms. She smelled of smoke. "Oh, angel."

The lace around the neck of Lauren's robe was singed, and Clara imagined that she had encountered the devil or somebody in the backyard, that the gates of hell had opened up back there and, for a minute or two, taken her. A few years ago, when Clara was eight, Sister Dympna at school had described what happened to bad people after they died, and the girl had lain awake after that for two nights in a row frightened by the spectacle of so many of the damned—kids included—tumbling into the flames of Perdition. The vision flashed into view once more, enlivened by these actual flames. But of course Clara knew that her mother would never go to Perdition. Ever.

Grandma Adela and Grandpa Mason, Lauren's parents, arrived a moment later in their Chevrolet. Adela was already in tears, and when she saw Lauren she ran to her and embraced her. The firemen were dousing the house with water, but really it was destroyed. Indeed a moment after Grandpa Mason escorted Clara to their car, the house collapsed. Clara sat in the back seat, shivering and astonished by the smoke rising from the ruins. Everything was gone.

2

At dinner six months later, Martin complained that, here it was summer already, and the new house plans seemed farther and farther away.

"Whole damned seasons change." The words slurred from his lips. He reached for his glass of wine. "Generations live and die." He lifted the glass to his mouth. The steak dinner before him had been wrecked by his attack of it. "For God's sake, it's not like these are the Middle Ages or something. It's 1955. We've got phones. We've got cars. But I can't get these architects to finish their plans."

Lauren cut into her own filet, slicing away a bit of fat that clung to the meat. "I think it's difficult to design a whole—"

"The architects don't call me back. The contractors don't call me. They bill me, and I don't know what for."

Cut off, Lauren lay her fork on the plate and sat back to listen.

"I think we're just going to have to live out of our suitcases for a while longer."

Clara wanted her mother to finish her thought, but she too was intimidated by her father, and afraid to interrupt.

"We'll be all right here, Martin," Lauren said.

Since the fire, they had been living on C Street in Eureka, in an old Victorian house they owned that had been a rental. The furniture was a confusion of stuff from Mason and Adela's basement and from Mina's house. Mina was Clara's other grandmother—Martin's mother—who lived in an enormous old Queen Anne-style structure that Clara loved. It had maybe a thousand rooms, she had once thought. And in the back garden there was a system of stone pathways that ran through the roses, in a circle around the pedestaled birdbath and between the hedges. She had played tag on the pathway, with friends after school, for as long as she could remember.

"Except I don't plan to stay here." Martin reached for his wine once more. He was fifty-three years old. He had lived in Eureka all his life and, until he had become engaged to Lauren in 1938, he had felt little need to leave the place. At the time, he had been thirty-five and living with his parents. "Damned best place there ever was, Eureka, California," he frequently said, an assertion that even Clara knew was not the case. Clara had been to Knotts Berry Farm, for example, and Balboa Island, and both those places, also in California, were much better than Eureka. Eureka was gray, sodden, and cold. Everybody walked around bundled up, so that they looked like totem poles with umbrellas, especially in winter when it rained steadily for months.

There had been a closet in their house, in the back bedroom where Clara slept, that was directly below a large oak tree that shaded the rear of the building. Even in July, when the temperature in Eureka gets up to as high as sixty or so, and the rain is replaced by a general fog—tropical by comparison—this closet was lined with mold. Lauren had to wash its walls down with ammonia twice a year. An old overcoat of Clara's father's had been in the closet for some time. Having forgotten about it for he last few years, and suddenly rediscovering it, Lauren took it out one day to donate it to the Saint Joseph's High School rummage sale. It was covered with a fine green dust. But the dust did not come off when Lauren beat it with her hand. She and Clara both began to sneeze violently.

Lauren looked up at her husband. "You mean you want to leave this house, too?"

That Martin could contemplate another move came as no surprise. He often said things on momentary whim that—unaccountably—he then actually went and did. As well, he made enthusiastic promises to Lauren and Clara that would cause great upsurges of joy—a suggested trip to the Grand Canyon, a new dog, that kind of thing—that at the appointed time he would deny ever suggesting. Clara had noticed that such declarations usually came during dinner, with the wine.

Martin looked about the dining room, then through the large windows into the backyard. "Yes. I don't like this house."

The tenants had not done much to care for the yard, so that it looked to Clara like a gray-green jungle. Rhododendrons bloomed everywhere.

A cherry blossom tree was just now going out of flower. It was a raggedy cloud balanced on a rumpled stick. An oak leaned against the fence at the far end of the yard, causing it to sag into Mr. Whipple's yard next door.

Lauren contemplated the baked potato on her plate. "Martin, how can you suggest a thing like that?"

"Because this place is a dump."

"But we're lucky to have it. We can't move in with Mina. We can't go over to my parents."

Martin leaned forward to spear another piece of steak from the platter. He was a graying man with a heavy face that his mother Mina had once characterized as "too black Irish, if you ask me." The description seemed odd to Clara, very disapproving, especially as Clara knew that her grandmother was fond of her son Martin. She complained a lot about him and how she thought he was too smart for his own good and so on. But on the whole Clara knew that her grandmother loved him.

When he sipped from the wine, Clara noticed how her father's lips so thickly embraced the thin rim of the glass. He pursed them as he swallowed. But this did nothing to make them smaller. They looked like puffed pillows filled with veins of blood.

"We could move into a hotel," Martin said.

"A hotel?" Clara's heart began beating with excitement. A hotel meant breakfast every day in the restaurant. Waffles. A swimming pool!

"Oh, Martin." Lauren looked across the table. It had seemed to Clara that her mother's heart had been broken by the fire, and Clara had accompanied Lauren's tours of the wreckage with considerable pain of her own. She hated seeing Lauren's tears because they were so clear an indicator of the loss her mother had suffered. Lauren too had wanted to get the house rebuilt as quickly as possible. But she had had to content herself with looking on as Martin had argued with the architect and the contractors over detail after detail. He had done so many additions to Foy's Arcade, the department store he owned in Eureka, that he sure as hell should know better than anyone else how to build a damned house. Martin said this frequently.

Nonetheless, Lauren and he had had long talks about what the new house would be like, and they had showed Clara what was being planned.

Clara very much enjoyed going over the early architectural drafts, especially to see where her bedroom was going to be. She imagined she could see, right there, the window box flowers she would have.

"It doesn't have to be a hotel here in Eureka."

Clara noticed the beginning of a smile on Martin's lips.

"But Eureka's the only place there is one," Lauren said.

"How about a hotel in France?"

Silence fell over the dinner table. A drop of blood from the meat on Lauren's fork fell to her plate.

"Paris, maybe." Martin busied himself rummaging his green beans. "The Ritz."

"Martin. Where we stayed on our honeymoon?"

Clara swallowed. "We're going to Paris?"

"Yes." Martin grinned.

"Paris Europe France?"

"Oh...sweetheart." Smiling, Lauren took Clara's left hand into her right, caressing the girl's ring.

"That's right, Clara. The City of Light."

Again there was silence. Clara didn't care what they called it, as long as she got to go there.

She didn't know whether Martin were being serious. He cut off a slice of steak and brought it to his lips. The thinning hair that stood up in strands above his head—defying gravity and the dampness of the air in the room—made him look scattered and hoary. But Clara's hopes had already begun to race.

What she knew about France she had learned from her mother. Lauren had told Clara many times about their honeymoon, a three-month sojourn through France in the summer of 1939. The way she told it, food and light and pleasure was what they had over there, especially in Paris. There were wonderful things to see, like Sacré-Coeur church on Montmartre, where birds flew around inside the dome above the altar, and the summertime ice cream shop—Berthillon, it was called—on the Île Saint-Louis, its long line of customers waiting to get at the delicacies inside.

But her father described long waits at Customs and fear of the Germans. Sure, he liked the food in France, too. A lot of cream and sauces, he said.

9

But in 1939, they had gotten out of France just months before the Germans had come in. Clara had seen movies about the Nazis, and she had listened anxiously every time to her father's telling of how he and Lauren had left Le Havre after the German attack on Poland, in the company of many hundreds of Americans and British, ordered to do so by their embassies. The story was thrilling, the ship leaving in the middle of the night.

Clara imagined her mother, so young, clinging to her husband's hand at the railing and looking off into the darkness of the North Sea.

Clara had read about Paris just this year. Sister Mary Magdalene had asked the children to do a report on some other country "less fortunate than ours, poor souls," and her mother had helped her, showing her pictures in magazines of people sitting around in cafes all day drinking wine, kissing each other, and standing in glorious sunshine in front of the Eiffel Tower. "Where they don't have the advantages God has given us," the nun had said, looking out into the cement playground. It had been raining at the time...heavily.

Martin caressed Clara's shoulder, looking into her eyes. "Yes. Paris." He sat back and glanced at Lauren. "These fellows doing the house aren't going to be ready for a month or two. And school's out in a couple weeks. So why don't we go for a vacation?"

Clara screamed her delight. But Lauren seemed dismayed by Martin's idea. She pushed a few greens around her plate, silent in the chaos of the girl's happiness. She stared with actual bitter-seeming distraction at her wineglass.

"What's wrong, Mom?"

Lauren began crying. She took the napkin from her lap.

"Is something wrong?"

She shook her head, wiping her eyes. Despair seemed to take her. Clara grew quiet.

"It's just that I'm so happy." Lauren looked toward Martin, and her eyes grew wide with regard. She reached her hand out onto the table toward him.

"Then why are you crying?"

Lauren did not reply to Clara, though tears streamed down her face. Clara took up her glass of milk, sipped from it, and replaced it on the table.

"We'll leave right after Clara's birthday, Lauren."

"Can't we go sooner, Daddy?"

Martin too was clearly surprised by Lauren's sadness. "It'll be like a present."

"Mother. Please?"

Lauren forced a smile, and it then was clear, at least to Clara, that she was indeed very pleased. It must have been the surprise that caused the tears. Why wouldn't she be happy?

So it was that, at last, a month later, when impatient Clara, seized with anticipation, was finally twelve, she went with her parents, excited and amazed, to Paris Europe France.

THE CABARET
D'ENFER

3

"Here's to Paris!"

Martin turned to Lauren and toasted her. She was at this moment rather nervous. She knew that Martin was happy, though...very much so, because although he disliked travel, he loved this city.

In general, Martin was not a romantic man. But he had a sense of ceremony and diversion, a spirit that caused him to bring large unannounced gatherings of roses to Lauren from time to time, or some kind of extravagant jeweled trinket. There was a photograph of him—a favorite of Lauren's—on one knee offering a laughing Clara a present for her ninth birthday. He was wearing a tweed suit. The gift was a white ceramic plate with a scene of blue ducks running past a blue cow, that he had brought back from an antique store in New York, the only other city that Martin enjoyed. He had learned to ice skate there, for one, during the winter of 1930, on his first buying trip for Foy's Arcade. Nowadays he stayed at the Waldorf and sent Lauren and Clara letters on the hotel stationery, something Clara particularly enjoyed.

Stepping down to the platform from the Le Havre-Paris express, Martin had turned and offered a hand to Lauren, taking the hatbox she carried into his free hand. He wore the same suit as in the photograph, and that was a mistake. Even in the shadow of the Gare du Nord's interior, it was a very warm July day. Lauren was dressed in a bright red Chanel suit, stockings, and patent-leather black heels. The suit was a favorite of hers, bought for her by Martin, also in New York, the year before. She recalled the pleasure it had given Clara when Lauren had first modeled it for her in her bedroom. Clara had stared at the suit, both directly and in the mirror, excited by the cut of it and especially by the luxury of the light wool of which it was made. She knew who Coco Chanel was, having read her mother's fashion magazines. And she thought that Lauren had made herself into some sort of beautiful star just by being given a suit designed by the famous French woman. When Lauren let Clara try it on (it was a size too large for her, and Clara had to hold up the skirt) she gazed at herself in the mirror as though she were some kind of frump, unable to come up with the stylish panache to wear such a thing. But Lauren saw that day that Clara was a beautiful frump, and would soon be just plain beautiful.

Lauren stepped down to the stool the conductor had provided, then to the platform, which was crowded with passengers moving to the exit. Ahead, steam from the engine swirled about a group of passengers and dispersed toward the ceiling. There were echoing voices and the rumble of announcements for arriving and departing trains, all in a gong-like, confused racket.

She looked up at the station roof, which was supported by metal beams, like old Erector sets, she thought. As they walked toward the platform exit, she took Martin's hand. Her anticipation of their arrival had now grown to the purest sort of joy. There were Arabs in fezes, German hikers, schoolboys from England dressed in shorts and blazers, great piles of baggage, and food hawkers in every part of the quay. Lauren's hatbox, secured in Martin's right hand, led the way, like a gold-embossed lantern from Bergdorf-Goodman, parting the crowds.

Martin insisted that they check their bags at the station, so that they could cross the street to a cafe he had spotted, for lunch. As they scurried through the intersection to avoid the traffic, a fleet of bicycles bore down upon them. There were many dozens of them, ridden by workers in white shirts and berets, students with briefcases slung over their backs, young women whose skirts fluttered in the wind. Derisive shouts from the cyclists, veering into one another to avoid the Americans, punctuated the drone of their bicycles wheeling past.

Clara looked up in the air, oblivious. "Where's the Eiffel Tower?"

A moment later, sitting at a sidewalk table, Clara and Lauren surveyed their menus, which were large hand-written cards. Clara watched everything around them. A group of nuns passed by, their headgear like swans' wings. A cart vendor stood behind a mound of peaches. A few of the pieces of fruit were cut up and glimmering on a plate, and the man's head appeared above the peaches like a bearded jar. The waiter, who was a small man of twenty or so dressed in a white shirt, bowtie, black slacks, and white apron, had already begun flirting with Clara.

"And here's to all of us being in Paris!" Martin raised his glass again. Clara was too distracted to notice.

Lauren wished to get to the hotel, her excitement giving way quite suddenly to a bad stomach ache. But she wanted to let Martin enjoy this moment. Once he had made the announcement about going to Paris, he had asked Lauren to make all the plans, and she was relieved now to see him so pleased. Martin did not like travel agents and the flurry of confusing details that surrounded a trip like this. For him, what he provided—the initial idea—was the important thing. What would actually happen, where they would stay, what sights to see, where they would eat…those things were better left to others. That is, to Lauren.

Martin did maintain the right, though, to criticize the plans she made, his snipes a kind of humorous patriarchal sabotage. In that way he could take credit for the fun, and not be responsible for anything that went wrong. This was behavior that mother and daughter had come to expect from him. Actually he found fault with plans no matter who made them, so that a picnic on a summer day was a failure because Lauren had brought the wrong wine. Or the Christmas card he asked Clara to make for Lauren every year lacked some detail…the ornaments on the water-colored tree, maybe, were to have been red and green instead of blue and purple. Sometimes even his own plans got faulted, when he forgot to remember that he had made them in the first place.

But Martin can also be so much fun, Lauren thought, as right now when he whispered to the waiter, pointing to the menu, that he wanted to order a grenadine soda for Clara. The waiter wrote the order on the ticket. His politeness was crisp, almost rude. When he brought the soda, he placed it before Clara with a few muttered compliments, and she was able, proudly, to say "Oh, Daddy, *merci*."

Lauren placed a hand on her tummy, trying to put aside the pain. She was caught among such confusing sentiments that she actually wished to be somewhere else. But the clash of colors and noise, the beautiful clothing on the women passing by, even the savory odors of the *croque-monsieur* Clara had ordered at her father's suggestion…all this made Lauren's heart rush.

Martin chatted with them, pointing out the brass *espresso* machine inside the cafe. The mirrors that lined the walls of the cafe made the terrace outside a part of the interior as well, so that inside and out were all part of the tableau.

Lauren touched Martin's hand where it rested on the table. *Love*, she thought. For her, the word was a watery, brilliant flame. She so loved her husband, and the affection she felt clarified how little his criticisms really cost her. *Look at him*, she thought, *how he enjoys showing Clara around so much.* Lauren was charmed by the *chantilly* eclairs he now ordered for them, and by his sneaking from Clara a piece of her sandwich when she was not looking.

They retrieved their bags and flagged a taxi. There was a long haggle between Martin and the driver, who spoke no English. The man finally understood that Martin wanted him to take a meandering route to the Hotel Ritz, by way of the Eiffel Tower, the Arc de Triomphe, Les Halles and Notre-Dame. The driver set the meter and started out, waving his hand before him and shaking his head. It was a fine day. Clara and Martin discussed with each other about what each wanted to see first. Martin sat in the front seat with the driver. Lauren, reeling from the negotiation, sat by herself in a corner of the back seat, feeling ill.

At the Hotel Ritz, she was finally able to lie down. Their room looked out on the Place Vendôme, and there was little traffic. Martin had gone out with Clara to the Place de la Concorde. There was another hotel there, he had said, the Crillon, which had bullet holes in the facade.

"And you're going to see a lot of that, Clara. I mean, the war ended just twelve years ago, you know. There are parts of this city that they haven't even rebuilt yet."

They were to go to dinner that night at Maxim's, and everyone was excited.

The hotel room pulsed with light, the curtains barely holding out the sun. The round table that filled the window bay was covered with white linen beneath a large, doily-like embroidery. A vase held a spray of summer leaves and roses. The room glared gold-yellow, brown and gold everywhere. Even the print that hung from the wall over their bed, of a milkmaid in flagrant repose with a boyfriend in the shade of a summer arbor...even the print glistened.

Lauren fell asleep, allowing the sunlight that fell across the end of the bed to warm her legs. When she awoke, the sun had disappeared behind the buildings, and the room had darkened. The curtains were no longer pure white, rather a shade of mottled, serene gray. There was no breeze of any kind.

She turned over on her side and joined her hands beneath the pillow. A spray of small peonies burst from a vase on the bed table. She reached out to finger one of them, and spread the petals apart, examining them individually. She sighed, letting the flower slip from her fingers. Turning away, she closed her eyes.

She dreamed of the Christmas fire. The tree burning in the front room had torn Lauren's heart. She had had just a moment to watch the ornaments exploding into flames. It had been so terrifying a moment that, as Martin and Clara ran from the house, Lauren had imagined them on fire themselves.

The recollection of that jolted her awake.

Jack Roman had given Lauren the wooden ornament that had disappeared in the fire. It was a carved figure from France, of an austere, bearded angel in a long caftan, the slim folds of which were forever filled with dust. He cast his eyes down, his hands folded before him. The only things that gave him away as an angel instead of as a dreary prisoner or a long-dead king were his gracefully crafted wings, which were outspread behind him. He was carved from some sort of hardwood that was pocked with age, and appeared very contemplative.

When Jack sent her the angel a few years after the war, he wrote in his letter that he had found it in an antique junk store in the Place des Vosges. He had sent the ornament to Lauren, with the hope that her family might enjoy it.

That was the first letter Jack had sent to her since the day, years before, that he abandoned her.

Now Lauren's mouth tightened with worry. In recent years they had exchanged a number of letters. The next day she would be contacting Jack, and she closed her eyes as she wondered what he would look like. She and Martin had avoided looking him up during their honeymoon in 1939. Martin didn't know the story (he still didn't), and Lauren had been too mortified to do so.

But she had gotten a note from Jack this afternoon when they had checked into the Ritz, a most welcoming note, filled with ideas for taking Clara and Martin around Paris. His handwriting was far different from in the past, with shaky and style-less notations, as though the thought were coming out far faster than his ability to put it down on paper.

Lauren was nervous about the meeting, and was glad that Clara was coming along, so that she, Lauren, could hide how she may feel about seeing him again.

Suddenly Martin stumbled through the door, startling Lauren from her reverie. He was pale, his eyes quivering with worry. "Clara's lost."

4

Clara had wanted to go right into the *cremerie*, but her father had been dawdling several yards back, looking for a gift for Lauren. Clara had just been ejected from the place next door, in which knitted wool baby clothes were being sold. Little jumpsuits, pants, and caps had been folded neatly on the shelves, and Clara had fingered several of them, exclaiming to herself about how lovely they all were, how well made, how.... The sales-girl—an otherwise charming-looking woman, about twenty-five, who was dressed in a blue cotton dress and open-toed high heels with no stockings, whose hair lay across her shoulders in a kind of perfect, curling repose, like Veronica Lake's in old movie magazines, yet who looked somehow, well, cheaper than Veronica Lake—this woman had come up to Clara and pushed her out the door with a storm of offended French.

What'd I do? Clara hurried up the sidewalk. *Did she think I was going to steal something?* She was offended, since she knew she had enough money to buy one of the outfits if she wanted to. She remembered something her mother had said, though, that the Parisians were often pretty rude. Lauren had told Clara that, if one of them ever yelled at her, she should just try to let it fall away, like water off a duck's back.

"You just have to get used to it."

But Clara knew that she would never go back to a shop like that. She wasn't a duck.

Just now, though, Clara wanted to explore the *cremerie*, and she did, leaving Martin behind, on the sidewalk at a flower stand.

She spent a few minutes examining the butter—which resembled a pale, carved tree stump—from which a clerk cut away small wedges with a wire held between two sticks. Also, there were packaged cheeses. Clara had never seen such labels in her life, being more accustomed to the cheese that was sold at Humboldt Bay Super at home. It was called Velveeta, and came in a yellow package. Here there were hundreds of brands, with labels showing laughing cows, goats, full-breasted milkmaids, trees, beret-wearing artists, kings, and biplanes buoyed up on windswept clouds.

When she came out of the shop five minutes later, Clara spotted her father a few doors up the sidewalk. She had felt liberated in the *cremerie*, her imagination jolted, as it were, by the abundant flurry of so many cheeses. Martin was looking at some birdcages that were out on the sidewalk, bordering both sides of it. Clara's curiosity overcame her wish to be on her own, and she joined her father.

It was a *boucherie.* There were chickens in the cages, rabbits as well, and the doorway to the shop was decorated with hanging birds of all kinds whose bright colors defied the notion that they were dead and waiting to be plucked. Inside the shop, the white floor glistened, except for the space immediately surrounding the butcher's chopping block. There, the small octagonal tiles were covered with gore. The butcher himself greeted Clara with a smile and a rough, grunt-filled voice. His white apron was smeared with portions of red handprints.

"Ugh," Clara observed.

They continued up the Rue de Rivoli until it became the Rue Saint-Antoine and they encountered the first of several blocks of fruit and vegetables carts. Passing across a side street, Clara glanced to her left and saw an arch beyond which was a fenced park and a statue of a knight on an enormous horse. Martin hadn't noticed, and had wandered ahead. Clara, knowing that this wouldn't take too long and that she would return to Martin's side once she had a look, turned up the street.

She walked through the arch into a plaza surrounded by decrepit brick buildings, all of the same design, the facades of which rose and fell in wavering lines depending upon whether the building had sunk a few inches into the ground. She got out the guidebook her mother had given her and looked up the place on the map inside. The Place des Vosges had once been a vacation spot for the nobility, she learned, and the statue was of a king named Louis XIII. She learned that another King, Henry II, had died here in a jousting match. Clara had no idea what jousting was. She thought maybe it was like telling jokes. But more probably it was wrestling or something. She didn't know. She entered the park and went to look at the equestrian statue.

After a moment, she turned to look for her father, and did not see him anywhere. She shrugged and walked through the square to the far side, where she spotted cafe tables beneath the arcade. She was very thirsty, and when the waiter arrived at her table she asked him for a glass of water. He understood a little English, brought her the water with a menu, and then stood with his notepad in hand.

Clara looked over the menu. It was a sea of French, and made no sense to her. She looked about and saw a woman spooning some whipped cream from the top of a peach melba. There were nuts and vanilla ice cream. She pointed at it and said she'd have one of those.

"*Oui, mademoiselle,*" the waiter said, ending his notation with a flourish. He took up the menu. "*Merci beaucoup.*"

She lingered at each spoonful, whelmed over by its many tastes. She gathered them consciously into her memory, deciding that this peach melba would have to be a Personal, as she called it, one of the secrets she had always collected for herself for her perusal only.

Her Personals had occasionally gotten Clara into trouble. For example, a year ago, Clara had locked herself into her bedroom—something she was forbidden ever to do—for an hour while she went through all her Personals. She secretly kept her most important stuff in little vanity kits and shoeboxes. She put them under her bed or at the back of her closet so that no one would find them.

She very jealously guarded the secret of their locations. But recently an accordion file in which she kept flat Personals had disappeared from a space behind her dresser. Her favorite was the picture of Roy Rogers lassoing Dale Evans next to a large cactus, with Trigger looking on. She had had it since she was seven. Rummaging through the entire room, bringing out all the Personals, she nonetheless couldn't find Roy and Dale.

"Clara!" Lauren rattled the doorknob. "Open the door."

Clara ignored her, hurrying to put everything away and worried that her mother might find out how many Personals Clara actually had.

Later, when Clara was sent back to the bedroom by her father without dinner (for locking her door), she lay starving on her bed in defiant silence, listening to the radio. She had gotten almost all her Personals re-hidden, and justice was hers, despite her father's not understanding the importance of the picture of Roy and Dale that she had finally found at the last minute, and that now rested on her bed along with the paper doilies Clara had made in the second grade, the fan photo she had of Annette Funicello and Mickey Mouse, and her most recent Personal, a photo of Jerry Lee Lewis with his right foot propped, heel down, on the piano.

Great Balls of Fire.

Personals were personal. They were an emotional self-caress, an object carrying warmth and memory, something Clara could hold to herself and her recollection without worry of ever being kidded about it. They were the things that, for her, for particular secret reasons, most made Clara Clara.

It was the secrecy of her Personals that caused them to be so pleasurable for her. Secrecy kept things from being rejected, since no one could laugh at things about which they did not know. So Clara's picture of Jerry Lee Lewis, for example, which caused her, every time she looked at it, to imagine what he must *really* look like when he played the piano like that… his foot in its black and white rubber-soled shoe, up on the piece of wood that bordered one end of the keyboard, his fingers arched and intent in the way they plunged down against the keys, the suit coat (Clara guessed that it was gray, probably silk) open and flailing out behind him, the collar of his white shirt open to his chest, his mouth mouthily open in an ecstatic lyric… *You broke my will*!…and his hair…his hair, she thought. *But what a thrill!*

So cute.

His hair was what Clara loved most about Jerry Lee Lewis. Elvis's was okay, but it was too metallic, and he wore it rolled-up like a shiny rug. *Too perfect.* Jerry Lee's was enormous and flew about. *And what if he were to brush it back, like an errant cloud, just as he was trying to kiss me.* Clara was sure he would. She had made up her mind: Elvis Presley didn't have hair anything like Jerry Lee Lewis's. It was too pomaded, too tall, like a waxed wave breaking on a beach.

Indeed Clara *was* in love with Jerry Lee. But how could she ever tell her mother that she wanted to kiss him? His lips, in that photo, were so disrespectful, so unorganized, so…big. A kiss like that….

Having finished the peach melba, Clara walked from the cafe up the arcade to a junk store. It was a dark cavern inside, with shelves that were lumpy with chipped china, bicycle wheels, tarnish, old clocks, dust and occasional filth. A woman sat at the rear, at a wooden desk, in a black dress. She barely moved.

Clara spent a half-hour in the shop. She pulled things from the shelves and examined them, minutely turning them about in her hands. She wanted at first to buy a coffee grinder from Frères Peugeot, made of mahogany, a corner of which was broken off. She could smell the remains of ground coffee inside, and wondered how many cups it had made. Then she came across a metal wagon made for children, in which the shopkeeper had piled numerous broken dolls. While looking them over, Clara spotted, in a dark corner, on a bottom shelf, a round mirror, the mercury dried and chipped, surrounded by a dust-clotted starburst of gold-painted wood. She knelt down to pick it up. It barely reflected her face.

She leaned against the wooden shelves, imagining that everything in the shop was someone's old secret.

Clara loved all hers. Secrecy that even the Confessional did not betray, although that was supposed to be the place where sins were admitted to and wiped clean. She would enter the confessional booth and kneel down to face the window, a wooden frame with some sort of translucent cloth that, when the slide was pulled aside, would reveal the shadow of the pastor Father Murphy's head on the other side…sometimes a few fingers laid across his temple or his cheek as he leaned forward to listen. He was a kind of sacerdotal ghost. The poor light allowed only the slightest difference between shadow and illumination. His head was a rounded semi-sphere, pale yellow and white, in the surface of which could sometimes be seen, illogically (given the lack of light), blue veins. It resembled an enormous, wisp-laden egg, Father Murphy's head did. His fingers looked like waxen bones.

The purpose of Confession was, of course, for Clara to free herself of the consequences of having sinned, and to receive absolution for her transgressions, so that she could continue her life with only a darkened soul, but no longer a blackened one. With Confession, the burden was taken from her. She was forgiven. (Though not entirely. She had learned that God forgave Catholic children reluctantly, and that Purgatory still awaited them, even though Hell may not. So, she would burn for her venial sins, although not eternally.)

Darkness hid the sound of her voice as she recited the litany of sins that, without the forgiveness that God would provide here in Confession, would result in her twelve-year-old soul perishing in Hell.

Confession meant forgiveness itself. But she also knew that news of her sins would go no further than the confessional booth. The priest would know about them. God would know. Of course, Clara would know. But the entire airing of her sins was hardly an airing at all.

Saying penance afterwards would lighten the air in Saint Joseph's, which was cold and, on Wednesday Confession evenings, dark. The other penitents were usually hunched over their folded hands, avoiding each other. She knew that they, too, had sinned, and she couldn't imagine what they had done, especially the adults. Of what particularly bad sins were they capable? Adults did things like murder and thievery. Had these people committed those sins? She recalled most recently a man in a gray over-coat in the second pew...Mr. Denman, who was the manager of men's wear at Foy's Arcade...whose graying hair had been so closely combed, whose hands were so thickly veined and ugly...the anguished, praying Mr. Denman.... Had he done any of those things?

Clara hadn't been able to tell, watching him shuffle from the church through the side door by the altar, after quickly reciting his penance. He still appeared ashamed, and afraid that someone in the church would find out what he had confessed to.

Clara went through a large box of celebrity photos. There were scenes from movies, with people kissing. There were fashion pictures in which models stood around looking luxurious in front of places like the Eiffel Tower. There were even photos of nude women writhing on sand dunes, pictures that embarrassed Clara and fascinated her. Lots of singers. The only one she recognized was Edith Piaf, and only because Clara had seen her a few months earlier on the Ed Sullivan Show, looking up at the camera with enormous hands opened before her chest, and anguished eyes that, on the television screen, had had the same gleam as had her little black dress. The fact was that Clara didn't like Edith Piaf much, whose voice reminded her of the busy-signal on the telephone.

She put the photo aside. There were none of Jerry Lee Lewis.

When she came out of the shop, the sun was nearing the horizon, and she hurried from the Place des Vosges. Walking back down the Rue Saint-Antoine, she could not keep her mind on her task, which was to get back to the Ritz in time for dinner. She stopped at bakeries, fruit carts, and butchers to look at what they had to sell. She paused outside the church of Saint-Paul-Saint-Louis to watch a sidewalk artist do a painting in chalk of Louis Armstrong. She moved on past a glove store (where she stopped a moment to look at some white suede formal gloves), then a hat store (a window filled with dyed feathers), and then an underwear store (with mannequins only slightly better dressed than the nudes on the sand dunes).

She approached the hotel just as the sun disappeared behind the buildings across the square. She was exhausted, yet filled with conflicting, happy recollections of everything she had seen. Her heart felt embraced by the colors, the rapid changes from church to square to tree-lined boulevard, and the gorgeous products in every shop, which were more plentiful and varied than she had ever seen in any shop anywhere.

"Clara! Where have you been?"

She turned about to see her mother hurrying up behind her. A handkerchief was wrung between Lauren's fingers. Her face was blotchy red and swollen with tears of worry.

"Your father's been looking for you everywhere."

"What for?"

"What for!" The relief Lauren felt at seeing that her daughter was safe seemed to do battle with her anger. "He said you'd gotten lost."

"I did not." Clara frowned, staring at the pavement.

"But he couldn't find you!"

Martin came up the sidewalk. "Clara. Where have you been?" Genuflecting before her, Martin shook Clara by the shoulders. "Damn it!"

"Daddy, I was just out walking." Clara's eyes washed with immediate tears. "Looking at stuff, that's all."

Lauren stared down at her, her lips quite pale. Her hair was messy, made more so now as she pushed a hand through it. Clara herself sniffled as she tried controlling the tears.

"There's no restaurant for you tonight, young lady," Martin said.

"Why?"

"Why! How can you ask a question like that?"

"Oh, Daddy! I didn't mean it."

"That may be. But it's dinner in your room and then to bed."

"But what did I do?"

"You scared your mother and me to death, that's all! You ran away—"

"I did not."

"You took off on your own, in this strange city where no one knows you. You didn't tell me where you were going. Clara, you can't do that." Martin waved a hand to the side, behind him. "Paris isn't Eureka, Clara."

"Daddy."

"You can't just disappear."

Suddenly the full weight of the fact that she was not to go to Maxim's settled upon her. She knew nothing about the restaurant, except that a lot of famous people had eaten there, like Frank Sinatra and Napoleon. Tears burst from her eyes as she realized she was about to miss what might be the high point of the trip. "I'm sorry."

"It's too late, Clara." Martin stood up before her. "No Maxim's, that's all there is to it."

"Daddy. Please!"

"Nope. I want you to go right to that room of yours and to sit there. Maxim's is out. It's room-service for you."

"Room-service!"

Martin turned away and took Lauren by the arm. They walked toward the hotel entrance.

"Daddy!"

Her parents turned into the hotel. Lauren, still in tears, looked over her shoulder at Clara, who followed behind. Clara was now a bit slave-like, in misery, and seeking forgiveness.

—

She sat on the bed in her separate room for the next hour, suffering from the silence that Lauren displayed as she got dressed to go to dinner. When her parents left for Maxim's (her mother giving her a surreptitious kiss and the whispered advice that she not worry), Clara remained on her bed. Lauren told her that she had ordered something nice from the hotel kitchen. Clara kept her mouth shut and stared at the wall.

Once alone, she changed into her robe. She turned out all the lights in her room except for the table lamp between the two single beds. Her mind turned to an uncustomary dark self-accusation from which she could barely imagine a return to happiness. *It isn't fair!* she thought as she threw herself onto the bed once more. *Just isn't.* And now she was going to get some dumb meal all by herself in secret. She folded her arms and imagined her parents raising a toast to each other and forgetting about Clara. Moaning, she leaned her head against the wall.

A quiet knock brought her from her thoughts. Clara stood and walked to the door.

"Who is it?"

"Room ser-vees, *mademoiselle.*"

Clara opened the door to a waiter, who stood with a cloth napkin folded over his arm, next to a double-deck wooden tray on brass wheels, with a brass handle at either end. The waiter bowed. As he pushed the tray into the room, the plates rattled against each other. The domesticity of the sound relieved Clara's mood, as did the odors coming up from tray itself.

A small gathering of yellow tulips hurried from a crystal vase.

There were four plates, each of them with a silver cover. The waiter removed the covers, revealing the dishes with a kind of prideful turn of the wrist. He was a very old man, shorter than Clara herself, dressed in a white coat with brass buttons. She noted the rickety grace with which he turned each dish about, in order to give her the most pleasing view of it.

The first was a bowl of tomato soup with a sprig of tarragon, like light green veins across the bubbled surface. Then there was *steak au poivre*, something Clara had never tasted before. But the sauce, made of brown cream dotted with pepper so that the steak resembled a kind of rustic pastry, gave off such a salted, remarkable aroma that Clara took a bit of the sauce immediately onto her finger for a taste. The fresh thyme leaves that decorated one corner of the steak gave it a look of rough-hewn finesse. There were some french-fried potatoes with the steak, of the consistency of lace. And, finally, a salad of butter lettuce, tomatoes, and sweet white onions. The tomatoes were the color of scarlet lipstick, but wet, so that they gleamed in the dim light from the table lamp. When the waiter made a dressing for Clara, of Spanish olive oil and red-wine vinegar with a julienned sprig of basil stirred in at the last, Clara could not wait any longer. She sat down at the table and unfolded a napkin, sticking one end of it into the collar of her robe beneath her chin. She took up a knife and fork and waited, impatiently, as the waiter tossed the salad.

At last, he revealed dessert, which was an apple puff pastry sprinkled with confectioner's sugar. It reminded Clara of a sugar bowl itself, but one from a fairy tale.

The waiter smiled at Clara's admiration of the pastry—at her delight— and took up a long slim package, wrapped in white tissue. From it he pulled a white rose, which he gave to her. Clara pretended that he was her long lost great uncle, who had traveled long distances from faraway lands just in order to please her.

"*Bon appetit, mademoiselle,*" the man said, and with an aged limp he wheeled the tray from the room.

Clara sampled the *steak au poivre*, and then took a few of the potatoes between her fingers. The tastes splashed into her mouth, so savory that she sat back in her chair and simply chewed. Suddenly there was no other, finer pleasure to be sought anywhere. The pepper warmed her lips, made slippery by the cream, a dollop of which dropped down her chin.

Clara paused a moment, imagining her parents at Maxim's. She wiped the cream away with a finger, and stuck it into her mouth. *I'll bet there are red silk curtains all over the place, and candles and diamonds,* she grumbled, still unhappy to be missing it all. She took the rose into her hand and put it to her lips. The faint odor of the flower was so elusive that she let it remain there for a full minute. She hoped her parents were sitting at the table in glum sadness, dawdling over their food, disappointed with themselves for the injustice they had done to poor Clara. She lay the rose down on the table, where it appeared to doze in quite significant, luxurious pleasure in the soft candlelight. She planned to let it dry out so she could keep it, as one of her Paris Personals.

5

The following morning, at the Café Deux Cygnes on the Rue Mouffetard, Clara and her mother sat at an outside table. There were few other patrons, it being quite early. The street meandered down a hill, and was bordered on each side by carts laden with fruits and vegetables. The vendors were still setting up for the day, and moved about the carts straightening their displays and calling out prices to the early-morning shoppers. Their voices all seemed to rasp.

Clara guessed they had to do a lot of shouting all day, so no wonder they sounded like Mr. Nash across the street in Eureka, who smoked too much and who, rather than speaking, barked. The light in the street had a smoky tinge. Indeed it was already hot out, and Clara had removed her sweater, which lay folded on her lap. Like her mother, Clara watched the activities in the street.

She was used to a market like Humboldt Bay Super, with its yellow linoleum floors, canned goods everywhere, and smiling Mr. Dilworth—a porcelain smile in a tan smock—who could not explain where anything was without sounding insulted. But here on the Rue Mouffetard, steam rose from the street where the shopkeepers had tossed their mop water. Occasionally a cart vendor was engulfed in the white-yellow mist, so that he looked like a smudged angel in a cloud, jabbering from an arranged pile of carrots.

At one of the cafe tables, a white-haired man smoked a cigarette while looking through a copy of *ParisMatch*. Elvis was on the cover, a color photo, onstage somewhere in mid-writhe, his right hand grasping the microphone. The man reading the magazine was dressed in a black beret, an old hounds tooth wool suit, white shirt, and grizzled black shoes. A scuffed Scottish terrier on a leash lay at his feet. Both dog and man had a similar air

32

of scattered decisiveness. At another table, next to the cafe's entrance, four French teenagers sipped from their coffees. The boy had a croissant that he tore into small pieces, which he placed in his mouth as the girls at the table talked.

The students were interesting to Clara because they were so different from the kids in Eureka. There was a kind of world-weary resignation about them, as though they were older and knew more. The boy's clothes had little of the crisp newness that Elvis's had, for example. And, of course, nobody in France had a duck's ass.

The boys here wore their hair in a nondescript cut that seemed altogether plain to Clara. Elvis looked like a juvenile delinquent, and that made him very cool in Clara's estimation, even though he was no Jerry Lee Lewis. Clara also wondered if French men went through the same ceremony that her father went through every morning. He tended to spend a lot of time in front of the bathroom mirror. One day, when her parents had gone out for a walk, she had snuck open Martin's medicine cabinet and studied it. There was a settled neatness about his toiletries. The Old Spice, the Gillette razorblades, and the Mum underarm deodorant seemed to belong there, all muscular, accepted, and lacking doubt.

Women's makeup was not like that. It was everywhere pink, and there was a certain hilarity to the myriad tiny bottles on her mother's vanity that made them seem sort of frivolous as well. When Lauren took Clara shopping at Foy's center aisle, for example, Lauren and Clara would have engaged conversations about which brands provided which colors and surfaces. Her father paid no attention when they talked about these things in his presence. He actually sold the products, but cared little about what they actually did.

Lauren was clearly worried as she looked down the Rue Mouffetard. "Where's your father?" Martin's half-eaten croissant sat in the middle of a plate, among many scattered crumbs and a large dollop of jam. He had left the Deux Cygnes after an angry exchange with Lauren that had started with a remark the severity of which Clara had not understood.

"Why is it so important to see Jack Roman?" Martin had said. "A guy you haven't seen since you were a kid."

Lauren opened her purse, her fingers pecking at its contents. "Oh, Martin, I don't know…."

"I'm going for a paper." He stood up and abruptly left the table.

"We're supposed to be meeting Jack," Lauren said now, looking at her watch. She was quite nervous, especially in the way her fingers took such tentative hold of the coffee cup before her. She wore a white sweater over a white summer dress. She had on curved, slim red earrings that rested against her neck. The purse, which was made of a kind of white-painted wicker and had a polished brass clasp, lay partially open on the cafe table. Among the pencils and matchbooks, there was a piece of paper with Jack Roman's address on the Place de La Contrescarpe.

Clara spooned a bit of jam onto the *croissant* she had ordered and spread it about, thinking a moment about Jack. She had never met him, knowing of him only through her mother's occasional stories. He was a very distant cousin who had been born in Dublin, Ireland. His father, a kind of itinerant political refugee who had once been a minor diplomat for the Irish Free State government…. Clara knew very little about any of this. What she knew was that Jack's father had been in prison during World War I, put there for some reason by the English. After his release, he took his wife and six year-old boy to France, fearful that he would one time be thrown back into jail.

The facts were that Jack's father Desmond Roman had fought in the war against the English, and returned to Ireland after the death of Michael Collins. He and his family left Ireland again in 1925, when Jack was eleven, as diplomats, and went to Dutch Indonesia, then to Mexico, and on to France. Desmond came to feel that De Valera's government was posting him to those countries so that they could get rid of him. He complained often to De Valera himself, about what Desmond called "this compromise the lot of you have made of the Irish dead." He had little patience with the new Irish accommodation of British interests in the north. It was all Collins's fault, he said. He continued to think that the Brits should be pushed, as he put it, "into the gray Irish Sea".

Lauren had explained to Clara that the Irish liked to argue a lot, and that they seemed to relish this sort of talk. She mentioned some of Desmond's other pronouncements, that it would be "a fine bloody day when the Irish finally get the respect that's comin' to them." Or that "the day I stand up to pay my respects to the King of England is the day that Jesus loves bein' up there on the Cross."

Clara may have understood little of this. But she enjoyed the way it sounded. Lauren told her, though, that Desmond Roman had been a brackish man who, when he was not making fun of the English, made fun of his son Jack.

Eventually, tired of having to deal with the new, conflicted Irish politics, Jack's father brought his family to Eureka at the behest of his American relations, Lauren's father Mason Cahill and his brothers.

Lauren had met Jack when she was in the sixth grade, at Saint Joseph's Church. Jack was almost sixteen at the time, a student at the adjoining high school. Lauren told Clara that, as a senior, Jack won the art contest that was held at the high school every year. Below the picture of him in the yearbook, there was a caption that identified him as the class of '33's answer to Rembrandt. Looking at the old yearbook, Clara thought that he looked a little more like Errol Flynn, which made her also think that Jack must have been pretty popular. He had a sideways way of looking at the camera, with a subdued, raffish, and very handsome smile. Clara thought his lips were actually pretty, in the way they formed so sculpted a grin. She wondered if Rembrandt had looked like Errol Flynn, too. Jack's eyes reminded her of ebony obsidian, and she asked her mother once whether they were indeed as large and dark as they appeared in the high school picture.

"That's not how he really looked," Lauren laughed. "Even though he was such a handsome boy. Big and disheveled, you know, with that elegant face. Just to look at him made you smile."

But then at the age of nineteen, Jack had gone back to France by himself.

This was an event about which Clara had heard quite a bit. Even now at the Deux Cygnes, as Lauren recounted the story to Clara again, she spoke of it with genuine sadness.

"We couldn't understand why," she said. "He wrote to his mother… you know, about how he felt he had to be an artist, that Europe was where Picasso and Dali were."

"Who?"

Lauren shrugged. "Artists. They're in the museums here. We'll go see what they did. Famous! Jack once met Picasso, I guess. He wrote to me that he did."

Clara nodded.

"He said that he just had to leave. There wasn't anything in Eureka for him, he said. Trees. Crab pots. Rain...." Lauren looked to the side, a little dismissively. "I guess artists don't care much for crab pots." She fingered the teacup before her. "Irish artists, anyway. But it really saddened his mother Grania, the way he felt about Eureka, because Eureka reminded her of home, she said, all the fog and the rain. And his father never spoke to him again, really. He said to my mother once that all artists had to be dummies, since they didn't make any money."

Clara sighed.

"I guess he thought it was funny." Lauren smiled. "But you know, everybody said that Jack was just a romantic. They dismissed him."

"Was he nice?"

"Oh, always, Clara." Lauren looked up and down the Rue Mouffetard once more. Martin was nowhere to be seen. Lauren took the purse between her fingers, sighing with impatience. Clara wondered whether there were more to the story. Her mother seemed so saddened with the telling of it. Her glance at the purse appeared to be a sign almost of mourning.

Clara tried conjuring up an image of what Jack must look like now. If he were an artist, he would have one of those pointy mustaches and a pointy beard, like the one in the illustrations in her mother's old high school French book. *Monsieur Le Roux*. He would have one of those things in his hand that holds the paints too, shaped like a teardrop with a hole for his thumb. A couple of brushes. *And a beret*, Clara thought. *For sure a beret*.

"Was he your boyfriend, Mom?"

Lauren squeezed her purse shut. "Clara. No."

Clara wondered what she had said wrong. Lauren continued looking for Martin in short-tempered silence. Finally she spoke once more.

"He was just the nicest, noisiest boy, that's all."

After several minutes, Lauren asked for the bill. Putting on fresh lipstick, she looked at herself in the small mirror she had brought from the purse. They were a half-hour late, and she did not want to keep Jack waiting any more.

"What about Daddy?"

"He'll have to fend for himself." Lauren took Clara's hand.

They walked up the street, passing through the crowds shopping at the food stalls and wagons. Finally reaching the small square at the top of the hill, in the middle of which were several shade trees, they paused a moment as Lauren took the slip of paper from her purse. She looked about the square for the right building, and then pointed to a brightly painted red door, number 57, to one side of the front of a cafe—the Cafe Contrescarpe. Placing the paper in her purse, she took Clara's hand and led her across the street.

Above the cafe on the fourth floor, an apartment with six windows looked out on the square. White lace curtains, semi-opened, sheltered the rooms inside. From the street, Clara saw an easel in one of the rooms, a cat sitting on the back of what appeared to be a large sofa, and a tall man looking down on the square. His hair was gray-white, and seemed to curl all about him like a storm cloud. He wore a suit and tie, although even at this distance Clara could see that the ensemble was badly mussed. Other than that, Clara could not make him out. For a moment, he remained motionless, like one of the mannequins in her father's store. Then, when he spotted Lauren and Clara, he waved and retreated from the window into the room behind him.

—

"Clara, this is Jack Roman."

He stood in the fourth floor entry to his studio, in a brown suit with a gray vest. The knot of his tie was faded. It was blue, though in places so wrinkled that it appeared two-tone, maybe three-tone. Clara knew that Jack was only in his forties, so his gray hair came as a surprise to her. His skin was lined as well, and there was an elegant reserve in his face that did little to mask his obvious happiness at seeing Lauren and her daughter. He was a large man. His body filled every inch of his coat.

He shook Clara's hand, welcoming her to the studio. "I hope it's not too much of a mess for you, Clara. I'm God's own worst housekeeper."

Clara broke into a smile. She enjoyed Jack's carelessness, and his voice, the sound of which she immediately enjoyed as much as everything else. His accent reminded her of her grandmother Mina, who was also from Ireland and who sometimes spoke in a similar way. There was a shine to his utterances, as though every part of it was intended to be funny.

Jack was clean-shaven, although Clara noticed a small patch of whiskers on his neck that he had missed that morning.

"I've got something for you." He turned to a small table behind him, which was littered with dog-eared magazines and unopened mail. A framed photograph hung from the wall above the table. It showed a younger Jack standing on a beach in bright sunlight. He wore a white shirt with the sleeves rolled up and a pair of white drawstring pants and sandals. His companion, a slim and very pretty girl of about fourteen, with black straight hair cut in bangs, held his hand. Attempting a happy smile in the photo, Jack still looked a little like a scattered and rather affectionate-seeming Errol Flynn.

There was also a small, creased snapshot that showed a bearded man in a straw hat, seated at lunch before a farmhouse. A little girl sat on his lap, about two years old. Her eyes were quite large, and shined with direct, glistening clarity.

As Jack took up a package from the table, wrapped in blue paper and secured with a ribbon, he noticed Clara looking at the pictures.

"She was the daughter of some old friends of mine. The fellow in the picture and his wife. Friends of my parents, actually."

He lowered his eyes to the package and fidgeted with it a moment.

"Can we meet her?" Clara said.

Jack continued worrying over the package. He glanced once at Lauren, who studied the pictures herself.

"No. I'm afraid not. She's…well, she isn't…." The silence that followed deadened the conversation, and Clara felt for the moment lost. She feared she had said something wrong. It sounded to her as though Jack were caught in sudden mourning.

"I hope you don't think this is foolish." Jack smiled, his eyes still fixed on the gift in his hands. He handed it over. The package was very small.

Hurrying to escape her discomfort, Clara pulled the giftwrap paper apart and dropped it in shreds to the floor. A smile came to her lips as, inside, she found a bracelet with a single charm, a small pewter windmill with lettering along the bottom.

"I hope you like it, Clara. I got it at Clignancourt, at the flea market. I go there every weekend." Jack smiled. "You know, there's nothing like doing a little shopping in the open air, is there?"

Clara nodded, thinking of her enjoyment of the Saint Joseph's rummage sale every summer in the church parking lot. "Is this a real place or something?" She turned the charm about between her fingers. The lettering below the windmill read *Moulin Rouge*.

"Sure it was, a famous dance hall. We'll go over there to look at it. I used to live in that neighborhood." Jack turned to Lauren. "When I first got here." He extended his hand to her. The gesture was very well mannered, Clara thought.

"Oh, Jack,"

Lauren brushed past Clara and put her arms around Jack's neck. Her sweater knocked the charm bracelet from Clara's hand.

"It's wonderful to see you."

Clara scurried about the floor, looking for the bracelet. She spotted it finally beneath the table, took it up and hurried it into the pocket of her skirt. Looking up, she saw how Jack's eyes had closed tightly and how joyfully he embraced her mother. The smile on his face was one of unsullied happiness, of love.

6

"It's just that I couldn't find any place open," Martin said, waving in the air the two newspapers he had brought. "Hello, Jack. I'm Martin Foy." He extended his hand. There was a note of disdain in his introduction. But he gripped Jack's hand with enthusiasm, so that Lauren could not be sure of what she was observing.

She looked about at the large paintings that cluttered the studio. She was very nervous with Martin's arrival, still angry with him, and not knowing how the two men would respond to each other. She did not wish a re-kindling of the jealousy Martin often expressed of Jack, especially now that her first meeting with him, after so many years, was going so harmlessly. And with everything that had happened in the intervening years—Martin's successful business, sweet Clara, the family the three of them had together, and the way Lauren so obviously cared for Martin—there wasn't any reason for jealousy.

Six large paintings, unframed, cluttered one wall of the studio, leaned up against it. A new one hung on the large easel opposite the windows, just begun so that there was nothing but a confusion of lines.

"I guess someone who lived through the war here," Martin said, "and who's alive at all must be doing pretty well."

"Oh, it was bad, Martin." Jack paused a moment, as though searching out Martin's intentions.

"You could have left, couldn't you? When the Germans went into Poland, maybe?"

Lauren's heart began to feel tight, as though it were in Martin's hands and he had the opportunity to suffocate it.

"Sure I could have. But I got caught here. There wasn't much I could do."

"I guess so. And none of us was here to...to see what really was happening."

Jack reached out and patted Martin's shoulder. "Yes. And there were personal reasons." He was a much larger man than Martin, and his fingers rested on Martin's coat with, in Lauren's mind, a nod to comfort and camaraderie.

Martin looked about the room and gestured toward the square outside. "But Jesus, there's no need to go into all that. Let's say that it's a pleasure to meet you, that's all."

Lauren felt her breath come back, and she closed her eyes, thanking Martin silently. No one seemed to have noticed her nervousness. Clara sat at a table looking over one of Jack's books, by a man named Lartigue, in which there was a number of photos of *fin-de-siècle* Paris. She studied a picture of an aristocratic woman seated at an outdoor cafe table. Her feathered hat made up a tableau of festive, arrogant wealth, and she held the coffee cup as though it were a petal between her fingers.

Lauren's apprehension eased even further as Jack declared, a mischievous smile on his lips, that he was to be in charge of Paris for "you Foys. You'll want to go everywhere." He gestured out the window into the sun-filled Place de La Contrescarpe. "Everywhere. And we'll get started early tomorrow."

—

He arrived at the Ritz the following morning, ready for a full day's touring. He wore a tailored blue suit with a white shirt and black tie, all pleasantly bohemian. There was authority in the gruff quickness with which Jack buttoned his jacket. He gave off an air of sophistication that made his poverty seem temporary, like a family downturn that would soon, and comically, right itself. His prideful humor made him appear moneyed, even though his polished shoes were cracked here and there. But the doorman deferred to him, laughing at Jack's French patter.

"You know, the Parisians are famous for being difficult," he said as they walked from the hotel. "But you chat them up a little now and then, and they're all right."

The first place he took them was to Sainte-Chappelle on the Île de la Cité.

"It's like a great sun," he said as they entered the chapel. He gestured into the air. Red-gold light colored the room, showering through stained-glass windows that surrounded it from floor to ceiling. Jack explained that the place had been built in the thirteenth century by King Louis IX. He rambled on for some time, about a reconstruction that had been done in the nineteenth century.

It was interesting enough to Lauren. But, finally, she went off by herself. She preferred simply enjoying the light's warmth. She had never been in a room that gleamed as this one did. The light seemed to lift through the air and to make it swirl, though not in a dizzying way. Rather, Lauren felt that she was floating in it, perhaps carried by the illumination from window to window as it warmed the large room.

From there, they went by taxi to the Eiffel Tower. This was at Clara"'s insistence, but really everyone wanted to go. As they rode up the elevator to the observation deck, Clara stood close by the window looking out. The girders passed from the top to the bottom of the window like pick-up sticks lying at angles scattered about.

"A lot of people expected him to cover it up with something, like ceramic or stucco," Jack said. "So when he left it like this, they complained that it looked like a railroad bridge headin' for a cloud."

All of Jack's explanations were made with an Irish accent, and were salted with humorous color and historic detail. He fascinated Clara...*all the stuff he knows*, she thought. Over the next few days, though, Lauren worried that Jack himself would become bored. Jack took them everywhere, and talked the whole time. At the Île de la Cité bird market, he intimidated the parrots with the finger he thrust into their cages. They tried pecking him, and Clara made a bet that one of them would succeed eventually. She lost.

At Les Halles, Jack introduced them to a butcher friend of his, a Monsieur Metoyer, who washed his hands in a sink before shaking everyone's hand. As he described the way the butchers worked, Clara turned her nose up at the vast collections of heads, entrails, hooves, eyes, and muscle in every direction.

In the café *Le Coq Rouge*, Jack described the history of the onion soup for which the neighborhood was famous. Several butchers sat inside. The red wine in their water glasses resembled the blood beneath their fingernails. "The soup's thick, eh, Clara?" Jack said. He floated the fingers of his right hand through the slight steam that floated from the surface of the deep bowl before him. "Lots of cheese, you see, and onions. So many onions that there's hardly room for the liquid."

Clara loved it.

She followed him about faithfully through the few very old Catholic churches to which he took them, looking up at the parapets to which he pointed, at the errant gargoyles and baroque abutments, the buttresses, vaulted transepts and apses as though all were unexpected, all were novelty. Which, of course, they were. There were dust-clotted crucifixes made of gold, obscure medieval chapels, grand gardens and aristocratic hôtel mansions in the luminous summer heat. Sorrow-ridden Christs stared at Clara from icons that were chipped and falling apart.

Napoleon slept. The Seine flowed. The sagging mansions and celebratory churches rose up in such grandeur that they seemed hardly subdued by the black soot that covered them all.

Jack's face was a mixture of fresh blue eyes and chunky humor. It sagged, blustery and attractive, so that his hangdog manner was often quite funny. By the third day, Clara was walking with him hand in hand as they made their way through the Tuileries. They sat at an outdoor cafe in the gardens, at which Jack entertained them with an ongoing translation of his Parisian patter with the waiter, in which the waiter described the famous stars who had stopped there. Maurice Chevalier, of course. The Argentine, Carlos Gardel. Marlena Dietrich. And, once, the Duke and Duchess of Windsor had paused for a lemon *glace*, in the company of Charlie Chaplin. Jack's translation matched the waiter's snooty arrogance at having served such notables. What made it humorous was the waiter's tiny delicacy translated by Jack into his own rough, even smudged, *joie de vivre*.

When they went to the Louvre, Jack took them straight to the Mona Lisa. A crowd stood before the famous painting, their heads bobbing back and forth for a look.

"No wonder he wanted to paint her." Jack stood with his hands entwined behind his back. Lauren noticed that Clara was watching him carefully, and following with her eyes his gestures toward the painting. Jack's tie hung before him like a rumpled kite tail. "I mean, look how beautiful she is." He shook his head. "Everyone talks about the smile, which they say is so enigmatic. But for me, this woman, Clara...this woman...."

The Mona Lisa's quiet fascinated Lauren too, because it was obvious to her that the woman was scattered with passion. There was, in the manner in which Mona Lisa's hands were folded across one another, the look of a faithful and thoughtful wife. But Lauren sensed a kind of adventuresome wander in the woman's look, as though she wished to ask a question that was, possibly, a compromising one. An inquiry about a bit of recent gossip, an assignation, maybe....

Martin became quickly bored at the Louvre, but Clara listened to everything Jack said. There were long discussions of particular paintings. A Giotto view of Saint Francis—in a swoon, receiving God's grace in the rays of light coming from the hands of a gold-white floating angel—made Clara feel that she was on a golden, light-drenched sacred field. She told her mother that Saint Francis seemed to be dreaming, so that she felt that she was being asked to walk with him through the vision.

When they meandered through the basement Egyptian collections, Jack showed his preference for the large guardian lions, dozens of them in yellow stone, which reminded Clara of the merry-go-round in Golden Gate Park in San Francisco. Lauren imagined Clara as Nefertiti riding around Cairo on one of them, whose reign Jack described while they looked at a bust of her. Nefertiti was a dark woman with glorious black eyes shaped like tears.

"But when can we look at some more of *your* pictures?" Clara asked Jack as they walked back out into the entry plaza of the museum.

"Any time, I suppose. But only if you really want to. They're just a lot of splotches, you know. Spilt milk." The remark was accompanied by a smile from Jack, and then Jack turned to Lauren and Martin. "You could bring Clara over tomorrow if you like, in the afternoon."

—

They arrived at Jack's studio at two the following day. A tropical humidity had settled over Paris, causing Clara to remark to her father as they trudged up the hill that she felt like a hot puddle. It was she who had looked forward with the most enthusiasm to visiting Jack's studio again, and now she led the way as they crossed the Place de La Contrescarpe toward his front door.

Jack ushered them up the stairs, and as they entered the studio, the light from the windows glared across Lauren's face, hurting her eyes. The studio was actually one single room, despite the six windows that looked out from it onto the square. It was painted white. The ceiling rose to an angled arch, with a rough, carved beam in dark wood running its length. There was a bedroom at the back.

The two men shook hands. Lauren shielded her eyes with one hand, causing Jack to walk to the windows to adjust the drapes. He was dressed in a dark green sport shirt, sleeves rolled up, and black slacks, as worn-looking as his other clothing. The hair on his arms looked like saw grass. The studio was very warm, and the air remained still when Jack opened a window at the rear, in the kitchen.

He walked to the wall opposite the windows and separated one painting from the others leaning against each other. It was made up of three splotches of color, dark blue-yellows and green, like an exploded triangle of glimmering reminiscences. It was very sad and very cold-looking.

Lauren looked at it silently. It was clear to her that the painting was filled with conflict, and it frightened her. She noticed Jack biting his lower lip as he too studied it. He appeared to disapprove of it.

"But what's it about?" Clara said.

"Water."

Clara's lips wrinkled with perplexity.

"Tears." Jack stepped toward the painting and scraped a bit of color away with his thumbnail.

Clara continued staring at the painting, trying to figure out what Jack could be talking about.

"What do you think it's about, Clara?" Jack said.

"I don't know. I guess it's—"

"How much is it?" Martin leaned close to the painting, as though attempting to study it.

Everyone looked around at him. He moved before the painting, dressed in a pair of tan slacks, a white shirt, and a linen sport coat. Sweat splotched the back of the coat.

"Pardon me?" Jack said.

"How much do you want for it?"

Jack's shoulders broadened as he took in a breath and considered his reply. "I don't know, Martin. I guess—"

"You do sell them, don't you?"

"I do, yes. I used to make a greater effort to do that, you know, than I do now. But I have my moments. I support myself." He smiled. "Especially just now there's a big painting I'm doing, that a woman named Madame Cleeve is looking at."

"What is she, a neighbor?"

"No! She lives in Saint Germain-des-Prés. A big buyer, famous here in Paris, of contemporary stuff."

"Stuff."

"Yes. Art."

"And she's serious?"

"Of course. She knows about those buyers in 1908 that had heard about the young fellow Picasso. Or that one poor sot who bought a painting from Van Gogh, the *only* one. She's like them. And she likes my things."

"Does she pay?"

"When it's finished, she will." Jack shrugged. "But it isn't finished." He suddenly grinned. "You know, there was a time when I painted for meals now and then, with a couple of restaurateurs I know." He turned again toward the painting. "Food and love, eh, Martin?"

"Do you have a job or anything?" Clara said.

"I sell my art."

Jack turned the painting aside, facing it to the wall, and pulled out another. It was of the same coloration, with quite similar shapes, this time lined up in a rough pile.

"But how much would you charge for one of these?" Martin said.

This painting gave off the same feeling of chilling termination and darkness. Lauren moved to the couch to sit down. She placed her elbows on her knees and gazed at it. Clara stood before it as well, watching the conversation between the two men. In her white skirt and dark, short-sleeved blouse, she appeared to Lauren delicately impressionable, as though she could be victimized by what had gone into Jack's work.

"I don't know," Jack said. His mouth worked as he contemplated the piece.

"A hundred dollars? Two hundred?"

The blues were made up of what appeared to be dozens of other colors underneath, which increased the profundity of foreboding that existed in the painting. They seemed to cause the composition to move, actually softening its darkness and making it, to Lauren's discomfort, quite lovely.

"How about two hundred?" Martin said.

"Sure, for God's sake." Jack turned to the side, glancing toward Lauren.

Martin pulled his wallet from a jacket pocket. He took several American bills from it and handed them to Jack. Turning to Lauren, he laid a hand on hers. "Do you like it?"

"It's beautiful." Lauren hesitated a moment, then realized that Martin wanted more of an acknowledgement from her. She leaned over to kiss him. "Martin, it's very beautiful. You're sure you want it?"

"Of course. Don't you?"

Martin had done this sort of thing frequently before, a spontaneous, surprising gesture like this. But just now Lauren felt his need to have the gift acknowledged, as though he were struggling to show that he could please her. But Lauren could hardly bear the dismay of the painting. She kept her hand in Martin's.

"Do you remember, Jack, you wrote to me once about some red paintings you had done? The ones that were so beautiful?"

"Yes. I haven't done any in years. Not since the beginning of the war."

"The way you described them, they sounded wonderful." Lauren took her hand from Martin's.

Jack's face brightened. He fingered Martin's money, and then tossed it to the table.

"You don't have any of those, do you?"

"No. The ones I hadn't sold got lost at the end of the war. It was a shame, too, because Max Ernst bought one just before the Germans arrived." Jack smiled and reached into his shirt pocket for a packet of cigarettes. Lighting one, he threw the match to the floor. "My most important buyer." He blew some smoke into the air. "He took the painting to the States." He examined the cigarette. "Although 'buyer' isn't exactly the right word." He chuckled. "I admire him so. He was here one day with a friend of mine, and he said my stuff had promise."

"Promise?" Lauren said.

"I sold that red one to him. I'd painted for a week straight before he got here." Jack looked out the windows at the buildings across Contrescarpe. "You know, I'd forgotten about those, Lauren." He sat down on a chair before the painting. Leaning forward, he placed his elbows on his knees and joined his hands. He was sweating, and there was the sense of a kind of steam coming from him. Something rasping in the way he breathed, the way his body was so brusquely taking in air. "They were all right, those."

—

The following morning, Lauren received a *pneumatique* from Jack, asking her to come to the studio by herself, if possible. This note was like the others he had sent, so hurried in its handwriting that she could barely make it out. Martin had planned to take her and Clara on a boat ride on the Seine, and Lauren excused herself, explaining that she wanted to have some time to herself, that she was exhausted by all the touring they had done. Clara went off with Martin, who was unhappy that Lauren would not join them.

Lauren went by *metro* to the Place Monge stop.

The door opened almost immediately, and Jack took her hand and led her up the stairs to the studio. His eyes skittered about. His shoes were spattered with paint, and the backs of them had been removed, revealing his heels.

"Look at this." The paintings from the day before remained against the walls. But now there was a new one. It leaned against the couch. It was red, and had been painted in an unreadable fury, a flurry of shapes floating in what appeared to be a carnage-filled sea.

"I did it last night." Jack stood before it, the morning light radiating across the wrinkles in his shirt. His eyes were dark, the skin around them puffed with sleeplessness. The smoke that rose from the cigarette in his hand floated through his fingers and dissipated in them. It seemed to come from the hand itself. "What do you think of it?"

Lauren removed her sweater and draped it over a chair. She stood next to Jack in the light from the windows. She held a strand of hair in one hand and feigned studying the painting. The fact was it horrified her. It was not ugly. Not intentionally offensive. But there was a kind of grasping terror in it that made her want to turn away.

"I made it for you."

Lauren sighed, a soft expression of worry.

"Because you said…I mean, you said it, didn't you? that you wanted red paintings." Jack pushed aside the newspaper that was opened up on the coffee table, and sat down. He appeared heated, so quietly savage that Lauren was afraid to look at him. But she did so, and felt from him the press of some kind of maddened love. It had no care for itself, and little wish that Jack's own senses be protected.

"Jack."

Rather, it wished to take him to pieces. And Lauren felt herself disappearing from view as well, even though it was for…*my love*, she thought, that Jack had made the paintings.

She whispered. "Please…." But the painting conveyed too brazen a sentiment, nothing like what Lauren had ever imagined as…affection, even. "Please, I've got to go."

———

She hurried down the hill, blind to the noisy Rue Mouffetard marketplace through which she passed. She felt trapped in the frivolity and shouts of the street, and imprisoned by the fine sunlight. It was clear that Jack was still disastrously in love with her. Even though everything between them had passed away years ago, when they *had* been in love. And she had had no wish to go back to that since the day so long ago that Jack had left her. The day Lauren had suffered the full twist and pain of abandonment.

Her heart had given itself to him then, as though it were valueless. And apparently she *was* without value, because he *did* just throw her away.

She stopped at the Deux Cygnes and ordered a coffee. Her chest hurt, and her breathing brought no relief. She felt enclosed and deadened by Jack's craziness. Staring at her hands folded in each other on the table, she wished the memories she had of him could be simple, secure recollections of a childhood love. But instead, the tawdry weight of her own obsessions in that time took her over.

—

Lauren recalled how Jack's hands were the first thing she ever noticed about him, while he was taking Communion at the altar rail at Saint Joseph's in Eureka. She had come up to the altar behind him and knelt at his side. It was in 1927, and she had just had her twelfth birthday. Although Jack had been pointed out to Lauren by her mother once when they had gone shopping downtown, she had not yet met him.

But she knew that he was an exotic. Before the World War, his father was with the Irish Republican Brotherhood, a fact that brought gushes of admiration from Lauren's father. Desmond Roman fought against the English and defeated them, her father said, although his labored explanations of the war against the English made little sense to Lauren. Lauren's whole family and most of her friends were Catholic. Why would the English be so mean to Catholics?

At the altar rail that day, Jack clasped his hands together, awaiting the priest. They were long, large hands, yet they lay across each other delicately, as a statue's would. They were almost ceramic-white and unmarred. Lauren glanced at them for just a moment, until the priest arrived to give her the Host.

At sixteen, Jack was a tall boy whose face had the same sort of imperfect clarity as his hands, especially in his eyes, which, despite their attractiveness, deferred to others, especially adults, as if manners were more important than self-knowledge. Too embarrassed to speak with him, Lauren watched him descend the church steps after Mass with his parents. It was obvious that Jack was different from the other high school boys. For one he was dressed in a suit and tie, and the suit appeared to fit him. This was unlike the others altogether who, when they wore a suit on Sunday, still looked like they were fishermen or loggers.

"Hello, Jack!" Her mother Adela called to him.

He awaited his parents, who stopped on the steps to speak with the priest. Caught taking an illicit peek at him, Lauren shook her head with embarrassment. When Adela introduced Lauren to Jack, the girl could barely address him. It seemed not to matter, since Jack paid no attention to her at all.

Jack and his parents drove away from Saint Joseph's that day in their old Ford coupe. As she watched the car turn the corner toward Myrtle Avenue, Lauren felt a kind of sudden, affectionate sickness. She tried to calm her heart, and could not. She thought something must be wrong with her.

"A nice boy, isn't he?" Adela said as they walked up the sidewalk toward their own car. She was busy fitting her missal into her purse. Lauren could not tell if her parents knew what she was feeling.

Her father had gone ahead, and now fiddled with his keys in the car door lock. A seagull flew overhead. Much higher, a bevy of seagulls turned about, reeling in imperfect circles. Lauren's heart felt scuttled within her. She imagined, to her mortification, being kissed by Jack, his lips caressing her eyes.

Lauren had to wait for three days after that, until Wednesday evening, to go to Confession. She knew it was a sin to feel so sick just for some boy. The trouble was that, now and then during those intervening days, she relished the sickness, and imagined all sorts of things she shouldn't have imagined.

When she entered the confessional booth the following Wednesday, Father Keller opened the sliding wooden panel, and in silence Lauren watched the movement of his hand as he leaned his head against it. He was an old man whose cassock fit his corpulent body like a black-buttoned tent.

Lauren was afraid of Father Keller and, as she crossed herself and asked the priest to bless her, that she had sinned, and that it was three weeks since her last Confession…as she did that, his head nodded with expectation.

"I've had bad…dreams, Father, about a boy."

"What kind of dreams?"

"I've dreamed of…kissing him. And it made me feel strange. I didn't know what was wrong, and it—."

"Has this happened often?"

"No. This was the only time."

Father Keller took in a breath. The exhalation sounded like his last. "God will forgive you. But you must put these things from your mind. Have you talked with your mother about it?"

"I'm afraid to."

"Well, you should. The Devil tempts girls not to tell their mothers when they've sinned like this."

Lauren shivered.

"Because he wants them to sin again, and knows that their mothers won't let them." The priest removed his hand from the side of his head. Lauren surveyed his sparse white hair, like dying thatch close to the screen. "So I want you to say ten Hail Mary's, ten Our Fathers, and then an additional ten Our Fathers, to make sure God hears you."

It was a drastic penance, more prayers than Lauren had ever been asked to say.

"And stay away from that boy."

"Yes, Father."

The priest reached up to close the wooden panel. His fingers clutched the latch like bent candles. "A boy like that is a bad boy."

"Yes, Father."

The panel clapped shut.

———

The waiter brought Lauren's coffee. She thanked him, saddened by her recollection of the old priest, who died a year later. She felt the same now as she had felt that day. Her breathing was inconstant. Her heart tightened, and she inclined her head toward the coffee cup.

How could Jack do this to me? Such a false memory. A kind of broken memory. He had given her that new red painting so violently that she felt it was a punishment. *But how could he punish me?* It seemed to Lauren that the painting was colored by simple madness. The red in it had little finesse. Rather it was dragged across the canvas, even smeared onto it.

She paid for the coffee, though she had only sipped from it once, and left.

7

"So we're going shopping?" Jack looked over his shoulder at Clara, who sat in the back seat of his old *deux-cheveaux*. Her purse was on her lap, and her eyes flickered as Jack reached out and touched her hand. "You ready?"

"I hope so."

He expected Clara had never seen anything like the Galeries Lafayette, and as he started the car and pulled into traffic toward the Place de la Concorde, he relished the fun they were about to have.

"How much money have you got, Clara?"

"I don't know. Nine dollars, I guess."

"No, I mean *francs*."

For a moment, there was no reply, and Jack waited as he sensed Clara's doing the arithmetic.

"I don't know." Clara fingered her purse. Her eyes were cast down. But there was a smile, and Jack realized that she was still doing the arithmetic. "How much do *you* think it is, Jack?"

"It's…uh…. Hang on."

"It's three thousand one hundred fifty *francs*."

Jack put both hands on the wheel and drove on, nodding his head.

—

The Galeries Lafayette went up for floor after floor, a glorious trove of clothing, drapery, millinery, make-up, and crockery. The store was filled with light that shimmered across city-like vistas of display, colors everywhere. There were female mannequins dressed in form fitting black wool suits, strings of costume jewelry, and fine black cloches. Saleswomen stood in the aisles, with atomizers from which they dispensed perfume onto customers' wrists. Clara waited in line for one of them, a tall blonde who reminded her of Grace Kelly. The woman murmured to Clara in French, Jack translating, about the properties of the perfume, how it would make all the boys love her, and that it was the perfect scent to go along with Clara's eyes.

Clara's face reddened with embarrassed pleasure.

She wanted to see the china, because her mother had told her that no store anywhere carried as many plates and platters as the Galeries Lafayette. When they arrived on the third floor, she stopped to look, biting her lower lip. The displays of decorated porcelain looked like terraced gardens, with level upon level of ivies, roses, French country scenes, and bluebells. There were French milkmaids, cows, windmills, and nasturtiums, all quivering on fields of bone-white. Overwhelmed with indecision, she moved toward the displays as though seized by them.

Jack pointed toward a stairway. "After this, let's go upstairs for a pastry."

"Pastry? They've got those here, too?"

"Everything. Ice creams. Pastries. Whatever you want."

Clara was not done yet with the china. She asked Jack what he thought her mother would like. But she had such a sense of Lauren's tastes that she laughed at Jack's suggestion that a yellow glazed Quimper teapot to which he pointed, with a blue peasant boy on the side, was just the thing.

"Jack, that's okay. But it isn't elegant enough."

"Oh. Sorry."

"But this one...." Clara held up a teacup and saucer. Checking the bottom of the saucer, she saw that it was Limoges. That too was a good sign, since Lauren had often exclaimed about the Limoges products she had once seen in New York. The cup was ringed about the fluted lip with a cloud-like line of blue, and surrounded below the line with a field of blue iris. She turned it about in her hands. The flowers appeared to be swaying in some sort of liquid-seeming breeze. "Mom would love this."

She touched the flowers, as though trying to feel the warmth of them in the sun. The way her fingers searched the cup's surface was a gesture she had inherited from her mother. It was the born wish to feel the very thing that was being represented. Jack, watching, knew how that was. Clara wasn't feeling the ceramic. It was the iris themselves, like light. Although it was blue light, Jack thought, and he bet that the flowers felt cold to her touch.

He had never expected to be so electrified by Lauren's appearance in Paris. When she mentioned the red paintings, memories that were unruly and nuts cluttered up in him. They possessed him through the afternoon despite his efforts to explain them away. Then, that evening, when the new painting came out of him like a floating spirit striving for the canvas, he knew that he still loved her.

The actual application of the paint to the gessoed surface meant nothing to him. He could barely remember doing it, his mind so racing with exhausting intensity. As the light appeared in the early morning, he succumbed to it altogether in ravages of guilt and love.

He hoped only that Lauren had forgiven him. But the longing he felt for her through the night was stifled, and encouraged, by the pain of what he remembered. Clara had intensified the difficulty because she so reminded him of Lauren herself when she had been younger. This was most evident in Clara's interest in the charm Jack had given her, and how she examined it so closely. The grace in her fingers as she turned the little windmill about was like that in her mother's.

But what had most intensified Jack's feelings was Martin's offer to buy the painting. Jack sold his paintings, through a few dealers he had known for some years and on his own, and was able to support himself with his art. But he was usually chagrined by the necessity of doing so. He knew how much they were worth, but he felt in his heart that the very question was impertinent. It distracted him whenever it occurred, especially when it came from people like Martin, who supposed that paintings were like suits. You legitimized the thing you didn't understand by buying it.

Such transactions…the begrimed commerce of them…was a mere necessity. Jack was not an impractical man, but neither did he care about business. Business was simple necessity. He could not tell whether he intentionally avoided thinking about money from resentment that it meant so much to so many people, or that it simply never occurred to him to care.

There was always money, somehow. It was true that he disliked his poverty. But he hated the idea of grousing for money even more, because it so clearly illustrated his disinterest in doing it. Thinking about money insured that he would think about the absence of it, and that conflict galled him.

He sold his paintings because he would be a fool not to. But he reveled in other conflicts, in the beauty of an abrupt swatch of complicated mixtures of red, say, and how it revealed the memory to him of his squandered love. There was blood in that.

Clara's questions about his paintings—the pleasured smile she gave him, as though she realized the complexity of what he was feeling—made him care for her right away. At that moment, Clara so resembled her mother that, to Jack, she appeared to be Lauren herself, the girl she was when they had first met.

—

Jack had barely noticed Lauren that day, introduced outside Saint Joseph's church, a few weeks after he and his parents had moved there. Lauren was very shy, only twelve years old, and barely able to look at him. There was little reaction on Jack's part. His own nervousness at meeting so many people had scattered him. He felt like a bulky tourist with his odd accent and woolen French clothes. People laughed at how Jack spoke. He quickly grew to hate what they thought of as the charm of his Irish accent. He effected that of an American as quickly as possible, and failed at it, never really losing his own.

He did not know what to make of Eureka, a foggy coastal town that was often drenched in rain. It was far from anywhere else, and he had already lived in several places far from anything. Ireland itself, for one. Southeast Asia. And France, for several years as a boy. But at least some of those places possessed real exoticisms, like strange natives and the Jeu de Paume, weird masks, Debussy, dances with flame, and feathered costumes.

Jack recalled going to school every day as a twelve year-old in Djakarta, when his father was an Irish embassy official. The boy walked with hundreds of Indonesian children on fog-washed mornings through the heat, their white school shirts and blouses making them float up the muddy road like gulls. That Jack had to turn off to go to the English school, up a hill into a gated compound, disgruntled him. There were no other Irish children there, and the chatter of the Malay language that Jack was trying imperfectly to learn from his mother's servants always pleased him. The laughter of the children floated into the morning as well, as they made fun of the strange *tuan* boy whose white skin and clear blue eyes were such exoticisms for them. So unlike their own eyes, which were so dark that they appeared to the Irish boy like pools of soft oil.

Jack and his parents had also lived in Mexico for two years, arriving there in 1925 on Jack's fourteenth birthday. Jack and his mother accompanied the bellboys at the Hotel Quetzal Negro, which was near the central plaza in Mexico City, as they scurried up the tile-lined stairs to their room on the second floor. There had been one scruffy, bare-footed bellboy for each bag, a total of seven. All the rooms opened to a passageway that looked down on the lobby. Jack stood at the railing, watching his father check them into the hotel. The lobby was ringed with ferns and parrot-perches, the birds quite menacing—green, yellow, and blood red—in silent perusal of the guests. Other guests read newspapers and chatted, the unfamiliar Spanish language rising through the lobby. A tiny, dark-skinned waiter dressed in a red woven shirt and red and blue pants, his head swathed in a bright red cloth, served a fruit drink to a quite fat Mexican man who was dressed in a white suit. Sweat gleamed from his face, making the skin around the tinted glasses he wore appear silver-brown, like tarnished coins.

Jack still had an Indian mask he had bought in the market at Oaxaca. There had been several displayed on the wall below the steps to the church near the *zócalo*. Jack remembered how the noise of the marketplace that day made it so difficult to simply watch what was happening. There were hundreds of Indians. The masks looking down at him from the white-washed wall—colored grotesques with bird-beaks, carved feathers, and crooked teeth—all seemed to be observing him directly.

A homemade rocket flew up from the church steps. An Indian lay face down in the square in a drunken sleep, and no one paid any attention to him.

Indeed the other Indians simply stepped over him as they made their way through the square. He appeared dead, his thickened lips wet with gummed saliva. An Indian reveler in a conquistador costume and a white-faced mask ran into Jack. He was slapdash and drunk, and his Spanish helmet was very much dented. He shouted at Jack angrily, and then ran into the crowd.

Looking across the market square, Jack wondered what it would be like to live here with these Indians, out in the hills in this kind of poverty and splendor.

When his mother's new acquaintances in Eureka first came to visit, they enjoyed the masks he and his father had collected, though in a tentative and very frightened sort of way. The women passed through his father's work-room, in a shed behind the house, with its displays of Indonesian shadow-puppets, jungle *parang* knives, and little Mexican wood-carved skeleton figurines in sombreros and tuxedoes, as though all these things were phantasms from disturbing dreams.

"But do they wear these things every day?" one of the women asked about the masks.

Jack explained what he knew of them. The reticence of the women, and their seeming inability to simply enjoy the objects or to see how humorous they were, surprised him. He felt oddly grown-up, a kid knowing so much more than they did.

When Lauren came to visit with her mother, she too asked to be shown the workroom. She followed Jack across the backyard in silence. Jack felt ill at ease, not knowing what to say to this girl who was so much younger than he. He barely knew her. Lauren found it difficult to converse with Jack at all. She had never been anywhere, she told him later, and she felt foolish around him.

He knew, though, that she loved him even then. Years later, she told him that he had seemed fantastic to her, a dream personage surrounded by all those things. She did not imagine he could ever care for her.

But he had cared for her. Finally, he came to love her, and to love her disastrously.

—

Clara held the Limoges up to the light.

"How much are they?" Jack said.

She looked at the price tag beneath the saucer. "It's eight hundred seventy-five francs each. That's—"

"Yes, uh…." Jack faltered.

"Five dollars for the cup and saucer." Clara continued surveying the cup, checking for imperfections. "I'm going to get them." She handed them to Jack, who beckoned to a saleswoman.

"Can I get them gift wrapped?"

"No, they don't do that at the Galeries Lafayette."

Clara's eyes darkened. Disappointment, like a shroud obscuring her pleasure, caused her to grumble. "But I want to make it nice."

Jack handed the cup and saucer to the saleswoman. Clara kept her eyes on the items as she carried them away. Jack put a hand on her shoulder. "They sell gift wrap here."

"You mean you buy your own?"

"Yes."

"In rolls? Like at Christmas?"

"No, they'll sell you just a single sheet."

Again, Clara frowned.

Jack took her up one floor to a small alcove in a corner of the store, where the walls were hung with displays of gift wrapping paper, some of it with a metallic sheen, other designs like mottled oil swirling across the sheets. Clara's unhappiness evaporated as the saleswoman showed her several different kinds. There were flowers and English riding scenes. Some of the wrap resembled pure gold. Chinese extravaganzas. Roman games. Clara chose a dark green paper on which was printed a flowering ivy. The ivy lay within itself in a voluminous embrace that was quite beautiful, with a verdant evening-like light.

Jack was surprised by the choice, having thought that Clara would prefer brighter colors. But he had noticed already how she cared for detail, how she noted, in the morning sunlight or a coffee filled with steamed milk, some change in coloration that made it newly interesting. She was the only child Jack had ever encountered who would sit in a park along the Seine just to watch the light change at the end of an afternoon. She talked with Jack about such things, referring to the darkening sunset broken up by the leaves overhead as "cool" or "neat." He knew that the pleasure she felt was far more complex than the words themselves.

What if she were my daughter? Jack thought as Clara watched the saleswoman roll the giftwrap into a tube and secure it with a bit of string. He imagined Clara in his studio, looking over his shoulder as he attempted, yet one more time, to make the color right in some recalcitrant abstraction. *Imagine having her there to help me,* Jack thought. *Me, her father.* He would wait for her, anticipating what she would say and the affection she would give him, with a smile like the one she offered him now as the saleswoman delivered the narrow packet into her hands.

"Can I just stay and look around by myself?" Clara's eyes turned toward more of the papers hanging from the walls.

"Sure. I'll go upstairs for a cup of tea?"

"Okay."

"Just come get me when you're ready." Jack headed for the staircase, passing by a display of crystal and glass that glittered in the bright store light like melting ice.

As he ascended the stairs, he thought again of Lauren, and the day they had finally, really, spoken to each other.

—

Christmases in Eureka were usually awash in cold rain. But there was the occasional day on which the sun would come out and the town would appear with a freshness that belied the mold-crust and old wood of so many of the buildings. On such days the light gave a very sharp edge to the buildings, so that each one appeared distinctly separate and isolated. Were it cold enough, frost and icicles would appear on the roofs and below the eaves, to last the morning. Even those warehouse buildings along the wharves that lacked for paint, appearing to list down the low-tide shore toward the water, glistened in such light, and the cold sharpened the air.

Jack's parents had become close friends of Lauren's, and it was at Christmastime, during Jack's senior year at Saint Joseph's High, that he fell very abruptly in love with Lauren. It was an immediate change of heart one morning, an innocent-seeming desire that neither of them could contain.

Lauren's father Mason Cahill was the manager of sawmill operations for a company called Arcata Logging, and he had gotten vacation jobs for Jack. Jack enjoyed the work, if only for the ferry ride across Humboldt Bay every day, from Eureka to the town of Samoa and back. The fog-shrouded bay water, in modulations of gray and charcoal, was iron-smooth in the morning and broken up in whitecaps by the afternoon winds. By the age of eighteen, Jack carried a sketchbook everywhere with him in a canvas shoulder bag. He drew the ferryboat, then different parts of it, along with landscapes of Gunther's Island and the wharf buildings along First Street in Eureka.

He also drew fabulous phantasms. He had read *Bulfinch's Mythology*, a book his art teacher Sister Agnes had given him. He imagined Bulfinch himself in the waters off First Street, his beard dripping with algae and seaweed as he came to the surface. And Charon, pushing Bulfinch away with a jab of his gnarled pole. Jack tried to imagine what Charon looked like, seeing him dark-skinned with a smoke-blackened shirt, and sweating through the mists.

As the ferry made its way across the bay, Jack would watch the smoke rising up from the chip burners at the lumber mills, and then draw pictures of them, like enormous badminton birdies, guarded at their entrances by Bulfinch's fiery creatures.

Walking toward the ferryboat dock Christmas Eve morning, Jack passed the entrance to Arcata Logging, across Second Street from the Carson mansion. He had drawn this place too. A kind of grotesque, the Carson mansion was a Victorian building of baroque proportions, with dormers and curlicues everywhere, all of it in redwood. It straddled the northern end of Second Street, overlooking the wharf-side sawmills where logs and cut wood were prepared for shipment to San Francisco.

He turned the corner to walk Second Street toward the ferryboat dock.

"Hi, Jack." Lauren caught up to him. Her father had given her a Christmas job at Foy's Arcade, wrapping presents behind a counter on the mezzanine.

Jack had noticed her there the day before, when he was shopping for presents for his parents. Lauren waved to him, though she looked quickly away as he passed by. Ascending the stairs to the second floor, he glanced back over his shoulder. To his pleasure, she remained watching him.

Just fifteen, Lauren had little of the shyness that had made her so quiet as a younger girl. Jack's mother talked about Lauren's reserve, and how she thought that it came from a wish to gather things together and to understand how she felt about them. Indeed Jack's mother perceived a dark contemplativeness in the girl, unusual for her age, which was now becoming hidden behind Lauren's very appearance. The irony was that, as Lauren matured and became more poised, her attentiveness remained in the background, nonetheless intentionally present.

"She's lovely, a real colleen," his mother once said, describing at the dinner table the conversation she had had that afternoon over tea with Lauren and her mother. "But she's so pretty that too few people realize how thoughtful she is. They stop at her eyes and at the smile." She shook her head. "And they don't go any farther. But there's more than that."

"Are you going to work?" Lauren said as Jack turned to greet her.

Jack wore a pair of dungarees, a T-shirt and a wool jacket. "You, too?"

"Yes, but I don't have to be at the store until ten, so I thought I'd come down here...with my dad, you know...." She brushed her hair back and looked out toward the bay. "It's so beautiful this morning."

The distraction in her voice, as though the remark made her feel foolish, gave way to a sigh. She had on a black beret, a white frilled blouse, and a black skirt and wool jacket. Her scarf was kelly green and tied in a loose knot about her neck. She had tossed it back over her shoulder.

"I'm going across on the ferry," Jack said.

The conversation wavered. They fell into silence. Neither of them was able to move it ahead. They continued walking, and passed through the blue shadow cast by a warehouse building. Lauren adjusted the collar of her jacket, shivering in the cold.

Jack took Lauren's hand. "Would you like to come with me?"

Lauren gripped his fingers, and they turned the corner at C Street, to go down to the docks.

As they crossed the bay, they sat next to each other on an outside bench of the *Madaket*. Jack held Lauren's hand in his jacket pocket. What he felt at this moment was new to him and unsettling. It was a kind of insistent pleasure and confusion, that Lauren was so obviously happy, and that she had waited for him and sought him out, while at the same time he felt her shyness and the wish that they be closer in some way. She caressed his hand inside the pocket as though she wished to examine it only by feel, only through the delicacy of touch. But Jack's eyes moved quickly from her lips to the fingers of her free hand to the cold froth of the water broken apart by the ferry's bow.

Floating through his life, forced to learn some part of one language, then to abruptly move on to another, to sail from Ireland to a palm-strewn country and on to a great high-plain Central American city, and finally to France, he had not experienced the sort of suddenness of intent and desire that took him over now. He interrupted Lauren's questions about whether people in Mexico went to the movies and did he write to any other girls anywhere, with a kiss to her mouth. She lowered her eyes. He touched her throat, leaned close to her, and kissed the skin of her neck, causing her to pull away, laughing. The ferry lurched across the wakes of several fishing boats headed for the channel, and the wind swirled about them like cold buffeting flames as they talked.

8

The day after her visit with Jack to the Galeries Lafayette, Clara insisted on going to Confession. There was no need for it, she being reasonably certain that she had sinned little since they had arrived in France. She smiled as she decided she had been too excited to sin. But she wanted to do Confession anyway, just to see what it was like in a place like Paris. Lauren agreed to take her.

As they approached Notre-Dame in the late afternoon, a flight of sparrows swooped in speedy disarray toward the plaza before the cathedral, and then climbed at an angle over the Seine. They turned up the cathedral's facade, climbed even higher, and disappeared above the roof. Though it was late, the sunlight was barely diminished at all. Lauren and Clara sat down on a stone bench, and the birds appeared again, clattering toward the river and the trees that lined the quay on the left bank. Notre-Dame itself rose like an ornate sailing frigate against the sky. Its centuries of soot made the exterior appear to have just come through a conflagration.

"Inside, it's different," Lauren remarked as they shielded their eyes against the bright light. "The cathedral goes up as high as you can see, and when the light is right, the rose window is like a star."

"The rose window?"

"You'll see. It's a round stained-glass window. Huge. There are more than one, but the northern one is really special. It's like the eye of God." Lauren glanced at Clara, who had clutched her missal close to her chest as she listened. "Heaven and earth."

Clara's eyes widened.

"Circled by the stars."

Lauren told Clara how you could get lost in the window when you followed its patterns, like the holy lines of God in illuminated manuscripts that lead everywhere forever. The rose window twirled about in the air, she explained, in blues, dark poppy-like reds, and metallic yellows.

"Sounds wonderful, doesn't it?"

"And we can see it?"

"It's filled with glow, Clara. Of every color." Lauren looked down at her own missal. "The softest kind of light you can imagine."

A moment later, Lauren crossed herself as she entered the cathedral. The inside of the holy water font was slimy, and her nose wrinkled as she noticed a ring of faded green running around the font, just at water level. Clara hurried past her. She paused at the slippery marble as well, pulled her hand from the water and shook it, and then surveyed her fingers. She wiped them on the side of her skirt.

Sunlight illumined the windows, so that the scenes of saints, courtly knights, and miracles were animated with gold. Light crossed the cathedral at an angle, in shafts of fine dust. The votive candles along the side-aisles gave off a drab vibrancy, as though it were a task to recall the dead souls for whom they burned. Still, there was considerable warmth as the light dispersed into the reaches of the cathedral. Above—way, way above—lighted chandeliers extended the glow into the vaulted ceilings, where Lauren imagined the angels reposed in the grayest corners farthest away.

The Cathedral of Notre-Dame grasped her heart. Her breath was taken by almost everything in it…by the sculpted tableaux of saints contemplating heaven, of dead knights laid out on coffins, and of skeletal Death itself surreptitious in its search for others to take away. All these things were obscured by the simple enormity of the air contained by the cathedral. Lauren felt she was in some kind of gloriously organized sky, simultaneously dark, bright, and surprising with candles, paintings, and altars everywhere she looked.

The thirty or so people who had come for Confession were dressed glumly, and remained isolated from each other. A few notes of organ music burst from above. There was a pause, and then a few more notes. Lauren and Clara walked part of the way up the aisle, to look back into the organ loft. The pillars, like fountains of water supporting the vaults, seemed to pull the gaze up past the balustrade walkways and high windows—numberless scenes of earth and heaven, the repose of saints, the voices of angels—to heaven itself.

Recalling Father Keller's descriptions during sermons, when Lauren had been a girl, of the apocalypse and the hordes of sinners it would send to black hell, she now wondered how it was that churches were not packed all day long, with people seeking to avoid the flames of Perdition. And this, in this cathedral, was such a beautifully illumined emptiness.

Clara's hands were clasped before her lips. She was occasionally religious, unlike the faithful, observant girl that Lauren had been at her age, especially on Holy Days of Obligation, when going to Mass was a real occasion. Church on Sunday was no such thing, of course, since it was simply a habit. But for young Lauren, getting up on a school day to go to an early Mass had imbued her with special grace. She loved the burden of faith that had rested so heavily upon her.

It amused Lauren to contemplate how Saint Joseph's in Eureka—so plain by comparison—served the same purpose as Notre-Dame. The gray walls of Saint Joseph's were actually brightened by Christ's agonies in the Stations of the Cross. The betrayal in the garden, His chaining to the pillar, and His struggle up the Via Dolorosa were all framed in golden myrtle wood, with a small pewter crucifix below each scene. The church's windows were made of translucent yellow glass that, on sunny Sunday mornings, gave the parishioners a malarial look. On the altar itself, a plaster statue of Saint Joseph held its hands up in an explanatory gesture. Two toes on his left foot were chipped. His head was turned to the side, as if someone in the distance had just yelled at him.

Her mother Adela had told Lauren that, whenever a woman died, she could insure a state of grace for herself by falling to the ground in the shape of a cross. So, as a little girl, Lauren practiced. Out on the front lawn, she would walk quietly about, then pretend she was being struck by lightning. She would fall to the ground in a pretend swoon, her arms straight out from her sides.

As she grew older—about eleven or so—worry threaded its way into her convictions. For example, what if you died in your sleep? Lauren knew that she slept in every kind of contorted position...her arms underneath her when she lay on her stomach; on her back, one arm supporting her head, the other lying on her chest; or, on her side, her hands clasped between her knees. What if you died then? Comfy and sleepy between the blankets, would you go straight to hell?

Clara arrived at the cathedral altar and knelt down at the railing. Her head bobbed as she prayed. She was so excited that she stood out for Lauren like a doll, her hands in a faraway blur as she crossed herself.

Kneeling in the first pew, Lauren laid her chin on her folded hands. She recalled riding back from Samoa on the *Madaket* on the Christmas Eve day she had fallen in love with Jack. Despite the cold, they sat outside the passenger cabin. The collar of her jacket fluttered against her face, and she kept her hands in the pockets to protect them. She did not know how she would tell her mother that she was in love. Indeed she had no idea at the moment how to define love, other than to sit on the bench and feel the joy of the last half-hour coursing through her heart. She kissed Jack goodbye on the dock, making him promise to call her that evening. Kissing him a second time, she lingered in the moment as long as she could, trying to study how it felt. The feel of his breathing on her throat caused her to lower her head to his shoulder, and the caress of his wool jacket against her cheek made her shiver.

A delicate, and difficult, unsettling ran through her. She felt lost, wanting just to remain with Jack. Her eyes could not rest on anything for more than a moment before darting away. Her breathing was incomplete. Going to work appeared as a dark barrier to her happiness. How could she put up with the nattering of her customers at Foy's Arcade, like that of her mother's friend Mrs. Jackson who, the day before, had not been able to decide between the red Christmas wrap and the green, or between the lollipop and the Christmas cane that could be tied into each bow? Of what importance could any of that be when Lauren wanted to be out walking somewhere with Jack, laughing in the cold air?

The masts of the fishing boats moored at the docks along First Street resembled stripped trees. She surveyed the black water. Love scattered her. For the first time in her life, Lauren faced the prospect of a Christmas day doting on her own unhappiness. On what usually was a wonderful occasion, Jack would be with his parents and Lauren would be with hers… lonely. Her heart already ached. All she wanted was to hold Jack's face between her hands, her eyes racing over his lips and eyes.

—

"Oh, Mother, it's so beautiful." Clara pointed at a pulpit that hung from an enormous pillar. "Is that where the priest gives the sermon?"

Lauren imagined, with warm pleasure, the gold vestments worn by the priest during a big Sunday High Mass here, hanging from his arms from the pulpit like emblazoned wings at rest.

A teenage girl entered the confessional to their left.

"God understand French, doesn't he." Clara whispered.

"Of course. Why?"

"I know He understands English. I just wondered whether He could do it in French, too."

Lauren sat back in the pew.

"Or if somebody had to translate for Him."

Amused, Lauren considered the possibility. "Who would He get to help?"

Clara smiled. "Joan of Arc?"

The organ began a dirge-like melody. With the music, the light seemed more precise to Lauren, and quite like a grudging processional.

"She heard all those voices, you know."

Lauren looked over her shoulder at the confessional booth. "Have you ever heard voices?"

"Me? No." Clara's smile turned to a grin.

"Really?"

"I don't believe in that stuff."

The organist began a long theme of solitary notes that soon were repeated. This time, though, he did not stop. It was a mournful fugue that, right away, grew bigger. It seemed to come from everywhere in the cathedral. Lauren laid her chin against her folded hands as she contemplated that slow contemplativeness.

She remembered the morning she had visited Jack, a few months after they had begun seeing each other. Her mother had already spoken with her, worried that she and Jack were getting too close. Lauren had told her mother not to worry, all the while barely able to wait until she could be with Jack again.

That morning, Jack's parents had gone for a walk on the Humboldt Bay jetty, and, without their knowledge, he had asked Lauren to come over. The bed clothing in his room had shined with the sunlight that came in the window. The wind pushed about the two Douglas firs outside his window, and they creaked as they moved. The light coming in the window illumined Lauren's green camisole, which was hung over the back of the chair in Jack's room. One of his shoes lay on the floor, on its side. She had never felt anything like what she was feeling at that moment.

Excitement washed over her, a voice hurrying through her heart, a kind of mad wish for Jack's happiness that swept her aside. The column of light fell half across Lauren's blouse, which was cast to the floor in a corner. She glanced at it, her hand grasping Jack's shoulder. She could barely tell where she was. Her body felt like it was sliding down a watery falls. The blouse was a luminous pool of light and shadow, white and veined in the sun. Jack caressed her back, and a jolt of sharp pleasure inundated her.

Interrupting Lauren's recollections, the curtain to the confessional was thrust aside, and the young girl came from it. She was weeping. The priest—a beefy man with glasses and a down-turned, slab-like mouth—stepped from the booth. He peered toward the altar, taking into his fingers the crucifix that hung from a cloth ribbon about his neck. He stepped toward Lauren and began speaking with her. He asked a question as he gestured toward the escaping girl.

"I'm sorry, Father, I don't speak French."

He spoke again, crabbily.

"I can't...."

The priest's face wrinkled with disapproval. He turned back toward the confessional.

Grumbling, Lauren heard gulps of breath coming from the girl as she approached a side door to the cathedral. Lauren descended to a confusion of brief, intense disdain for the priest.

WHEN CLARA WAS TWELVE

"What happened?" Clara looked back at the priest, who appeared insulted. "What'd he say?"

"I don't know." Lauren turned away, angry at herself for not being able to intervene for the girl. Clearly, she had confessed to being quite sinful in some way, and the priest had punished her with some snippy admonishment.

Lauren tried suppressing the swirl of rage that possessed her. So exposed in such a holy place, it would be even more sinful than usual to swear at a priest. No matter what the girl had told him, he did not understand the reason she had done whatever it was she had done. A priest couldn't possibly have a clue. *What a fool he is!*

It was always a surprise to Lauren to see how blurred priests could be. She would like to respect them without question, the way she had been told to as a child. Such grand, important men. But they were often so peevish. As during the Sunday meal Lauren had served to Bishop Hartigan from San Francisco just a year ago, who, while carrying on about the sins committed by Hollywood in those awful movies of theirs—"You know, that tramp down there, that what's-her-name, Marilyn Monroe."—also complained about Lauren's gravy. The gravy made Lauren feel a little cheap herself.

The trouble was, a priest could complain about anything he wanted to, but you could not complain about him. As a girl, Lauren had had such respect for the priesthood that she could not imagine arguing with one of them. But now...this Frenchman, chiding that poor girl for whatever indiscretion or foolishness she had told him about.

Lauren pondered the probability that the girl didn't speak English, a language that, had she confessed herself in it, would have rendered the priest dumbfounded. Lauren glanced at Clara. *And maybe God would have been dumfounded too.* Lauren smiled.

She remembered the frightened start she received when Father Keller opened the wooden panel in the confessional, the day she had gone to him to confess the mortal sin she had committed with Jack. The priest was an abrupt man, his graceless kindness a subject for joking among the parishioners. There was no subtlety to him, so that he did not lay the Communion Host on your tongue so much as he tossed it there. On occasion during Mass, he publicly chided an altar boy for missing some cue or other. This caused no difficulty with the parents of the altar boys, because Father Keller was a favorite of the servers themselves. He made them squirm with considerable good humor. But on that day in the confessional, as he leaned close to listen to Lauren, his head appeared to her like a dried-out skull, propped against the screen.

She struggled to control herself. She was there to tell the priest what had happened, and, worse, to seek forgiveness for it. She knew that the moment Jack touched her legs and caressed their skin—skin that she had been told so often by her mother she should never let any boy ever, ever even see—she knew that she had committed a terrible sin. But the bile in Lauren's throat was not simply the result of her fear, because she found happiness in the memory (also a sin, she worried) of Jack's embarrassed hugs and his own obvious nervousness.

She loved how kind he had been. She had been told that pleasure like she had felt with him, and the arrival of what she knew without question was real love...that all that was for married people, and even then it was only for making a baby. Otherwise it was a transgression against the word of God. But she could not believe that, for Jack and herself, sin was the only possibility.

So the heavy rasp of Father Keller's breathing intensified her embarrassment. In the same moment that she knew she had to tell him about it, she found she could not. She could not muster the appropriate self-condemnation. She began trembling as she wondered whether it would also be a sin to tell Father Keller that she regretted making love to Jack. It would be a sin because it would be a lie. She felt her heart race.

Her silence in the confessional finally angered the priest. "What is it, young lady?"

His impatient whisper terrified Lauren. "Oh, Father, I...I don't know."

"Speak up. What is it?"

Moaning, Lauren stood and hurried from the confessional out into the street. The knowledge of the sin remained hers alone.

She stood and took Clara's hand. The memory of Father Keller had deepened her resentment of the priest who had treated the Parisian girl so roughly. They moved toward the center aisle, intent on leaving.

"Oh, Mom." Clara nodded to the rear as the French priest approached them. They paused in the aisle next to the pew.

The cathedral had darkened as the sun had lowered, and was now filled with gloom. The priest spoke, holding his hands out before him. Lauren began to quiver, her eyes widening. As the priest murmured in French, he actually shrugged and placed a hand against his chest. His head nodded up and down, the wrinkles in the cloth of his cassock hardly visible at all. The shadows in his face resembled pieces of wire.

Lauren was frightened. But after a moment she sensed that he was trying to make some kind of amends. The tone of his voice softened, and a second shrug, accompanying a smile, implied a wish to explain himself.

Clara grimaced as the priest patted her shoulder. His teeth were quite crooked, and the thick plastic rims of his glasses obscured his eyes.

He's apologizing, Lauren thought.

Finally, the priest turned away. He returned to the confessional booth, where a line of parishioners still awaited him. He exchanged a few words with them, motioning toward Lauren and Clara. There was a grumble of deferential laughter.

Lauren led Clara toward the exit. Their hurrying up the main aisle felt to her like a passage through mud. She imagined herself as Moses stumbling over the bottom of the Red Sea, sea animals and salt-sludge clinging to her clothing and legs. Suddenly, Clara pulled Lauren to a halt. "Mom. Mom." She was whispering, her breath grainy with anxiety.

"What?"

"Where's that rose window, the one—"

"I don't know. It's…." Lauren looked up behind her, scanning the walls of the cathedral. Now, in the highest ceilings, there was no light at all.

"That's it." Clara pointed to the north wall. A great circle, intertwined throughout with curving stone and plaster, dominated the view. It was like a star, though the glass was gray and gray-black, with little of the color Lauren had mentioned. It seemed to have collapsed in upon itself, like a flat plane of mud and shale in pieces.

They hurried from the cathedral.

9

"Here we are." Martin entered Clara's room followed by a waiter in a white jacket carrying a tray. "Just for you."

The waiter laid the tray, which was lacquered in swirls of black, on the table in the bay window. There was a shiny tea service for one, made up of a pot, sugar bowl and creamer, all in silver. Gold *fleur-de-lys* formed a ring around the outer edge of each cup and saucer. Martin had also ordered a *mille feuille* for Clara, and she sat down at the table to study the pastry as the waiter transferred everything from the tray.

He laid out the folded cloth napkins on the table and carefully arranged the silverware. His smile was quite yellow. He looked to be about sixteen, and Clara did not find him in the least cute. He slouched, with sloping shoulders and very nervous eyes. He attempted practicing his English, which was no better than Clara's French. Only Clara understood it to be English, and she helped him pronounce the word "tip," which came out "teep." Irritated, Martin gave him a teep.

"Do you want some, Daddy?" Clara pointed to the *mille feuille*. She knew he was waiting to be asked.

"Sure, I'd have a little."

Clara took up a knife and fork and addressed the pastry. But the beauty of the thing put a momentary halt to the movement she made toward it. Her hands hovered over it. The pastry itself oozed. The confectioner's sugar that lay in a wintry dust across the top was of a desert-like dryness, while the creamy innards appeared to pulse.

Clara held the pastry secure with the fork. She pushed her knife through it, and the cream came out the sides in a deluge. The *mille feuille*'s layers ended up broken, like parts of a destroyed wall.

Satisfied, Clara picked up the plate and handed it to her father, with a fork.

Martin scraped a few pieces from the plate, and savored them. He watched Clara a moment as she continued dissecting the pastry. His caring for her was evident in the smile that flashed across his lips.

Martin left, giving her a light kiss on the cheek. It pained Clara to worry, as she had so often before, that she was not nearly as attractive as her mother. Martin was always...*Gosh*, Clara thought, searching the word...enthralled by Lauren's beauty, a fact that always made Clara feel a little lumpy by comparison. Lauren herself did not agree with Clara, and lauded her looks whenever the two of them were looking in a mirror together. Clara fretted that she did not have blonde hair, as her mother did. Also, some of Clara's friends at school really *were* pretty, and seemed so confident of the things they talked about that Clara wondered if they ever got mad at themselves or got spinach stuck between their teeth or came in third or fourth in whatever race they were running in P.E.

He's so sweet to her, Clara thought. Her mother often told her how nice Martin made her feel, before a party or when they were going out to dinner. He frequently complimented Lauren and brought her flowers, or took her arm at odd moments in a simple exchange of affection. The strange thing, though, was that he often was so...well, *not* sweet to Lauren as well, especially when she was indulging him.

Lauren took remarkable care of Martin, making sure everything was right for him before she did anything for herself. Clara thought this was as it should be. A wife is supposed to be nice to her husband, Clara thought, and give him things, like the right kind of cereal in the morning and bacon cooked well done. All sorts of stuff. Shirts ironed. Compliments paid. All the women did those things for their husbands. It was kindness.

Though Clara sometimes thought to herself how lucky her father was to have married her mother. Lauren was so beautifully slim, a model in a magazine, while her father was like a vibrant factory, with such serious intent. He was eighteen years older than Lauren. When he ran his fingers through her hair, he was quite attentive to her, thoughtful of her. So Clara knew that her mother loved her father. She saw it every day. There was a glance, a look on Lauren's face, that showed an active tenderness and regard that warmed Clara's heart whenever she saw it. And she saw it frequently. When Martin announced a family trip or brought a present home to Lauren, or when he presented her with the special Christmas gift he gave her every year, the one for which he asked Clara to prepare the card, it was love. Clara knew it was.

She felt it for her father herself when she watched him polishing the Buick in the driveway in Eureka or standing up to shout when the San Francisco Forty-Niners scored a touchdown on the radio. She tried to imitate the look Lauren gave him, hoping that her eyes brightened like Lauren's did, the lashes standing out like shining petals.

Love.

The white curtains blew from the window in a breeze, and then settled, luxuriously, back down. Clara looked out and spotted Jack's *deux-chevaux* pulling up before the hotel. It was black and spotted with rust. He got out of the car and walked around to the other door, which he opened. A young woman in a long black skirt and sandals got out. She and Jack spoke with each other a moment, until Jack took her in his arms and embraced her. She laughed, kissing Jack on the cheek, and walked alone up the sidewalk.

Who is that? Clara leaned out the window to watch. The woman turned the corner onto the Rue Saint-Honoré, and Clara remained in the sunlight a moment, dazzled by the dark blue sky above. *Is that Jack's girlfriend?*

Clara turned and stepped toward the armoire mirror. Her long hair, which was much more curly than her mother's and dark brown, was gathered up into a ponytail in one of Lauren's tortoise-shell barettes. She glanced over her face. It had none of the perfection of Lauren's, and little of its soft openness, with her almost ceramic skin. Clara's eyes pleased her, however, as large as they were, with a light-filled clarity that everybody talked about. Clara felt she had that, at least.

She looked down at the legs coming from her white undershorts. She turned to the side, to see if anything were shapely, anything secretly new. But there was nothing new. Except, she sensed, for the feeling of her mother and father racing through her in her blood and the warm sunlight of Paris and the loveliness of her own eyes.

The phone rang.

"*Mademoiselle, Monsieur* Roman is here," the operator said. "He is in the lobby."

"*Merci*." Hanging up, Clara reached for the skirt on the bed. She thought it must be fun to go around painting all day and sitting in cafes with *mille feuilles* everywhere. She imagined herself as one of those women she had seen in the Lartigue book in Jack's studio, sitting at a table in front of the Cafe Deux Cygnes in a big flowered hat, beautiful beyond all description.

—

A children's playground formed a kind of noisy stage set below the buttressed rear of Notre-Dame. Jack parked the *deux-chevaux* in front of the Café Saint-Regis, the tables before which looked out on the cathedral and the Left Bank beyond.

"I'll just be a minute," he said. He pointed to a street corner in the direction of the right bank. "This is the street… the Rue Saint-Louis-en-l'Île."

Seated in back, Clara attempted adjusting her knees, which were jammed up against the front seat. "Where the ice cream store is?" A cloth bag next to her rattled with bottles of wine.

When Jack turned to smile at her, she saw for a moment the regret in his looks that her mother had once noted to her. He ran his fingers through his graying hair. His eyes were finely structured, with sagging lines and shadows here and there. Indeed for Clara they were not necessarily unhappy. So blue that they reminded Clara of the sky itself, they contained a watery lilt and movement that was rendered romantic by the enormous beret he was wearing. They glimmered when he laughed, and sunk into sea-like darkness when he was chagrined by something. That his dress was so elegantly shabby made him even more attractive to Clara. His cravats, suede shoes, and turtleneck sweaters were unusually dashing, even though they sometimes needed mending.

He pushed the bag of wine bottles to the side, to make more room for Clara to get out of the car. "I got these for tonight. It's wine from an old friend of mine. An Algerian, over by where I live. Malouf's his name."

Clara smiled at him.

"Berthillon's up there." Jack pointed ahead into the street, and then secured the car brake. "On the right hand side. But go to the Pont de Sully, at the far end. There's a park there. Beautiful view of the Seine. And then I'll meet you at the ice cream store." He opened the door. "I'm going into the Regis here to make a reservation for us, for tonight." He nodded toward the cafe.

Clara walked the Rue Saint-Louis-en-l'Île. She had on a bright blue skirt with petticoats, and a white blouse with a lace-bordered bodice. She wore the new sandals she had bought a few days before at Galeries Lafayette, the ones that, she hoped, made her look like a French girl herself. It was a sunny day, the air itself so hot that there seemed to be a kind of baked tension in it. There was no discrepancy in the blue of the sky. It formed a metallic canopy over the soot-blackened buildings that ran up either side of the street.

She came to the Pont de Sully and passed through a low iron gate into the small park. Above, the trees moved about slowly in a hot afternoon breeze. They caressed one another, moved away, and touched once more.

Clara walked to the end of the park, which was a tight triangle that overlooked the end of the island. Below on the quay, a shirtless Frenchman fished in the Seine. He wore long pants and leather shoes. He had a tattoo on his arm, a mustache, and a cigarette hanging from his lips. Cargo barges passed by, moving so slowly in the heat that even the clothes that had been hung out to dry by the wives of the barge men seemed barely to move.

Clara turned toward a bench that faced back into the park. The trees continued moving, and the sound of them made her dreamily lazy, the way she would be at home in a hammock at their summer place on the Eel River. Watching the aspen trees quivering gold to green to gold, swirling against a backdrop of Douglas fir and redwoods, solemn trees that barely moved with the wind far away, she would fall asleep suspended in the warm, pure air.

From the corner of her eye, she noticed a young couple—high school kids, she guessed—seated several benches down from hers. The boyfriend was kissing his girlfriend's throat, and he had his hands inside her blouse.

She herself seemed dazed. She leaned back on the bench, her eyes closed. Her tongue wetted her lips, and she caressed the bench arm with the fingers of her hand. Her book bag lay crumpled on the ground, and one of the books had fallen out onto the sand. The boyfriend kissed her hair, and his hands fumbled within her blouse like small, excited animals.

The girl sighed, almost as if she were in some sort of pain.

Clara imagined, briefly and astonished, how she would feel if a boyfriend touched her like that. Even just the idea of it had to be a Personal. She pursed her lips, looking down at the ground. Her face reddened. This was something about which she could never talk to her mother.

Clara glanced again at the couple, a little guilty for doing so. A kind of shudder seized the neck and shoulders of the girl as her boyfriend kissed her lips.

Clara felt that the girl should knock her boyfriend's hands away. But to Clara's astonishment, she actually extended her own hand about the back of his neck, pulled him toward her, and kissed him back, lost entirely in the privacy and secret of her wish for him.

Trying not to look, Clara fled from the park, intent on Berthillon.

A long line of people stood outside a shop halfway up the island on the left. Dressed in shirtsleeves, they fanned themselves with newspapers, read books, and conversed. Other customers came out of the shop door with ice cream cones in their hands, and the line progressed.

When Clara arrived at the end of the line, she was startled by a brash whistle and laughter coming from across the street. Three Frenchmen leaned against the side of a large black truck. They were coal deliverymen who were everywhere the same color. They wore no shirts, though each of them had a black apron that covered his chest and the front of his pants. Their skin was caked with coal dust, and their eyes seemed to be hidden within their faces...small, devilish fissures. Taking a break for a smoke, they had been watching Clara's arrival. They surveyed her as if she were an exotic peacock in a zoo. Clara shrugged, looking away, and grimaced at the rise in laughter as one of the men made some rude French remark that she did not understand.

Leave me alone.

There was another whistle, and one of them pointed at the front of his pants.

Just don't look.

She worried that she must have done something wrong, that maybe American girls did not know how to act in France. Clara glanced once more at the men, angry at their rudeness, and turned away as she saw that they wouldn't leave her alone. The line moved very slowly. She examined the cracks and ruts in the wall of the building before her, still tersely aware of the men across the way. She looked up the line, to see how far she was from Berthillon's doorway. There, she figured, she would find relief from the workmen, who had now grown sullen. They were involved in their cigarettes, though they continued looking at Clara with lowered heads, silent glances, and lewd, crummy smiles.

Up ahead in line, a man and woman were kissing each other, oblivious of the others. They were in their twenties. The man, who was very good-looking and sort of dark, Clara thought, with too much curly black hair and a small beard...although he *was* good-looking...opened his lips and secreted his tongue into the woman's mouth.

Clara looked away. But she glanced back at them. The woman leaned against the building, put her hands around the man's waist, and pulled him close. She wore a light short-sleeved blouse and a long black skirt. Her sandals were like Clara's. A cloth bag hung from her arm, in which she carried some books.

Clara recognized her. The shape of her eyes, and their clarity—a light green intensity and directness—seemed quite familiar. But, for the moment, Clara could not remember where she had seen her.

She studied the cigarette in the woman's hand, and how her fingers rested so comfortably on the sleeve of her boyfriend's long-sleeved shirt. The cigarette was a natural-seeming part of the tableau, a sophistication that thrilled Clara. It represented a kind of un-sinful lasciviousness. The woman's fingers traced the stitching along the rear belt loops of his pants. She pulled him toward her.

The line moved on. When the couple stopped arm in arm at the doorway to the shop, Clara watched how the woman moved her hand lower, over the back of her companion's slacks. She smoked her cigarette with what seemed to Clara to be unaffected self-assurance.

"I hope she knows," a woman behind Clara muttered in an American accent, to two teenage girls standing with her. They were watching the couple with the same veiled intensity as Clara's.

"Knows what, Mom?" one of the girls said.

The woman scowled, changing her shopping bag from one hand to the next. "What men do."

Clara's face grew hot.

"You girls need to remember that. Pregnancy and so on."

Clara became embarrassed. People who got pregnant were like her mother...older, congratulated whenever it happened, showered with presents, and always married. Of course there were the bad high school girls who suddenly disappeared and whose fate was then discussed by all the other girls, and the boys, too, laughing about it. Sadly, there were the poor girls from broken homes who ended up at the Florence Crittendon Society, to which Lauren donated ten dollars every year at Christmas.

"Don't ever do things like that, you girls." The woman pulled a cigarette from her purse and lit it, suddenly turning from the conversation with her daughters, who, like Clara, looked on with surreptitious intrigue.

Clara arrived at the head of the line. There was movement across the way. One of the workmen crossed the street toward her. Very young, he carried a cigarette between his index finger and his thumb. An eye was disfigured...half-closed and very puffy. The other men watched his progress with gleeful rudeness. Clara turned toward the building, her back to the street. When the workman approached her, his voice was high and thin, and Clara realized he was only a few years older than she.

He said some French things that she couldn't understand. But his tone of voice was lurid, and the downturn in his mouth very disrespectful. To Clara's surprise, a tear slid down her cheek. It infuriated her, and she punched the boy in the arm. "Go away!"

He flinched and threw up a hand to protect himself.

"Creep!"

The boy dropped the cigarette. Glancing at it, he muttered a few things in Clara's direction, gesturing at her.

Clara wiped a sweaty splotch of coal dust from her knuckles. But now it stuck to both hands, so that she felt even more soiled. She felt very foolish. "Go away" meant nothing. That was what you said to a fly buzzing your ear, even though in that moment her voice had sounded surprisingly sharp to her, unkind, even aggressive. She had been struck by its acidity. To be sure, no one had ever flinched at anything she had ever said. Certainly not some dumb teenage idiot.

A few of the people in line protested the boy's intrusion on her, and he retreated across the street. He shook his head, and his companions broke out laughing once more.

Clara was astonished by what she had done. Before, she had always thought the best thing to do was to ignore things that bothered you. That's what her mother always said. If you get all steamed up about things, Lauren would say, men won't like you.

Clara had agreed. But just now, with a kind of new, brazen.... Clara felt soiled. She felt victorious.

When she entered the shop, she took up a crumpled copy of *Le Monde* that a previous customer had left on a table inside the door. She wiped her hands, and the coal dust smirched the photo of Nikita Kruschev, who was smiling gat-toothed from the front page.

The young couple passed Clara by, heading out the door. They each had an ice cream cone, and Clara noticed right away that there was only a single scoop, and that it was drearily small, not at all like the huge ice creams Clara got at Bonboniere's in Eureka. But the only flavors at Bonboniere's were vanilla and rocky-road, neither of which had such profoundly vivid colors as the ice creams the couple had. The woman's was very dark blue, and reminded Clara of the glass milk pitcher Lauren had gotten on her honeymoon. Her boyfriend's ice cream was blood-red, like early blackberries.

The couple passed out to the sidewalk.

The woman behind the counter addressed Clara in French. Clara contemplated the flavors. She did not know the word for blueberry, and reached into her purse for her pocket dictionary. Hurrying through the pages, she found the word just as the woman behind her in line received the tiny cone she had ordered. Clara looked up from the book.

The counter-woman was about forty, quite short and plump, wearing a brown cotton dress with a dark blue apron. Her hair was carefully curled and blonde. She wore vivid, burgundy-colored lipstick.

Clara pronounced the word for blueberry, and laughter broke out in the shop.

"*Comment?*" The woman chuckled.

Clara looked around and found that all the customers were watching her, all of them amused by the way she had spoken. Her throat seemed to seize. She could not say it again.

"*Vous desirez, mademoiselle?*"

Clara gathered herself and struggled to get the word out once more, and it came from her in a strangled sort of way. There was a cloudy look on the woman's face.

"You know," Clara said, embarrassed. "Blueberry."

The woman smiled, but it was clear to Clara that she didn't understand.

"Oh...." Clara groaned and looked again at the book. She placed the dictionary on the counter and pointed at the word.

"Ah! *Myrtille!*" The woman looked toward the man working with her behind the counter. "*Ces jeune anglaises, Jean-Paul. Comme elles sont mignonnes!*" She turned back to Clara. "You are from Lon-dohne?"

"No. From Eureka." Clara said, relieved by the woman's turn to English.

"That is where?" The "z" with which the woman pronounced the first word gave it a kind of electric zip.

"California. The United States."

"You are *americaine?*"

"Yes."

"Oally-wood?"

"What?"

"Uh...uh, Jean Wayne? Coh-boys?"

"Yes," Clara said. "Hollywood."

The counter woman smiled, then opened the freezer before her and scooped out a quadruple portion of blueberry for Clara. The ice cream cone was enormous, the equal to anything served up at Bonbonierre's.

"Then, this is for you." The woman smiled, handing the cone to Clara. "We luf the coh-boys."

Clara surveyed the cone.

"*Vive les americains!* They help us so much in the war."

"Wow." Clara reached into the pocket of her skirt and brought out money for the cone.

"*Merci,*" the woman said, drawing out the last syllable into an aspirated remnant.

Clara, grasping the change, turned toward the door.

"*Au revoir, chéri!*"

"Eh, *mademoiselle*." The voice startled Clara. She looked back over her shoulder. The coal delivery boy had followed her. His friends remained on the opposite sidewalk and watched as Clara hurried her pace up the street.

The boy kept on talking, as though the cold shoulder that Clara so obdurately gave him was something he could not believe, or understand, like what she now said to him in English.

"Go away, twirp."

He reached out and knocked Clara's ice cream to the pavement.

"Leave me alone!"

The boy began laughing at her.

"Get out of here!" Clara's face brimmed with liquid, and she began quaking. She could no longer speak.

The boy kicked the ice cream cone aside, then moved about to face Clara directly, cutting off her path. He spoke as he had spoken before, some kind of nasty-sounding French drivel. But he spoke this time with passion, and Clara realized he was actually angry. Clara wanted to sock him once more. But she was afraid to, as the boy now put his hand up on the front of the building to block her way completely.

"Get out of here!" she said once more, her voice muddy with fear.

But she got pushed aside. Jack grabbed the boy and forced him backwards. In the struggle, Jack's beret fell to the sidewalk. Clara cried out as she stumbled against the building, and the boy threw up his arms. Jack pushed him toward the curb, and he fell back against a Citroen sedan that was parked like a black bathtub in a space before the shop. Jack gripped the front of the boy's apron and uttered a string of epithets in French that was spattered, just once, with a word Clara had never heard. She nonetheless understood it simply from the ferocity with which Jack shouted it out.

"Fecker!"

Clara laughed and covered her mouth.

The boy batted at Jack's sleeve, backing away a few steps into the street. He made a sign…his left hand grabbing the bend of his right arm, the right fist straight up in the air. He sniveled at Jack in a gravelly voice.

Jack appeared at this moment quite storm-tossed. He had prevailed. He grew bigger as he glared at the retreating boy. His hair flew everywhere. To Clara, his head seemed weather-scarred and buffeted by a tempest. The other workmen remained where they were, obviously intimidated by him.

"And you're a gobshite," Jack said. He brushed his hands of coal dust.

Again, Clara giggled.

The boy approached his friends in a saunter, muttering some insults. Clara feared he might return with them. But to her relief they climbed into their truck and began driving away.

"Where *were* you?" Her hands curled into fists at her sides. She glanced at her ice cream, now a piled up puddle on the sidewalk.

"I was trying to make a reservation, wasn't I?" Jack checked over his coat.

"That boy was bothering me."

"I know, Clara. Frenchmen are like that. But, I saved you. So, all's well that ends—"

"Why didn't you save me sooner?"

Jack reached back to finger a tear in his coat. "Clara, I'm sorry I left you here on your own. I shouldn't have taken so long, but the owner of the cafe didn't want to give me a reservation. The idiot's been an idiot for years. It's just that he runs the best kitchen on this end of the island, and I wanted you and your parents to at least get one good meal while you're here." Jack straightened his tie. "And he never did give me a reservation."

Clara pointed down the street. "But that boy…." The coal truck rounded the corner.

"Were you scared?"

"No!" Clara grimaced. "Well…yes."

"Are you scared now?"

Clara tightened her lips, wishing to somehow get away from Jack.

"Come on. I'll get you another ice cream and take you to the hotel."

"I don't want to go back."

"Clara—"

"Can't I just walk around? I've got my Metro tickets."

"Clara."

"Oh…" Clara's lips bunched tightly.

"I'm not going to leave you alone again."

"Oh, all right."

10

A few days later, Clara and Martin visited the Jardin des Plantes, and she asked him if she could ride back to the hotel on the Metro alone. "I want to see if I can—"

"Figure it out. You think you can do it?"

"Daddy...."

Martin shrugged. "Okay. But be careful." He pointed toward the Quai Saint-Bernard. "I'm going to walk back."

They parted at the gate from the gardens, having looked over the map in Clara's *Michelin Guide.* She crossed the Pont d'Austerlitz and headed for the Quai de la Rapée Metro.

At the end of the ride, Clara felt flattened, as though her face had been shoved around by all the lumpy shoulders pressing against it. The Metro pulled into the Concorde station. As she exited the car with hundreds of other people, a residue of dog-like odor remained on her, making her feel very beat up.

She scurried up the station stairs and walked toward the Place Vendôme. She wanted to take a bath. She turned down the Rue de Rivoli where, at the end of the first block, a cafe sprawled out onto the sidewalk. The waiters went in and out the door with trays over their heads. They reminded Clara of scurrying statues of liberty. Some of the patrons sat alone reading newspapers, but at most tables, groups of people sat in close conversation, unaware of the surrounding noise.

Clara's eyes paused on one couple at the far end of the terrace. The man's large hand rested on the woman's, and he leaned forward to speak with her. The woman was very agitated, as though she did not want to listen. She was extraordinarily lovely. She shook her head, but her hand remained beneath his. She listened carefully, and her eyes widened with intent, almost painful, interest. Then, in a slow movement that was barely perceptible from such a distance, she turned her hand palm up and took that of her companion.

She wore a long green skirt and white blouse, with a gold star-shaped pin and black pumps.

Clara retreated to one of the pillars near the curb, which supported the arcade. She peered around it at the couple once more. Her heart was in actual pain, a hurt of near panic as she watched her mother steal a glance at the passing traffic.

Lauren removed her hand from Jack's. For a moment she could not look at him. Jack leaned forward again, speaking intently, his hands held out before him in further explanation. Lauren shook her head. Clara could tell what she was saying, watching her lips form the simple word "No," followed by "Please, no."

She could not take her eyes off them. The design of Lauren's Dior skirt and the blouse seemed informal enough for the afternoon, even though their stylishness was not lost on a few of the other women seated at other tables. Lauren stood out from the rest of the cafe clientele. Indeed, she was isolated from them by the intensity of her startling eyes and the vernal Irish green of the skirt she was wearing and the puffed short sleeves of the white blouse. Others in the cafe were watching her as well. Lauren reminded Clara of a slim, opening rose, a demure, definite coming-to-flower. Most of the patrons were dressed in blues, browns and blacks despite the warm weather. The small marble table at which Jack and Lauren sat, the two cups of coffee, and the small plates—one in front of Jack, with the remains of a cream pastry like little scraps of tawdry laughter making fun of Clara's confusion; the other, with one of her mother's favorite foods, an artichoke, untouched—caused Clara to close her eyes, feeling betrayed, yet trying to expel the betrayal from her heart. When she opened her eyes again, Jack had folded his hands before him on the table. He remained silent. Then, slowly, he ran the fingers of one hand through his hair. His eyes were cast down sadly, his head at an angle.

Clara lay her cheek next to the pillar. A smudge of dirt rubbed off on her chin, which she wiped away. Lauren placed both her hands on Jack's. Clara's heart fell into chaos as Lauren leaned forward and kissed his lips.

Then, to Clara's dismay, the kiss lingered, their lips parting so slowly that the tenderness of it appeared to grow even as it ended. Lauren sat back in her chair and looked out into the street. Her eyes appeared feverish and very happy.

11

The lobby floated downward from the hotel lift, which was a curved cage made of shiny brass metalwork. The window in Clara's room had been opened slightly by a maid, for the air, and yellow dusk sunlight shined across the table inside.

A note rested on the table, next to a vase of roses that Clara was certain had been ordered by her mother, especially once she read the note itself. *Clara... We're going to dinner at 7:30 for dinner. Jack's choice!*

Lauren had neglected to sign it.

Clara ran a bubble bath. When she stepped into the tub, the bubbles settled about her like clouds. She had brought nothing to read. She wanted just to lie in the water and dream, not wanting to think about what she had just seen.

But she could not dream.

The kiss she had witnessed had taken Clara's heart, as it constituted a flame that made her heart recoil. Jack and her mother had been like the couple in the park. They were careless, free.... No one else knew about it except Clara, and she wanted to run from the responsibility of it. How could she tell her father? How could she talk to her mother? What could she say at all?

She grimaced, shoving the thought from her mind.

Then the recollection of the kids in the park came to her again. Clara thought young women were supposed to be demure and resisting, like they were in the movies with Doris Day. *But that girl... the way she just grabbed him. And especially the way she looked when he was....*

Clara shivered.

When he was feeling her up.

When the girl's eyes were open, which was not often, they had a glazed look that lacked any kind of focus. *It's like she was having some kind of vision,* Clara thought. *Sighs flying around.*

Clara pushed the water about with her hands, her nerves relieved by the warm swirl. She took a clean washcloth from the rack next to the tub and dried her hands with it. It was white and very soft, and the hotel's initials "HR" were embroidered in it, in a medallion-like script. Clara dropped the cloth into the water, wrung it out, and washed her face with it.

That the eyes of the girl in the park had been closed had made her appear to be in a dream, despite the dishevelment of the blouse she wore, which was partially pulled from the waistband of her skirt. Her face was entirely composed, and her lips were made up into a smile of such clarity that Clara herself had felt guiltily envious of it.

When Clara walked from the park, her stomach was tingling. At the iron gate, she glanced once more at the couple. The fingers of the girl's hand made a circle about her companion's cheek as he kissed her wrist.

Clara imagined her father's face, were she to tell him about her mother and Jack...his large eyes hurt and his mouth turned down, hidden by his right hand. The fingers would curve across his lips, and he would let out a silent sigh. Martin did all these things when he was unhappy. But this unhappiness would be terrifying, and Clara could not possibly know what he would do. *He might get mad at me!* she thought, and she fretted that he would slap her or tell her to shut her mouth, that she was lying.

She couldn't tell him.

Clara tried putting it all out of her mind again. But her anguish remained, like a vice imprisoning her in the tub. She lay back and let the water turn about her. She wetted her lips with her tongue and flicked away a bead of sweat from her forehead.

She lay the washcloth over her chest and raised herself out of the water. The cloth was glued to her by the soapy bubbles, and she thought she looked like Marilyn Monroe, maybe, when her dresses just covered her secret places.

But Marilyn Monroe's not it, Clara thought. She wanted to be more like Audrey Hepburn. Grace Kelly. Clara wanted a more elegant look, with jewelry and soft light and flowers. Like her mother. So, as she readjusted the washcloth and sunk back into the bath, letting the cloth float on the surface of the water so that it just caressed her—which caused her this time to tingle all over—she imagined herself in the City of Light, dancing at the foot of Sacré-Coeur with some handsome man, taking his hand just as Lauren had taken Jack's....

She pushed the washcloth aside.

—

After cocktails in her parents' room, the family descended the lift to wait for Jack in the lobby. Martin was dressed in a dark brown suit and tie. Lauren had put on a black silk dress that came down to the middle of her calf, nylon stockings with a thick black seam down the back, and black pumps. She let Clara carry the light silk jacket that she planned to wear to the restaurant.

Clara sat with Lauren in the lobby, but was unable to get her mother to say much. Lauren was distracted, and Clara's efforts to speak with her brought only hasty replies. She held Clara's hand. But Lauren's own hand was sweating, and there was so little to the affection that Clara worried that her mother was angry with her.

A few minutes later, a taxi pulled up before the hotel, and Jack walked into the lobby. He smiled at Clara. Taking Martin's hand, Jack shook his head back and forth. "You know, Martin, Clara's fearless."

"I know. She negotiated the Metro today by herself."

Lauren sighed and fiddled with her purse.

"I could have used her today when I was making the dinner arrangements." Jack looked down at the floor. Clara noted that he had not yet paid any attention to her mother. His eyes actually glimmered as he brought a small card from his coat pocket. It was from a restaurant called *Les deux palestiniens*, on Boulevard de Clichy. At the top of the sheet it showed two crossed curved swords.

"It's Arab," Jack said, watching Martin peruse the card. He glanced briefly at Lauren. "Stuffed grape leaves. Spinach Pie. Goat cheese."

As the taxi approached the Place de Clichy, Clara rolled down the window. Traffic crowded past in a roar. The neighborhood appeared to be filled with restaurants and cafes, and all were filled with customers. The interiors were yellowed by the light. Each was jammed with festivity.

At Jack's suggestion, the driver pulled to a stop.

"I thought we'd walk a block or two to the restaurant, because the crowd here is interesting." Jack turned to Clara. "But hold on to your purse."

Thrilled, Clara grabbed hers and looked out the window again as the taxi stopped at the curb.

Walking ahead with Jack, Lauren glistened with laughter. Men walking in the opposite direction glanced at her, and then turned to watch as she continued up the sidewalk. Clara stuck close to her father. There were so many men in the street that she worried for her mother's safety. A lot of the men laughed to each other about Lauren, moved by her beauty. They were rude and gruff, in French and Arabic, and they did not seem to care that they could be heard. Clara did not understand them, though she knew very well what they were saying.

But in the partial light of the street, Clara could see that Lauren had become pale. Clara wondered if she were afraid as well. Her animated talk covered up the fact that she did not look very well.

"So Clara, what do you think of Paris so far?" Martin took Clara's arm on his own. He had shown real interest in her enjoyment of their trip, and just now he was very happy, Clara thought, though the lights from the street threw shadows across his face that made him look even older than he was.

Clara was crazy about him, wanting to please him in everything. But she lamented his occasional disinterest in her schoolwork and the projects she had. Apparently Martin thought that those things were to be shared only by women. Art projects, Jerry Lee Lewis and riding a bike to the store were matters of no importance to him.

Indeed, he had once observed to Clara when he had found her in a hammock reading a novel—*The Wizard of Oz* by L. Frank Baum—that he didn't like to read novels himself because they had nothing to do with life.

"Politics and business, Clara. That's what I like. If you were a man, you'd understand that."

The trouble was that Jack Roman was a man, and he did not seem to care about either of those things. Surrounded by the clutter of his studio, where there was color everywhere, and where, it seemed, a windfall of a few extra *francs* resulted in a visit to some quaint cafe for a coffee in the afternoon sun, Jack never even mentioned politics and business.

But here in Paris, Martin did seem more willing to have such a coffee himself. He had even gone with Clara to explore the junk store she had found in the Place des Vosges. He had waited for her, seated in a chair while she examined a chipped porcelain doll, covered with grime, that she had discovered on a lower shelf in a back corner. The empire style dress the doll wore was threadbare with age.

Martin told her that he guessed the figure was from the turn of the century. "You can tell from the costume."

"Oh, no, Daddy. It's from a long time before that." Clara tapped the doll's wig, which was piled up over her head in many levels. Dust flew about, and small parts of the wig fell to the floor. "She's like that lady in the painting we saw at the Louvre. What's her name? The Duchess of Devonshire?"

Clara wanted the doll badly. It would be something she could keep in the closet of her new bedroom, to be brought out when she was by herself simply for the memories of Paris it would bring to her. She glanced at her father.

"Oh, yes." Martin took his wallet from his coat. "I guess you're right."

The warmth in his eyes as he paid for the doll surprised Clara. She placed a hand in his as he awaited his change, her other hand holding the paper-wrapped doll. Her father was often distracted. He seldom gave Clara much time. But she knew he loved her anyway, and she felt that all she had to do was to love him in return in order to have his affection forever.

"You know, I love Paris," she said as they strode now up the Boulevard de Clichy. "Especially when we all get to do things together."

They passed a club called the *Cabaret d'Enfer*, and were distracted by music coming from the entry. A curtain covered the left half of the doorway, but Clara glimpsed what was going on inside.

A woman danced on a small stage, her body barely covered by chiffon scarves and flashing gold costume jewelry. She was barefoot, and she shook her hips so slowly, in such circles, that she reminded Clara of the winter seas off Humboldt Bay and Eureka. The chiffon the dancer held to her face hid everything but her eyes. The eyes themselves flashed with such black intensity that Clara abruptly stopped in the doorway to watch.

A dark man in a fez stepped out from behind the curtain, shaking his head at Clara, and she moved away. But she was held back by her father. Martin continued watching the dancer. The woman's skin was lit by red and gold spotlights. Her belly, hips, and breasts all seemed to be the same size, and they moved in even more contemplative surges of seawater.

"Come on, Daddy." Clara pulled at his hand.

But Martin wished to remain a moment longer. Clara looked up at the facade of the club. The entrance formed a kind of face, with two bloodied, crazy eyes staring out at the street above a set of enormous teeth. The plaster had disintegrated in places, so that rusting wire broke from the gums. The doorway formed the figure's mouth, down the sides of which hung fake stalactites that were fallen apart as well and covered with street dirt. Small relief sculptures represented sinners, dozens of them, writhing with terror as they tumbled down into the inferno.

"Daddy."

"Okay, I'm coming." They continued up the street.

Sammy was the *maitre d'* at *Les Deux Palestineans*. He had very large lips and was exceedingly charming. He showed them to a window table. Sammy spoke English as well as French, and Jack explained that he was Christian, and had gone to a British colonial school in Jerusalem as a child. After seating everyone, Sammy retreated to the kitchen. He came back after a moment with one rose each for Lauren and Clara. "For the most beautiful women in Paris." He walked about the table. "Monsieur Roman knows our food very well. He is, *alors*, a connaisseur, as we say." He tapped Jack's shoulder. "That is so, no?"

Sammy snapped a finger toward the kitchen, and several waiters came through the door bearing trays laden with food. Clara was struck by the richness of the light that came up from the small dishes as they were placed on the table. The first was a circle of *taramasalada* in a swirled pattern, with an enclave of black olives in the center. There was a salad of red lettuce, red onions, blood-red tomatoes and white cheese, sprinkled with olive oil. Then, for each person, a tiny dish of *hummus*, in the center of which was a pool of olive oil sprinkled with red-orange paprika. Sammy himself took a platter of grape leaves filled with rice and lamb from one of the waiters and placed it in the middle of the table. They looked like green cigar butts, Clara thought. After sampling one of them, she let the cigar idea go, and took two from the platter.

Looking around at the other dishes, she chose a *spanokopeta*, some wrinkly green olives that were dotted with shards of garlic, and, following Jack's lead, a piece of the soft round bread that was piled up like doilies on a separate platter, glistening with olive oil.

"Don't eat too much, though," Jack said, "because the main course is coming."

Clara could not imagine a main course, because the food on the table was already of such festive proportions. The tastes of it were like the colors. The *tarama* was pungently sour, yet so soft on her palate that she took a second portion of it right away. All the other foods were quickly sought after by everyone.

After several minutes, a waiter brought out a platter piled with chicken and vegetables, on some kind of yellow rice. The chicken had been overcooked, so that it was a yellow-white slickness impaled on slippery bones. There were sliced tomatoes, like sagging lips, all around the edge of the platter.

"It is *cous-cous*." Sammy armed himself with two large serving spoons. "I will serve you." He placed one such spoonful on the plate before Lauren.

Suddenly, Lauren brought a handkerchief from her purse and began wiping her brow. She leaned forward over the table. Her skin appeared to be covered in clear oil.

"Mom, what's wrong?"

"I've got to go back to the hotel." She whispered. Her face sagged.

Clara took the handkerchief from her and daubed her brow with it. The others stopped eating as well, quickly concerned about Lauren.

"Come with me, will you, Clara?"

"Sure, but are you okay, Mom?"

"No, I feel awful."

Lauren took the handkerchief back and brought it to her lips. She was breathing quickly, and her skin was very cold. Clara looked around the table. Martin and Jack had been talking, and only now did Martin notice the crisis. He stood and came around the table, his napkin hanging from a hand. He put an arm about Lauren's shoulder.

"Don't touch me."

"What's wrong, Lauren?"

"Just leave me alone."

"But what did I—"

"It's not you, Martin. I just have to go." Lauren stood, taking Clara by the hand.

Sammy beckoned to a waiter and pointed to the entry. "Yes, we'll have a taxi for you right away."

"Lauren—"

"She's just sick, Daddy." Clara took up her purse and, readying herself to leave, looked across the table at Jack. Ignored all this time, he sat quite still. He too was pale, though his eyes were intent...indeed, motionless as he watched Lauren's distress. The plates of food were arrayed before him in ruined festivity.

Martin reached for Lauren's coat. "Come on, I'll—"

"Just leave me alone. I want Clara to take me back to the hotel."

During the silent ride home, Lauren almost fainted. While Clara went to the front desk for the room keys, Lauren sat down in the lobby, exhausted. She leaned her forehead against the fingers of one hand, and Clara sensed that she wanted to hide, to be left alone, the way Clara herself wished to be when she was being criticized by her parents. Clara wanted to get her mother into bed and to have the hotel call a doctor.

Once they arrived in her parents' room, Clara helped her mother get undressed, and then hurried back to the lobby.

"My mother needs a doctor, please."

The clerk, a doleful man with dark bags beneath his eyes, looked down at her in fidgety silence. The bags appeared to be sweating.

"Could you call a doctor?"

This time the man responded, though in French. Clara interrupted him. "Speak English!"

The desk clerk shrugged and simply continued speaking. His fingers rested on the countertop like knobbed pencils. He gestured to a room behind the desk. He pointed to his watch, shook his head, and folded his arms, finally paying no attention to Clara at all.

"Don't you see? My mother's sick." It was almost midnight, and Clara was worried that something terrible might happen to Lauren if she did not get help soon. Biting her lower lip, Clara checked her purse for money and the *carnet* of Metro tickets, and ran out the front door of the hotel.

She went to the Concorde station. Hurrying through the gate, she entered the quay just as a train plunged into the station. When she arrived at the top of the steps at Place Clichy, she immediately had to fend off a bum pushing his hand out toward her. The man was wrecked, his face appearing to have collapsed about his toothless mouth. His hair and beard were all of the same length and soil. He raved in a voice that sounded like gravel.

Clara avoided his hand and ran up the street.

She hurried along the sidewalk, looking for the *Deux palestiniens*. The lights of Boulevard de Clichy seemed to leap out at her as though they wanted to hurt her. After three blocks, she stopped at a corner. An Arab in a black coat jostled her, his dark eyes appearing to be ringed with blood. The collar of his coat was up around his neck. He muttered something mean-sounding at her and continued on his way.

She remembered that there had been a sign in front of the restaurant, showing two men with large mustaches, in fezes. She walked back to the Metro stop, looking for the sign. But it had disappeared, and Clara wondered if she were on the wrong street altogether.

A prostitute spoke to her from a doorway, a smile on her face. Clara did not understand her, though she knew the language was not even French. She could not tell from the woman's costume—a kind of showgirl thing with open-toed, scuffed high-heels—where she was from. The kindliness in her voice was marred by her eye-makeup, which looked like multi-colored cement.

Clara feared that she would be taken away in a swirl of claxons and flashing lights. There was music everywhere up and down the boulevard. But it was jangling music, bits of French lyrics from jukeboxes, the long wail of Arab songs coming out of the doors of smoke-darkened cafes, and the singing of a pair of drunken men emerging from a *pissoir*. Their rude voices sounded like smut, and the smell drove Clara away.

A guitarist, his cap lying open on the sidewalk before him, sung in English, something in a dead voice about sweet home Chicago. Clara thought to ask him if he knew where the *Deux palestiniens* was. But then she noticed he was barefoot, and that his feet were smeared with dirt. His toenails looked like blackened, broken seashells.

Maybe she hadn't gone far enough, she decided. So she walked a few blocks more, past black shop entries and alleys. Glancing up one of them, she saw candlelight and bodies sleeping beneath filthy bedding. She felt a rising of tears into her eyes, and struggled to suppress them.

"Please, God, help me find them."

She crossed the boulevard, hurrying away from a man who actually touched her. He was very fat, and his smile was like a yellow, crooked smudge breaking from his little beard. His hand moved quickly across Clara's chest, and she slapped it, running to the next corner.

Suddenly, the sign appeared before her. *Les deux palestiniens* was written in wobbly script. In fact the men weren't wearing fezes, rather some sort of cape, like in the picture Clara's grandmother had shown her once in *Life* magazine, of Rudolph Valentino. But Clara did not care what they looked like. Whispering thanks into the noisy air, she entered the restaurant.

Sammy smiled with surprise. "No, I do not know where your father is. He and Monsieur Roman left about a half-hour ago, you know, to go see some other places."

"Oh...." Clara turned toward the doorway.

"But, Mademoiselle, it is not safe."

"Do you know where they went? Is it around here?"

"Monsieur Roman, he likes *La belle algerienne* in the next block. You go there. Maybe they are there."

"Thanks." Clara headed out the doorway.

"Mademoiselle, you must be very careful."

When she got back out to the sidewalk, the fat man was waiting for her.

"*Viens avec moi, ma petite?*" he said, reaching for her arm.

"Get away from me!" Clara pulled her arm from his grasp, but the man persisted.

"Oh, you speak English, do you?"

Clara noticed that his feet were very small, and that his pants cuffs were gathered into bicycle clips. He spoke with some kind of accent. He smiled, and his teeth were brown near the gums.

"Where'd you pick that up?" he said.

Clara began running.

"No, it's all right, m'love." The man's voice sputtered behind her. "Come back!"

Clara ran on. Every cafe she passed was a threat to her, each alleyway a soiled path to some frightful kidnapping.

"I'll be nice."

The doorway to *La belle algerienne* was like the entrance to a cave. Indeed, the stairway to the cafe itself descended through rock walls with a curved ceiling. Clara ran down the stone steps. Pieces of paper blown in from the street littered the stairway. At the bottom, there was a fog of gray cigarette smoke, from which the sound of droning violins emerged. But they were violins as Clara had never heard them. The sound trudged slowly, interrupted by heavy drums and a woman's voice climbing through some kind of mad, dreamy verse that Clara could not understand at all. Her knees quivered, and she bit her lower lip as she reached the bottom of the stairs.

The cafe was filled with Arab men, and there was a good deal of laughter. The patrons at the bar looked about to see who had arrived. Their dark coats and pants looked like slabs of a broken wall. They all leered at her, and Clara felt suddenly that she had no clothes on. She turned to run back up the stairs.

Traffic noise inundated the night. She looked up the street, and the fat man spotted her. He began walking toward her, waving to her. Tears of fright welled in her eyes, and Clara ran away, headed for the Clichy Metro station.

She passed the *Cabaret d'enfer*. The belly dancer was up on the stage once more, and, despite her fear, Clara stopped a moment, distracted by the gorgeous colors that cascaded down the dancer's hair, her belly and legs. The doorman himself was watching her, and did not notice Clara. The men in the club applauded the dancer's movements.

Clara spotted her father and Jack standing at the bar. Abruptly she entered the cafe.

"*Mademoiselle!*" the doorman said.

The music immersed her in languid swirls and turns. Passing by several tables, she kept her arms close, not wanting to be touched by any of the men. The doorman pursued her.

Martin gave a surprised smile as he spotted her coming across the room.

"Daddy, you've got to come with me. Mom's sick."

But it was a troubled smile as well, as he looked beyond Clara. The fat man had followed her into the club, and now stood glaring at her. He gave her a sniveling smile, as he tried to understand who these two men at the bar were. He almost held out a hand to greet them.

But then Clara took Martin's hand and pulled him from the bar. "Come on!"

Martin had had quite a bit to drink, and his face was puffed up, yet appeared a little collapsed. The surprise on the faces of the two men was dispelled by Clara's insistence. She pulled again at her father's hand.

"We've got to go now!"

The fat man paused, looking like he wished to be of service. "Gentleman, I see that you already...."

The saliva in Clara's mouth tasted like iron. She felt the sweat beneath her arms.

"Who are you?" Martin said.

"An Englishman, mate, making his way about. And what about you?" The man surveyed Clara.

"I'm this girl's father." Martin glanced at Clara. "Who is this guy, Clara?"

"Daddy, I don't know!" Clara tightened her lips, hurt that Martin did not seem to understand why she was there. "He was following me. I mean, you know, bothering me."

The Englishman frowned. He was suddenly quite angered.

"But Mom's sick. We've got to go!"

"How'd you find us, Clara?" Jack said.

"I don't know. I just looked for you, that's all."

Jack buttoned his jacket, shaking his head. He looked down at Clara, his face warm with admiration, and placed a hand on her shoulder.

She hunched, pulling away from him.

"Okay." Martin pushed the whisky glass away from him. "Let's go."

He stepped from the bar, still holding Clara's hand. In the smoky darkness, Martin's face formed a mask, pocked and lined with anger. The Englishman moved to step aside. Without warning, Martin let go of Clara's hand and pushed him. The Englishman staggered, fell against a table, and knocked it over. Arabs at the table began shouting, their voices scattered in the sound of breaking glass. One of them kicked the Englishman, who rolled over on his side, protecting his head. His voice rose in a frightened wail.

Clara pulled at her father's hand. Jack followed along and, as they cleared the doorway, a din rose up behind them. It was a clamor of shouting anger, in which the Arabic sounded to Clara like machinegun fire as fights broke out around the Englishman.

Returning to the hotel in a taxi, Clara described her mother's collapse. "And nobody knew what to do. Nobody understood me."

"Jack'll be able to help us." There was a kind of drunken burr in Martin's voice. Sitting in the backseat with Jack, Clara noted his silence. He seemed intimidated by Martin, as though the suggestion were also some kind of accusation. Jack waved his hand in reply. He sat against the door, looking out. Then, with abrupt impatience, he turned to Clara. His eyes searched for hers, looking for some kind of relief from his own worry. He looked away.

When they arrived at the hotel, Jack immediately told the clerk to phone a doctor. He remained at the desk, arguing with the clerk, jabbing at the man's chest with a finger, as Martin and Clara went up to the room.

Jack followed them a few minutes later, and, when the physician arrived, he explained to him what had happened.

Lauren lay in bed, her eyes closed, and the physician asked everyone to leave, except Jack, whom he needed for translation. Martin objected to this, saying that no doctor could throw him out of his own hotel room. The physician gave in to him, and Martin told Clara to wait in her room.

"Daddy—"

"Now, Clara."

After several minutes, the three men came to her room.

"The doctor says your mother's all right," Jack said. "There's something…." He surveyed his hand a moment, searching for the correct words. "She's very upset about something, he says."

Clara sat on her bed, her back to the wall. Her legs were curled beneath her.

"Something that frightens her."

Clara's shoulders quivered as she listened to his explanation.

Martin interrupted. "I couldn't…Clara, we couldn't get her to say…." His words faltered, and Clara leaned her head against the wall. The kiss she had seen appeared in her heart, and she knew that Jack must be thinking of it as well, the moment with Lauren during which, he had thought, they were alone.

"Can I see her?"

The doctor and Martin assented. Clara accompanied them into the hallway. Jack excused himself, saying that he would call in the morning. His voice was very fatigued. He turned down the hall.

Clara watched him as Martin and the doctor re-entered her parents' room. Jack waited, slouching, for the lift. His entire body appeared to be hanging from his large shoulders. He pushed a hand through his hair, and then looked back up the hall. Worry affixed itself to his face like a decaying mask.

Clara turned to her mother's room.

Lauren's clothes were scattered on the floor, and Clara picked them up. She put the skirt on a hanger. The slip was damp with perspiration, and very wrinkled. Clara carried it into the bathroom and ran a basin of water, pulling the door half-closed behind her. She began soaking the slip.

"So I'll pay the doctor," Martin said after a moment. Clara heard him opening the door to the hallway. "And then I think we should all get some sleep."

Clara pushed the slip deep into the water, and, as the door shut behind Martin and the doctor, she reached up to take a hand towel from the rack. Water dripped from her fingers onto the tile floor.

"Oh, Jack." Lauren's voice was barely discernible.

Clara's hand remained suspended above the sink. She turned toward the door. But then she paused, and peeked through the crack between the door and the jamb. Lauren's right hand held a handkerchief, and it rested on the pillow next to her cheek. Her hair lay in scattered curls on the pillow. "Jack." She turned her head toward the lamp. She brought the handkerchief down to her stomach, where she grasped it, opening and shutting her hand around it.

The towel dropped to the floor from Clara's hand. Isolated in the bathroom, afraid to move from it for fear that she would be discovered, she stood in the bright light. She barely breathed, despite the fact that her mother, so close to her in the next room and so isolated herself, began to weep.

12

The following morning, the shouting from her parents' room imposed a gray nervousness on Clara. There was no purpose to her movements. She was simply waiting for the end of the argument between Lauren and Martin to come, as it always had on other occasions.

But this one went on, and Clara grew more and more upset by it as the morning passed. Muffled, barely decipherable rises and falls of language came from the next room. She wanted to demand that her parents stop arguing, but was frightened especially by the ferocity of her father's anger.

Finally, Martin came to Clara's room and asked her to join them. His shirtsleeves were rolled up, each at a different height. The shirt was very badly wrinkled, and the cuff of the right sleeve, partially sticking out, resembled a broken wing. Martin's eyes were cast down, dejected and red-lined. His hair appeared to Clara to be more gray than usual. His forehead shined like a mottled tray.

Preceding her into their room, he motioned to Clara to sit down, and she moved to the loveseat.

Lauren herself sat on the side of the bed. The sound of her crying seemed far away, and alarmed Clara. She wore a dark brown cotton dress. A string of amber beads hung from her neck. The beads were roughly tear-shaped and of different sizes. Clara noted the imperfections in them and how they were cracked here and there internally, like melting ice. Lauren's hands were joined in her lap, and a handkerchief was crushed between them. The smears of lipstick that spotted it resembled splotches of blood.

"Clara, I've asked you here because…." Martin placed his hands on his hips as he gathered his thoughts.

He knows! The betrayal and its secrecy sickened her.

"Because your mother has decided that she's in love with Jack." Martin's voice grew hoarse at the end, and he cleared his throat.

Lauren brought her hands to her stomach, and a groan of immediate sorrow came from her. Clara slouched on the loveseat. Her eyes ticked back and forth between her parents, though they lingered more often on Lauren.

"They've been carrying on since we've been here."

"Martin...." Lauren gripped the handkerchief with both hands. "We haven't been carrying on. We've—"

"And now she's decided to abandon us." These last two words were uttered with tight precision, each syllable distinct from the others. "So I want you to make a choice."

Startled, Clara turned her head toward Martin. "A choice?"

"It's your mother or me. I'm going back to the States."

"Home? Now?"

"In a few days, Clara. The next plane to New York is Thursday, and then we'll go on to Eureka. Right away. And of course I want you to come with me."

"Martin." Lauren sat up straight, and the handkerchief fell to the floor. For a moment no one moved, and she reached down finally to take it back into her hand. "This isn't fair. You can't ask Clara to—"

"It's as fair as what you've done." Martin's eyes softened with dejection. Clara was terrified by his authority, sensing that he was on the verge of attacking Lauren. There was real pain in his look, the kind of pain she herself felt when she was treated badly in an undeserved way. Told, yet again, by her father that her room was a wreck. Or angered by her own reflection in a mirror, when she was convinced she was just a plain-looking girl. Those times, Clara felt that she was being asked to disappear into a dark hole where she would no longer be bothersome to her victimizer. Her victimizer was herself, and at such moments Clara felt no longer noticeable.

The way Martin's eyes darted away from Lauren's, as though he could not bear her replies, was countered by his need to be told that she loved him and that this business with Jack was all a mistake. So even though he looked away, his eyes as often came right back to Lauren's. "And Lauren, you should tell Clara what's been going on."

"I can't."

"Tell her."

Lauren brought the handkerchief to her eyes, and then wiped her cheeks with it. When she spoke, her voice wavered. "It's true, sweetheart." There was a pause. "We do love each other. We've always been in love."

Clara wanted to get up to leave the room.

"You know that Jack lived in Eureka when we were children. We fell in love then, and now it's happened once more, and—"

"Mother."

"And I can't lose him again."

Clara gestured toward her father. "But what about us?"

"I want you to stay with me, Clara." Lauren brought the handkerchief to her eyes. For a moment, the silence in the room was broken only by her whimpers of anguish. "I can't bear losing you either."

"Clara, you have to choose," Martin said. "Because I'm not staying here."

Clara was so angry with her mother that she wanted to take her by the lapels of her dress and shake her. This was senseless. Her mother loved her father. Her mother had always loved her father. How could she love Jack, or anyone else?

"But, Daddy, how can we—"

"Please stay here." Lauren, isolated on the bed, appeared to expect a rejection from her daughter. "Stay with me, Clara, please."

Clara thought that it wasn't fair to have to make such a choice, even though she already knew that she would go home with her father. Her father lived where they had always lived. He wanted to go on being a family. He wasn't being dumb, like her mother was. But she felt a dark isolation in her heart, with the thought that she may not see her mother for…for how long? Forever?

Lauren held a hand out before her. The fingers glistened. They were bent and even fractured-seeming. "It may sound insincere to you, Martin—a broken promise—but I do love you"

"Oh, Jesus."

"I do. But don't you see…Jack has just…. It's been so difficult to live without him for so long. Especially after what happened between us so long ago."

After what happened! Clara thought.

Martin waved the utterance aside.

"Even with everything you've done for me. And for Clara."

"Then, if you love us, why…." Martin was unable to finish.

What's she talking about? What happened?

"But I didn't think this would take place," Lauren said. "It's been so long since Jack and I….You see, I thought you and I and Clara would come to Paris just for a visit. And then we'd go home. That's what I thought would happen." She lowered her head and took in a breath. "But I see now…." She closed her eyes, as though confessing a secret misery. "I see that I was always in love with him." Lauren looked to Clara. "Everything I feel for you is the same, sweetheart. It can go on, just like always."

Martin's posture, as he leaned against an armchair, was one of offended accusation. He folded his arms before him. "You just decide on your own to stay here, Lauren? You don't ask us about it? You don't think about our wishes. You just go off on your own." He looked to the side with disgust. "What are you? You want to be a starving bohemian like him?"

"Martin, please."

"You consign yourself to a poverty-stricken garret with no money… and you won't get any money from me, Lauren. You do all that just because you love this worthless fool and his worthless art." Martin twisted the cloth of his shirt between his fingers. "Art. Great Christ!"

"Martin, I love him."

"Your head is turned by him, that's all. You've been dreaming about him all these years, the great artist living in Paris, the romantic lover, as though he's some kind of ideal." Martin stared at his hand. "While I go about building a business, building a store and a house and a country place for all of us. Dull, maybe. You probably thought it was boring."

"Martin, I don't."

"Look at what we've done." He pointed to Clara. "And you're giving her up for Jack Roman, a dumb mick who now and then sells a painting. All he's got are his mick paintings." Martin's head turned aside. He placed his hands on his hips, striding back and forth. "You're selling yourself to him...some kind of courtesan. And you want Clara to do that too. You'll live with him. Run your fingers through his hair. Live on wine and the occasional two hundred bucks. It's all false promises, Lauren."

"Stop it, please."

"Jesus, like some kind of whore."

"Martin!"

Clara took in a deep breath and held it. She wanted to shout, to get them to stop.

"Martin, I had his baby."

Martin stood in abrupt silence. Lauren's words hung in the air, like a pestilence. The sound of them reverberated in Clara's mind, over and over. It was a sound covered with the offal of a dug up secret. A disastrous Personal, all her mother's own.

Martin held his hand out, as though it were paralyzed. His wordlessness, a paralysis of its own, accompanied a look of surprise riddled by betrayal.

"I had his...daughter." Lauren was unable to pronounce the last, and it came out as a gargle. It was a half-word. A half-baby, Clara thought.

"Lauren."

Clara grasped her hands on her lap.

"It's true, Martin. I'm sorry."

"Lauren, I...." Martin's voice seemed to dry out, as though his surprise drained him of any speech.

"It's true. And I have to tell you, because it will explain why I want to do this."

"I won't allow it."

"You have to. I love you, Martin. And Clara is *our* baby, yours and mine. You have to let me tell you."

To Clara's surprise, Martin did not reply.

"She won't ever understand it...you won't understand it...if you don't let me tell you."

Martin's shirt was dotted with sweat. Swaths of it stuck to his skin.

"When we were children, Clara…. When Jack lived in Eureka, we…" Lauren crushed the handkerchief between her fingers. "I was fifteen, and I became pregnant."

Clara closed her eyes. She could feel her father's descent into defeat.

"Jack was almost nineteen."

Clara took in a breath.

"My parents sent me away." She brought the handkerchief to her eyes. "For a year. No one knew about it, except my mother and father." Lauren sighed, and laid the handkerchief back on her lap. "And Jack and his parents, of course. We kept it a secret. I was so ashamed. I was just…" Lauren's shoulders sagged once more. "Ashamed."

"But did Jack say he'd marry you, Mom?"

"No." Lauren began weeping. "Jack left me. When he found out I was going to have the baby…it was then that he left Eureka and ended up here. It was awful."

"He should have married you."

"Oh, Clara, he was just frightened. He didn't know what to do."

"I'm going with you, Daddy." Clara had been afraid that she would be alone with her father. But now, despite what she had just said, she worried there would be even more unhappiness. She turned to Lauren. "Mother, please don't…don't do this." She stood and sat down next to Lauren on her bed, placing her head in her lap. "Please."

Lauren's shoulders slumped. A long, descending moan came from her.

For a moment, Clara did not know what to do, despite the hurrying of sympathy for her father. Her mother was going to be abandoned. She imagined Lauren at the cafe on the Rue de Rivoli, years from now, with her hand in Jack's. Both of them would be elderly, served by elderly waiters. Despite their declared love for each other, they would be isolated completely over the crumbs of their shabby croissants. Who would know where anyone else was?

The family was going to be destroyed.

In Clara's heart, there was nothing left except what she perceived to be the smell of ashes on her mother's clothing. But this couldn't be possible. There were no ashes. She could not bear the sound of the sobs that were constricted now within Lauren's throat. The dampness from the tears on Lauren's fingers slid about Clara's palm.

Clara's thoughts fell into very dark, uncomplicated certainty. She was suffering the shock of extraordinary surprise. She considered it a moment, and the darkness shrouded everything. She yet spoke, as though she were tossing herself away.

"I'll stay."

"Clara!" Martin stepped toward the bed and blocked Clara's view of the room. She immediately regretted her decision, fearing her father's rage. But Lauren's fingers grasped hers in a quick movement. Lauren's felt powerless, as though the bones had been taken out of them.

"I'm not going to leave my mother." Clara's stomach felt filled with mud.

"Goddamn it, Clara."

"I don't care. I'm not going to leave her."

13

Sister Monica pulled back the bed sheet and blanket for Lauren. The movement was peremptory, as though the nun were attempting a show of kindness despite her disapproval of the young girl. Lauren's mother Adela remained in the doorway, her daughter's suitcase in her hand.

Sister Monica pointed to her left. "This is the sink. You'll receive a towel a day. Your bedding will be changed once a week, and you're expected to make your own bed. Meals are at seven, noon, and six." She turned to Lauren and folded her hands together. She wore glasses, and reminded the girl of Lon Chaney. Her voice was quite high, so the monstrosity of her appearance was made even more shocking for Lauren by the nun's girlish trill. "As your time comes, of course, we'll serve your meals here in the room." She smiled. She seemed to Lauren, on the surface of it, actually nice, though of a sepulchral temperament and nervous. Lauren herself continued shivering, even though the temperature was about eighty degrees, and the view out the window was of the New Mexico desert.

"And after your time, of course, we'll serve you and the baby here as well."

Lauren grimaced. She still had not admitted to herself that she was pregnant. During the train trip to Albuquerque, she had waited for some indication that all this was simply a passing dream. The Home of the Little Sisters of Mercy did not exist. Nor did the Little Sisters of Mercy themselves. Jack Roman did not exist, or at least, if he did, he had not left her. Albuquerque did not exist. Above all the little baby growing in the darkness wasn't there at all.

"Thank you, Sister," Adela said.

"After you get settled, come up to the front office, by the chapel, and I'll show you the dining room." Sister Monica touched Lauren's cheek, though Lauren did not look up at her. The nun's finger rasped against her. "You'll like it here, Lauren. All the girls are from the right kind of family."

Lauren, feeling dirty and contrite, as though she deserved the worst sort of disapproval from her mother, Sister Monica, and everyone.... Lauren remained silent. Adela placed the suitcase next to the wall. She put her arm around Lauren, who suddenly crumpled against her and grasped her.

"Mother, please don't make me stay here."

Adela held to Lauren, but there was not the usual caress to the embrace, the warmth of real love in it to which Lauren had been so accustomed. Indeed, there was so much reserve that any kindness Lauren had found in the moment—from Sister Monica's sweet officiousness, the cleanliness of the room, or the lovely wild-flower view outside, a courtyard filled with trees with a silvery-watered fountain in the center—deteriorated immediately into the certain truth that she was being abandoned.

"We can't let this get out, though, Lauren," her mother said. "It's such a...shame, sweetheart."

Lauren felt her mother's heartbeat. "Mother. Please—"

"Isn't it, Sister?"

The nun folded her hands. "Oh, yes, Mrs. Cahill. It is that." Her habit appeared to hang from her with no folds at all, as though there were no room in it for privacy of any kind, sequestered affections, or intimacies. "But we can keep a secret."

Six months later, Lauren held the newborn in her arms. She was a jewel with mottled skin and a red face. Lauren loved the little girl from the start, and when Sister Monica took the child away from her, Lauren wept for days. She had abundant milk. But the nuns strapped her breasts, in order to stop the flow.

14

C lara stood with her mother on the sidewalk before the Hotel Ritz. Two suitcases and a large valise were lined up at their feet like memorial stones. It was well before sun-up. A few taxis were parked several yards away, and Martin stood in the lobby.

Clara gripped Lauren's hand, keeping her eyes on her father through the glass doors of the hotel entry. Martin seemed barely recognizable to her. He was determined in what he was doing, single-minded, the way he always was when he was nervously rushed. But this morning he was even more so. He paced back and forth, the belt of his open overcoat swinging about behind him. He placed his hands on his waist as a bellboy arrived with his luggage. Hurrying a tip into the bellboy's hand, Martin glanced at the luggage on the sidewalk, looked about him, checked his coat pockets... anything but address his wife and daughter.

The hotel lobby provided the only light. But surrounded as it was outside by gray dark everywhere, the lobby seemed joyless. The luxury of the furnishings, the gold-threaded curtains, and polished brass were all, for Clara, just an insincere smile.

Martin came out to the sidewalk finally, to beckon to one of the taxis. He carried a half dozen yellow tulips in his hand. The large Citroen moved up the curb toward the hotel. The black hugeness of the car and the sputter of its diesel engine made Clara think of iron-dark vaults and war movies. Lauren caressed the back of Clara's head, trying to ease her sadness. The cabdriver loaded the suitcases into the trunk, and moved to open the back door for Martin.

Martin's eyes changed to an expression of dismayed loss, imploring Clara to help, to do something to put a stop to this. He knelt and grasped her in his arms. His sigh dismayed Clara's heart even further. After a moment, during which neither of them took a breath, he let her go.

"Are you going to write to us, Daddy?"

He took her into his arms once again and kissed her cheek. "Clara, I'll miss you." Standing up and stepping back, he held the tulips before him, proffering them to her. "I stole these from the vase in our room." He smiled. "Just for you, Clara."

"Oh, Daddy." Clara grabbed the flowers from him and brought them to her chest.

Martin swept her from her feet into his embrace and held her. She threw her arms about him.

"Goodbye, Clara. I'll write to you. I'll send you things."

"Daddy...." Her heart actually hurt, and as she laid her head on his shoulder, she felt taken over by the darkness of the Place Vendôme. The square closed in on her, smothering her. The smell of her father's coat further agonized her. It was the same overcoat he wore to work, and she had always enjoyed its rich warmth when her father took her in his arms on his return every evening from Foy's Arcade.

Now, it felt to her that the coat enveloped her, so that she would not be able to escape to her mother's side. She pushed at her father's shoulders, trying to get away from him. But he held on to her, and his resistant arms felt suddenly like rope clawing at her arms.

"Daddy!"

"Clara. Stop it."

Clara twisted about, unable to free herself.

"Clara."

She could not escape. But, grabbing her father's shoulders, she embraced him once more. She was terrorized by her own confusion.

Martin released her. She stepped away from him, and her breath caught in her throat. She was dazzled as the lights of the taxi came on. The tulips were beginning to wilt. They glared in the light. Martin stood between her and the car, and his coat formed a monolithic veil through which she could not see. He was monstrous. He was a glistening pillar in the darkness, and his head disappeared into the black, as though it had been swept away by a sudden blade.

"Mother?" Clara turned to Lauren, who stood several feet away, silhouetted in the darkness. Her body formed a gray line against the gray buildings beyond the square. Lauren did not reach out. It appeared that she could not.

THE ANGEL OF
PÈRE LACHAISE

15

Only one other student at the Ecole Saint-Simon spoke English, an Irish girl named Mia Phelan. She spoke in a very formal way, in an accent that reminded Clara of a butler in a movie, although she seemed to enjoy swearing. Mia giggled whenever she used a bad word, causing Clara to do the same. She giggled the loudest when she used the worst word, the one that caused Clara's face to get rosy and her eyes to glisten with guilty enjoyment. But Mia pronounced the word "Fook," as though it were a Chinese restaurant. And she used a phrase "Fook off," which Clara had never heard. She knew, from the wave of Mia's hand and the disdainful grimace on her face, that it meant something like "Would you please go away?" Smiling, she loved the fact that it was quite a bit more rude than that.

For her part, Mia laughed at Clara's accent. Mia had never been to the United States, although she had wanted to go there badly since the day she had first heard Elvis Presley's "Heartbreak Hotel", which had been released the year before. She had seen the pictures of him in a magazine, and was therefore wildly in love. She occasionally quoted from the song, with longing sighs, in whispers..."Lonely-hearted lovers...."

Mia often broke into laughter when Clara spoke, especially when she used some American colloquialism that reminded Mia of mobsters in the movies. "I don't get it," "Can't be beat,"...that sort of thing. Once, Mia broke into a gale of chuckles at Clara's declaration—using a phrase of her father's—that "Notre Dame's no slouch, as cathedrals go." Mia's abundant blonde hair swirled about her face as she shook her head. "It's just so funny, you see?" she said, bending over to laugh.

Clara and her mother had been living in Paris for six months, and she was finally getting used to the idea of having to speak French all day at school. When she arrived there one cold January Monday morning, she spotted Mia across the yard, playing jump rope with some of the other girls. Clara would have loved to join them, but she feared the usual cacophony of French that would result. Actually, though, she wasn't doing too badly with her own French, and Mia was helping her with it.

The day the previous August, when her mother had first proposed her attending École Saint-Simon, Clara had objected. "I won't be able to talk to anybody."

"Clara." Lauren took Clara's hand in the way she always did when she didn't want any back talk. "The English school is too expensive, and we don't have the money for it."

"But, Mom—"

"And your father wrote to me and said he won't pay for it. He says the French school will be good for you."

Shocked, Clara sat back in the chair. "Daddy said that?" Her eyes surveyed the ruin of the half-slice of toast she had been eating.

"Well, Clara, at least they're Catholics there...at the French school."

It was awful that her father would say something like that. Clara had written letter after letter to her father. She missed him with an aching, emptied heart. She worried about the way they had parted, her father so hulking and anguished in the darkness of the Place Vendôme. Clara had wanted to continue embracing her father, while terrified that what he really wished to do was to abduct her. And now this, that he wouldn't help her go to an English school. She loved him so, that this news came as a hurtful shock. She suddenly felt blamed.

On the first day of school, the girls had made fun of Clara for a number of reasons. For one she was an inch or two taller than any of the others. One girl especially—a chunky, intense, and very noisy little sixth grader named Jeanne-Marie—actually followed Clara around the first morning of school, trying to get her to say something. She poked at Clara with her fingers. When Clara told her to cut it out, Jeanne-Marie started making fun of how she spoke. She mouthed a phrase in some kind of gibberish. Mortified, Clara turned and walked quickly away. *Can't they leave me alone? Just because I can't speak their stupid French.*

Clara sat in the back of the classroom in silence. Recess and lunch, which in Eureka had been moments of great fun for her, were at Saint-Simon torturous embarrassments. She was not able to talk to anyone, and when some of the other girls approached her, she did not understood a word they said. The experience of passing up and down the hallways hardened Clara's stomach. She stuck to the walls as though she wished she could vaporize into them.

It was during lunch on the third day that Clara met Mia. As it happened, Clara had just gotten into a fight. Jeanne-Marie had brought a group of girls together to bother Clara while she sat on a bench eating her sandwich. They made faces at her for how dumb she was. Jeanne-Marie held her hands above her own head and stood on her toes, straining to make her neck look longer as well. All the girls laughed. Their uniform white blouses looked like flags bouncing on a line, and Jeanne-Marie's voice was very raspy.

"Stop it," Clara yelled, and when Jeanne-Marie continued, Clara threw the sandwich at her.

The sandwich made a direct hit. It was meat loaf with a great deal of catsup, just the way Clara liked it. It broke up in mid-flight, and the catsup splattered across Jeanne-Marie's chin. The slab of meatloaf itself got caught in her hair.

Clara stood up and pushed Jeanne-Marie to the ground. "You leave me alone!"

Suddenly she was surrounded by girls, all jabbering so loudly that Clara could barely hear her own voice. Jeanne-Marie lay on the ground crying. She had scraped her elbow, and held it gingerly at her side with her free hand. The catsup was marred with dirt from the playground. The shouting filled Clara's ears. It was French noise, nasal jeering. She gritted her teeth, terrified that she was going to get beaten up. She tried pushing her way from the circle of girls, but they would not let her through. Their voices pierced the air.

Sister Madeleine arrived, waving her hands about to disperse the crowd. Right away Clara began crying, certain that the nun was going to punish her too. *It isn't fair*, Clara thought. *I can't even talk to them.* And

now Clara was going to get thrown out of school altogether, and in French!
Her stomach clutched with fright.

Sister Madeleine shut the girls up. She addressed Clara, who once more
could not understand anything. Holding the fingers of one hand to her lips,
the nun stared at her in silence. She was a very fat older woman. There
were pouches of skin to either side of her mouth, others beneath each eye,
and a large one, like a pearl-colored wattle, beneath her chin. All of these
shook as she spoke. Her jowls were very much larger than the restrictive
wimple she wore. So, Sister Madeleine's face resembled a circle of folds
and flops with glasses.

She belonged to the Carmelite Order, and the cornet of her veil spread
out from her face like the manta ray in a photo Clara had once seen in
National Geographic. The comparison did not hold up well, though. Despite
her fear, Clara recalled the nun's sweetness when she had first come to the
school, babbling at her kind-heartedly in French as she gave Clara, Lauren,
and Jack a tour of the classrooms.

Now, though, the nun appeared stricken. She had to do something to
restore order, and she did not have the words to do it, at least for Clara's
benefit.

"You are...you...." The English words were pronounced slowly, with
precise, inept diction. "You are...very bat?" Sister Madeleine's eyebrows
rose up inquisitively. She appeared just as friendly as before.

Clara's heart sunk. She did not feel "bat." She felt victimized. A surge
of unhappiness came into her face.

But very quickly one of the girls stood out from the crowd and began
speaking in rapid French, gesticulating at Clara.

"Zees ees true?" Sister Madeleine asked after a moment.

The other girls protested, and were shushed by the nun.

"Is what true?"

"I told her you were just sittin' there," the girl said, "eatin' your bleedin'
sandwich." Clara blinked as Mia placed her hands on her waist and stuck
out her lips. "And that these girls were bothering you and you didn't deserve it, and that it wasn't fair."

A fresh, grateful sigh pushed from Clara's lips.

"And that you told them to leave you alone."

Gratitude cleansed Clara's heart. "Yes, I…" She didn't know how to explain to the nun what had happened. "Please tell Sister that I was just having my lunch. And that I can't help it that I can't speak French. I wish I could. And that that girl was being mean."

Mia translated, and Jeanne-Marie yelped, defending herself. She held out her scraped arm as proof that it was all Clara's fault. But then a few of the other girls began to speak, and it seemed to Clara that things had suddenly begun going her way. Mia held her ground, and the nun turned her attention to Jeanne-Marie, who jabbered in an attempt to interrupt the Irish girl. But two other girls interrupted her, accusing her, and quickly Jeanne-Marie turned and ran from the circle. Her leather shoes clopped against the cobblestones of the playground. Clara noticed that one of her laces was untied. Her blouse came out of her skirt in back.

Sister Madeleine turned to Clara and spoke with her a moment, then gestured to Mia for a translation.

"She says you can get on with your lunch."

Clara looked down at the ground. The slice of meatloaf was covered with grit. The nun muttered a few words.

"Maybe you can go with her to her desk just now, she says." Mia grinned. "And get a couple *franc* for a cheese sandwich or something."

———

After school, Clara and Mia went to the Café Deux Cygnes, where Clara asked for a hot chocolate. Mia ordered coffee.

Clara was drawn to Mia because she seemed to know so much. Just in the way she ordered the coffee, for example, she treated the waiter as though he were simply supposed to bring her whatever she wanted, no questions asked. Clara's mother had always told her to be respectful of everyone, and that included such people as waiters and gas station attendants. Even bums. So, to see Mia ordering the coffee with a flip of her fingers, as though she were brushing the waiter off, seemed to Clara very sophisticated.

Clara asked Mia many questions about herself.

Her father wrote books, Mia said. "But he writes things they don't approve of in Ireland, he told me. He's been banned there, you know.

"Banned?"

"I guess so. It's a sin to read what he writes. It made me cry when he told me that. But he also told me that it's not a sin just to know him. Or to be one of his kids. That's all right, he told me."

"That's awful."

"I asked my mum about it. She told me that my father makes fun of priests in his books. I guess he shouldn't do that."

"I guess not."

"And he told me that if you aren't banned in Ireland, you're hardly a writer at all."

Puzzled, Clara shrugged her shoulders.

"Yeh, I know. It makes no sense." Mia spooned some sugar into her coffee. "What does your father do then?"

Clara's hand hovered over the cup of chocolate. "He's in the United States."

Mia's eyes widened as she sipped a bit of the coffee. "They're not divorced, are they?"

Mortified, Clara shook her head. Divorce was such a terrible sin, as well as being so embarrassing, that she could hardly bear considering it. Worse, she imagined how aimless her parents' lives would be after a divorce. She saw her father wandering around the kitchen scratching his head as he contemplated how to cook an egg. No picnics. No playing in the swimming pool with his daughter. And now...how could she explain her mother's sleeping every night with someone who wasn't even her husband? How would she explain it to Mia?

"No, they're not divorced." Clara hoped the moment would pass.

Mia, however, pressed on. "Are you with your mother?"

"Yes."

"Just the two of you?"

Clara sat back.

"Have you got brothers and sisters?"

The silence was marred by the sound of a car horn from outside. A waiter wearing a white shirt, black bow tie, and white apron hurried past their table.

"No," Clara whispered.

Sensing Clara's discomfort, Mia asked no more questions.

The two girls went to the Deux Cygnes every day after school. Mia was very amused by Clara's insistence on calling it The Swans' Café, or, more specifically, The Swans'. It was there that Clara could ask Mia for help with her own French. It was a fiendish language. Clara tried to say whatever she could, and got laughter as a response. That is, when people were being kind. More frequently she was simply abused when she attempted speaking French. It did not seem right to her that the Parisians made fun of people who tried to talk to them. *How would they like it if they came to Eureka,* she wondered, *and walked up and down the aisles of Foy's Arcade, trying to get waited on?* Clara suspected, though, that few people in France knew where Eureka was.

A few weeks after their first meeting, Mia introduced Clara to her parents, Domnhall and Mary, who lived in a flat in the Rue Soufflot. Domnhall was in his thirties and had bright orange-red, curly hair. He was a very humorous man with a square face and big chin, who wore glasses, and who made fun of Mia in the same way Mia made fun of Clara. He did not seem at all profligate as, Clara thought, someone who was banned must be. Indeed he took quite a bit of time to tell Clara about her own family name, and how there were Foys in north Connaught that were famous for their fine, sweet voices. He wondered was her father capable of carrying a tune?

Clara's breathing quivered.

She also noticed a couple of the paintings that Mia's parents owned. "My mother," Mia said. "She sells them. These are Irish artists."

"Who's that one?" Clara pointed to a small apparent portrait of some man. She assumed it was a man. The sitter's face was all a-swirl, as though it were being scattered by a small cyclone.

"His name's Bacon." Mia laughed. "Imagine that, will ya'? Bacon! Like at breakfast!"

"He's famous now," Mary said. "He owed my father money, so he gave this painting to him. He wasn't famous then."

There were a few others, whom Mary identified as they walked around the apartment. "This is one of my favorites," she said, pointing to a framed piece of stained glass that was lit from behind, and showed a woman who Clara guessed was the Virgin Mary. "Harry Clarke's his name. I wouldn't sell this one for any money, poor man. He's been dead for a quarter century. Way too young."

"And who's that?" Clara pointed to an unfinished oil portrait of a young woman looking directly at the viewer. Above her neck, the painting appeared to be finished. Below, there was a drawing of shoulders and an indication of a dress. A design for wallpaper appeared behind her, although none of it was yet painted. She wore a brooch, though, at her throat, that, like a ceramic wonder, exhibited a small gathering of flowers lushly colored.

"Margaret Crilley," Mary said. She reached out and removed some dust from the outside of the frame. "Harry Clarke's wife. Wonderful painter. She has a following still, but not like that Bacon fella." Mary smiled, shaking her head. "No one's as famous as he is."

Her visit with the Phelans was so pleasant that Clara asked Mia to come to her house after school the next day. So, as Clara hurried across the schoolyard now to join her friend, she looked forward to the plan she would make with Mia. There'd be things she could show her. Her old Empire doll from the Place des Vosges, for which Clara had bought newer, fresher clothes. Her books…she was reading *Gone With The Wind,* and almost done with it. The little painting in red that Jack had given to her for Christmas. And Jack's studio, with its beautiful view of Contrescarpe and the fresh light coming in.

School that day was even more contrary than usual. The lessons crawled by, each moment a snail-like yearning on Clara's part. Mia sat at a front desk, the reward for her being one of the best students. But she turned around now and then, when Sister Madeleine was at the blackboard, to sneak a glance at Clara. There was a Geography lesson. Then Math. Then Reading. The book's illustrations showed a boy and a girl on a farm. Clara followed along as the others read out loud. She was surprised by how much of it she actually could get, even though she looked out the window quite a bit. At last the day ended, and Sister Madeleine dismissed every-one. Clara moved excitedly toward the door, but then saw that the nun had asked Mia to stay behind a few minutes. Clara stayed behind also, until Sister Madeleine told her to leave. Groaning to herself, she went out into the hallway.

By the time Mia finally did get away, the hall was empty. Its dark brown walls, scuffed badly by the passage of so many girls for so many years, re-minded Clara of a long, empty closet. The crucifix that hung over the entry gleamed in the semi-darkness. There was an old painting hanging to the right of the doorway, of Mary praying in tears at the foot of the cross. It was so dark a picture that the Mother of God looked like a ghost in a cave.

"Sister told me she wanted me to speak French with you every day," Mia said as the girls passed out into the sunlight. "And I told her we already were."

The trees up and down the Boulevard Saint-Michel had turned to fall yellows and browns. The sidewalk was strewn with leaves.

"She said you're already talking pretty well."

Clara blushed with pleased surprise. The girls walked out the entry to the school playground and turned toward the river. It was a roundabout way to get to Contrescarpe, but the air seemed to brighten the trees, especially as, in the late afternoon, it began turning warmer gold.

"So we'll just go to my house," Clara said, "instead of to The Swans'?"

She did not want to waste time sitting around over a cup of chocolate at the cafe. She imagined how pleased her mother would be with the surprise of Clara's new friend. Lauren would make the coffee and chocolate herself. Best of all Clara was sure that her mother would sit down with the two girls to have a cup of coffee with them.

The booksellers' stalls were still open along the quay, and the activity of all the patrons, thumbing through the books and talking with the ven-dors while Notre Dame rose up forbiddingly black beyond them, thrilled Clara. The ivy hanging down the wall over the river remained dark green, even though the trees everywhere were turning color. Eventually the girls walked up the hill toward Contrescarpe, and at each corner Clara's heart warmed a bit more at the prospect of introducing Mia to Lauren.

The girls paused on the stairway leading up to the studio. One of Clara's shoelaces had come undone, and she bent over to tie it. She heard Lauren laughing. Her voice, muffled beyond the door, had the kind of silvery glee that Clara had often heard in her mother's moments of joy. The talk that followed was punctuated with more laughter.

Her shoe tied, Clara proceeded up the stairs, taking the latchkey from the pocket of her skirt. She turned to Mia and smiled.

Hurrying through the door into the studio, Clara stopped short just inside. She lifted her hand to her mouth, trying to hide her surprise, and her shoulder basket dropped to the floor.

"Mother!"

Mia bumped into her from behind, then gasped as she looked over Clara's shoulder. Clara's schoolbooks slid onto the parquet. Her mother lay on a couch, resting on one elbow in the late afternoon sun. She wore a pair of heavy gold earrings and an orange silk scarf about her head. A swatch of blue silk lay entwined about her lower legs.

Otherwise she had nothing on at all.

—

"Clara." Lauren's voice trailed away at the end from embarrassment. She appeared milky in the sunlight. Her skin was unblemished.

Jack's brush hovered above the canvas. He looked over his shoulder toward the door as Lauren pulled the smock from behind the couch and covered herself. She glowered at him, and he stepped to the paint-spattered table where his brushes, bottles of turpentine, and scrapers lay scattered. Clara turned away, bumping into Mia, whose eyes skittered back and forth between Clara and her mother.

"You see, I...." Lauren stammered. "Jack is doing a new one of me." She pointed at the immense canvas that hung, unstretched, on the wall opposite the windows. She sat up and put her arms into the sleeves of the smock. She tied the belt and made a brief attempt to straighten her hair.

"Mom, this is Mia."

Lauren smiled, wishing to be gracious.

"I suppose…." Mia turned back toward the door. "I guess I should go."

Clara did not know what to say. "Oh…" Her cheeks burnt.

"Bye." Mia hurried toward the stairs, clattered down them, and went out the door into the street.

Clara knelt to take up her books.

"I've never done this sort of thing, Clara," Lauren said. "So I thought…."

Clara ran to her room. Her book bag pummeled her legs. Jack had cleaned out a small storage space for her, where he had been keeping some of his completed paintings. The room was larger than a pantry…slightly… and was well lit by a window that looked out on a courtyard. A friend had leant Jack a bed and some extra blankets, and Jack had painted the room for Clara, decorating it with some old stone-lithograph food posters they had found in the flea market at Clignancourt. It was a very bright, grotto-like refuge.

Clara threw the bag onto her bed, and sat down on the wooden chair. A few seconds later, Lauren entered the room, fidgeting with the front of her smock. Her hands were quite long, and her fingernails polished. Lauren still wore her diamond wedding ring, which resembled a sliver of polished water. Her right hand was nestled against the colors in the smock and, to Clara, appeared entangled in them, like an anemone overcome by flowers.

"Clara, please, I—"

"Mom."

"Jack wanted me to do it. He asked me to."

"You're not supposed to show yourself like that to, to—"

"Clara, I'm sorry."

"To boys! I mean, what about poor Ladeen?"

Clara had recalled the conversation Lauren had had with her about Ladeen Muscovy, after Ladeen, a neighbor girl in Eureka, had been sent to live with her grandmother in Tuscon. She had been caught by her father with Howard Phipps, who was a senior at Eureka High, a football letter-man and very cool, in the backseat of Howard's 1952 Ford convertible. A terrible scandal had ensued, and everybody seemed to know about poor Ladeen's being dragged from the car by her father, that she had forgotten her brassiere in the backseat, and that Howard had displayed it to all his friends the following Monday.

Ladeen had stayed home from school for a week, too embarrassed to make an appearance. Even at that, the day she did return she went home crying at lunchtime. A boy had made fun of her in the cafeteria—something about "Phipps's tits"—taunted to it by his friends who sat at a table watching. Later, Ladeen learned that she was going to have a baby and, abruptly, she disappeared. Her friends were forbidden by Ladeen's parents to write to her in Tuscon, which had been especially difficult for Clara who, though she was four years younger than Ladeen, was a neighborhood friend.

"So you have to be very careful about boys," Lauren had counseled Clara. "Because you can't really defend yourself if you get pregnant."

"Mom, I wouldn't do anything like that."

"Even though…" A kind of joyous sadness had appeared in Lauren's face. The memory of that moment now was refined by Clara's knowledge of Lauren's own scandal as a girl. "Even though love makes you forget yourself sometimes." She looked at the floor and sighed. "And the boys… their parents, too…they won't help you."

"Clara, this is different," Lauren said now. "You've got to see that Paris is not like Eureka."

Disgruntled, Clara got up and left the room. She walked to Lauren and Jack's bedroom and sat down noisily on the bed. Lauren followed her. Sitting next to her, she put a hand on Clara's knee. "There's a whole history that's different here. People do things differently here."

Clara's skirt came up about her thighs, and she reached down to lower it. "But what about Daddy?".

"Your father wouldn't understand this."

"I guess not!" Clara's hands were clasped together on her lap. She stammered a moment as she tried to speak.

"Don't you see? Clara, I love Jack."

"But—"

"And I've always wondered what it would feel like to do what you just saw."

Clara took in a breath. She pulled her hands away.

Lauren's speech began wandering, as though Clara were not even there. "I'm sure you think it's crazy. But being with Jack…" She paused. "And I love your father, too. At least I always thought I did. But your father, Clara, isn't a man who gives up a kiss very…easily." Lauren covered her mouth, as though mortified by the admission. "But I never realized how hidden away I was with him. How…." Lauren turned away from Clara a moment. "How hidden I was."

Clara protested to herself once more. She remembered the evening, when she was eight, when her mother had come upstairs to tuck her into bed. Lauren and Martin were going to a dinner party. Lauren was wearing the new fur jacket Martin had bought for her in New York. She wore the fur over a green wool dress, the simplicity and formality of which had dazzled Clara. She also wore a gold brooch, centered just below her neck, a pair of shell-shaped gold and pearl earrings, and short black suede gloves. As she leaned over to kiss Clara goodnight, Clara smelled the Chanel perfume her mother wore, a kind of faint applause for her beauty. The fur against Clara's cheek made the girl stir with pleasure, and the scent remained even after Lauren adjusted the sheet about her shoulder and moved toward the light switch.

"Mom, that's not fair," Clara said now.

Clara's father *was* mean sometimes. He could make Lauren cry if she interceded for Clara at the dinner table. But he was Clara's father. You didn't talk about fathers like they were guards at the jail.

"Please don't be angry with me, Clara."

Lauren's eyes pleaded for kindness. But Clara could not give her such kindness. Indeed she pulled her hand away as her heart tripped about inside her. Lauren clutched the smock tightly and lifted her hand to her throat. The fingernails scratched at the skin.

"Please don't treat me like this." Lauren lowered her head. "Don't do this to me."

Her voice seemed to grow smaller as she spoke, to drain. She laid her head in Clara's lap. She grasped her about the waist. Clara's fingers, caressing Lauren's hair, felt airy, even ghostly. Her eyes fell across the small wooden trunk at the end of the bed.

Jack had told Clara when she had first moved in that this contained the greatest treasures of the world, and that someday he would show them to her and Lauren.

"Magic things?" Clara had asked.

"No. But beautiful things."

She ran her fingers over the trunk latch. "Can't you show them to me now?"

Jack shook his head, rolling up the sleeves of his shirt. Smoke from his cigarette floated into his eyes. He closed them and waited for the irritation to pass. "No. Not now. They're things you may not think are so special, anyway. But someday you'll see them."

Amused, Clara had imagined exotic dreams floating from the trunk's dried-out wood. It was like something in one of the storybooks she had read with her mother as a very little girl, a magic box that contained secrets yearning to get out. All it needed was the secret words or the proper caress of the hand, like a genie in a bottle.

Did Mom's baby die? Clara looked down at the trunk as she continued caressing Lauren's hair. The thought had come from nowhere. A phantom.

Clara caught herself before the question blundered from her mouth. Lauren's gaze wandered out the window. The question fluttered about Clara's mind so violently that it made her feel sick, as though she were caught in a sudden whirl.

Her sister would be twenty-five or so, now. She wouldn't even know who were real mother was, Clara thought. She'd have another mom and another family. A boyfriend. Pretty eyes. She'd look at herself in the mirror and wonder where, in her eyes or her smile, she looked like her mother.

16

In the isolation of Jack's studio the next day, Clara lay on the couch reading *Gone With The Wind*. She wore a pair of dark red pedal pushers and a cotton shirt, no shoes.

Propped up on a couch cushion, she placed her hand behind her head. She was very involved in the book, a yellowed copy that Jack had gotten for her, used, at a store around the corner from the Square Viviani. She loved the smell of it, like old cloth from a mothballed drawer, almost as much as she loved the book itself. Even the color of the paper on which it was printed—a stained tan…someone had spilled water on the book some years ago—gave her joy.

She was using a folded letter as a bookmark. She lay the book down on her stomach for a moment to read the letter once more.

> *Dear Clara,*
> *I know you weren't very happy about going to the French school.*
> *I could tell from your letter that you were upset. But it sounds now*
> *like you're enjoying it. You'll be able to say things that no one in*
> *Eureka can say. I love you, sweetheart. I miss you, Clara.*
> *Love,*
> *Daddy*

Clara worried about how he had mentioned only *her* name in that last sentence. She refolded the letter and put it back in the book. She wanted her father to miss her mother just as much.

The late January sun coming through the window caused her to drowse. Out the window itself, Clara could see the dormer windows of the buildings across the Place de la Contrescarpe. Jack had told her that those were the windows of maids' rooms, and that they were the rooms hardest to get to because they were so high up. Clara thought they had to be the best ones, then. For one there would be complete privacy, since no one would want to go all that way just to spy on the maid. The windows themselves were so unusual, sticking out from the slanting roofs and giving the maid a view of all the other roofs with their charming crockery chimneys and angled mansard slopes.

Clara nodded several times, unable for the moment to concentrate on Scarlett's conflicted annoyance with Rhett. The light that warmed the couch ran through her body, and the cloth of her pants caressed her legs. She fell asleep a few minutes, and then woke up again, attempting to concentrate. But soon the print doubled and blurred, and the book fell from her fingers.

She dreamt of the Christmas fire, and the gold chaos of the tree ablaze in the front window. When she awoke, her shirt stuck to her stomach with sweat. The windows glared silver, splintered with light, and her shoulders felt covered over in grease. She sat up, and *Gone With The Wind* slid down her legs to the floor.

She walked to her mother's and Jack's bedroom and passed through it to the bathroom, where she splashed cold water in her face. As she dried herself with a towel, she sat down on the bed. Lauren's toiletries were arranged to one side of the vanity, like a neat city of bottles and atomizers. In the open closet, Lauren's few things took up a narrow space, while Jack's ragged clothing filled the rest. Every suit, cravat, and shoe was an antiquity.

She moved to the end of the bed and placed a hand on the trunk. Its dried, old wood was held together by black-tarnished brass sleeves at each of the corners. After a moment, Clara stood and walked to the bedroom doorway. Peering out into the studio, she listened for footfalls on the stairs. *Gone With The Wind* remained on the floor, and the sun now illuminated only half the couch. She realized that she was still quite alone, and she stepped across the room to the vanity.

In the top drawer, Jack kept a shallow straw basket half-filled with notes to himself and odd mementos. He had picked through them one day, surprising Clara with a silver charm—a silver rowboat—that he had given to her. There were also several keys in the basket, of which only one was small enough to fit the trunk's lock. She took it now, and turned back toward the trunk itself.

When she opened it, the faint odor of smoke rose from the articles inside, causing Clara to wrinkle her nose.

There were two levels. The top was a shallow shelf filled with sheet music, some with names that Clara recognized from her mother's piano music in Eureka. But, while her mother had one or two pieces by Beethoven that she played badly after months of desultory practice, this trunk had all kinds of things. Stuff Clara had never heard of...sonatas, etudes, divertissements. Bach. Debussy. Best of all there was music by someone named Clara Schumann.

When Clara removed the shelf and looked into the actual trunk itself, she found a thick photo album that seemed devoted to vacation pictures. As a younger man, Jack had gone to the mountains quite a lot, that was clear. To the beach too. And in many of the photos he was shown in virtually the same pose, seated in a wooden chair outside a tent or under an umbrella, a book in his lap and a hat on his head, his legs crossed. There were pictures of Jack sitting in cafes, apparently with other artists, all dressed in coats and ties, but coats and ties that seemed ragged or dog-eared. Many wore scattered beards. There were women, too, either in disconsolate sadness or making a spectacle of themselves, leaning over some cafe table flourishing a cigarette or kissing someone with quite obvious relish. Clara was not sure whether these were the wives of all those artists, or maybe their models. Maybe even their girlfriends. *Or maybe even artists themselves*, she thought, recalling Margaret Crilley. All she knew for sure was that she found the pictures, and the adventurous diversion that they showed, thrilling.

But none of the pictures interested Clara as much as the one toward the back of the album, a creased, yellowed photograph that showed Jack and Lauren as teenagers standing on a small wooden dock. It was the wharf at the end of C Street in Eureka, where the Samoa ferryboat was still moored every night. They were hand in hand in the photo, and Jack was whispering in Lauren's ear. Lauren actually looked like Clara herself, smiling at the camera and brushing her hair back with her left hand.

Clara leaned over the picture, examining each detail of her mother's dress. It must have been a cold day, since Lauren was wearing a short wool jacket and a wool scarf. The little white socks she wore with her black leather shoes, the dress skirt covered with flowers, and the long-stemmed daisy in her hand gave the scene the appearance of carelessness and fun. A sailboat was moored to the dock, along with two fishing boats. The house-strewn shore of the town of Samoa across the way was at a tilt.

Clara felt that she could hear Jack's whisper, although it was obvious that he intended the secret message for her mother only. Clara also wondered if her mother's lost baby were swirling about inside her, a tiny face, arms, and legs in a tiny sea.

There was a packet of letters in the trunk, tied with a string.

She took out a large single envelope that had been seared at one end in some sort of fire. Inside, Clara found several flat pieces of card paper that were lithographed with images of Greek pillars and, on the largest piece, a scene of a countryside with a pastel-colored castle. There were thin, hovering clouds. Two other pieces presented a framework of poplar trees. The printing was faint, faded, and old.

From a smaller wax-paper envelope, Clara pulled out several paper dolls...angels, mostly, and a man dressed in pantaloons and a shirt with baggy sleeves, and a shiny vest. There were also two women with high white wigs and beautiful gowns. Both were singing. Clara had to remove the dolls carefully because they were so dried out. It was difficult to say what the man actually looked liked, since half of him was so badly charred.

Clara put the painted pieces together. The walls supported a ceiling hidden behind a proscenium arch that had been painted with gold stars. In the center of the arch, a laughing mask was shown, on a meringue-like frill of cloud. Lettering beneath the cloud spelled out a loopy, curved phrase... *Cosi fan tutte*. Tiny eyelets in the angels' heads showed that they were to be hung from the ceiling. Clara found her mother's sewing kit in the vanity and, after measuring and tying pieces of thread, she put the angels in flight.

Completed, the stage was a foot and a half high. Closing the trunk, she placed the stage on top of it, and then put the paper figures inside, supported by the cardboard pegs glued to their legs. In the case of the man, there was such a sense of movement in the doll's raised arm that it reminded Clara of a burnt Gene Kelly.

She took up the letters. The one on top was dated September 21, 1944, below which was written *Dublin, Ireland.*

Dear Jack,

It's time you knew something about the little girl who was born to Lauren Cahill. Your mother and I kept this from you, because we didn't think it appropriate for you to know. But now, our worry about the war and that baby's welfare has convinced us that you should know about her, because she may soon be in very grave danger.

Clara put a hand to her mouth, and then looked back over her shoulder. There was no noise on the stairway. Her heart trembled, as though it were sickened and could not beat calmly.

We arranged, with Lauren's parents, for the girl to be given up for adoption as soon as she was born, and we knew a fine French couple— called Dusel—who live in the east of France, in the Vosges, outside the town of Riquewihr, near Colmar. They are vintners, and your mother and I had known them well when we lived in France, when you were a small boy. They had no children. They're fine Catholic people, and we felt they would raise the little girl well. We didn't want her to be given up just to anyone, to wander through the world lost.

Clara felt that her breathing must be so loud that anyone could hear it out on the stairway. She hurried on through the letter.

She lives there now and she's twelve years old. Her name is Emma Dusel. Your mother and I understand that she has fine green eyes, like Lauren herself.

Clara put the letter down on the floor and leaned over it, placing her chin on one hand, her elbow touching the floor. There were instructions in the letter about how to contact the Dusels, and further instructions for finding their winery.

I'll tell you the truth, Jack. I wasn't sure that I should write this letter.

I'm still not sure. But I hate to think what will happen as the Germans retreat to the Rhine. She and the Dusels lie right on the path to Germany.

They've had a bad time of it with the war. And I'm sure that getting around in France these days is difficult, even though Paris is back in the right hands. But if you can get down there to Riquewihr, and find her, try to convince her and the Dusels to leave, maybe to come back to Paris with you. Jack, it's your chance to do something to help that poor child.

Da

Clara glanced from the letter at the play-theater. She could barely think about what she had read. The letter lay open before her, but she could not bring herself to peruse it once more. The theater offered her some relief from the information that it contained. She fingered the paper doll.

"Clara!"

The doll flew from her hand.

"What is this?"

Jack strode into the room, taking Clara by the arm. Panicked, she slapped around for the doll on the floor.

"Who told you you could do this?" He picked her up off the floor.

"Let go!"

"Who told you?" Jack dropped her to her feet.

"Nobody! I just—"

"Jack, stop!" Lauren had followed him into the room. She took Clara into her arms as Jack began taking the theater apart.

"What is that?" Lauren held Clara's head against her chest.

Jack's face had tightened and was now gray-white. "None of your business." The angels flew around like scattered flames. "These are things I want kept private." He slid the separate pieces of the model into the envelope. The angels became tangled in the threads. "Damn it, Clara."

His hands were like those of a giant, ruining a little girl's plaything. His voice was gargly and filled with anger. Clara held her mother close. Jack sounded crazy to her, and the quick movement of his fingers was so destructive—twitching and clenched where they were caught in the threads—that she closed her eyes and buried her face in her mother's blouse.

Clara ran to the living room, taking up *Gone With The Wind* and tossing it onto the table before the couch. The book slid across the glass and fell to the floor again. Moaning, she sat back against the cushions. The sun had just gone down, and a few lights were beginning to show in the dormer windows. She feared that she had invaded Jack's privacy so completely that he would never forgive her.

Yet she had noticed how he very carefully replaced the flat pieces of the theater-set in the envelope, despite the speed with which he did it. Even the tearing apart of the thread was done with agitated care. She had been terrified that he would destroy the theater and the doll figures. But the fact was that he even examined the pieces—swearing while he did it—before replacing them in the envelope. His affection for them saved them from destruction.

—

The threads were tangled and inseparable, and they stuck to Jack's hands. He swore at the angels, the pain of their being discovered by Clara like some kind of choking cut into his heart.

How could she do this? He placed the paper figures in their envelopes and took the theater apart. Folding it, he replaced it in its envelope as well, relieved that there was no damage.

But as his anger subsided he realized the care with which Clara had constructed the theater. Each piece had been examined and wiped free of dust. The angels were attached with precision to the threads, at different heights so that they resembled a tableau arranged for a real stage.

Putting the theater back in the trunk along with the other things, and securing the lock once again, he carefully removed the remnants of thread from his fingers. Holding one of them up before him, he surveyed the light that fell its length. It was a filament of nothing. It was like the past he had so successfully abandoned, and it caused him to shiver. He had left Lauren, and now she was with him again. He had made terrible mistakes. Now, a moment ago, he had punished her daughter, thoughtlessly so, destroying the threads she had tied with such care.

—

139

When he was twenty-two, he had been living in Paris for three years, in his studio in Contrescarpe. The rent was difficult to make every month, and the concierge did not trust the young Irishman who spoke French so well. Irishmen were supposed to be lorrie drivers and laborers, just passing through, and Jack's facility in French always surprised her. For the first year or so she had waved him away, pretending not to understand anything he said.

He had little furniture in the beginning, simply a pair of chairs and a table that he used both for work and for meals. That the table in time began to look like a palette as well, and to smell like one, led him to a second, larger table on which to eat. After a year he bought a sofa at a flea market, and an iron bedstead.

He lived alone and had little money. He did not care about that, as long as he was able to sell a piece here and there, to make his rent, food, and some art supplies. Indeed, Jack cared a great deal for his own impracticality. He had no particular political objection to money. He simply seldom thought about it.

At first he received little word from his parents, although he had written to them as soon as he had arrived in Paris. Then after several months he started receiving regular letters. They wrote about the weather, mostly about the rain in Eureka. His father made occasional remarks about political events, particularly the rise of the Nazis in Germany, and "that eedjit Hitler", whose demise Desmond predicted with each letter.

Jack replied to them. But his heart darkened whenever he thought about the United States, infected by the memories he had of his own cowardice, as well as the anguish he felt when he realized that he would not be allowed, ever, to make amends to Lauren.

After she told him she was pregnant, his father said that he could never see her again. Jack called Lauren many times, but her mother hung up on him. He could not go anywhere in Eureka without some whisper or smile of knowledge appearing on someone's face, the raised eyebrow that told him that everyone seemed to know what had happened and why Lauren Cahill was away for the while.

"You may think that life can go on as it was before, Jack," his father Desmond said one night. He was a tall man and very thin, with graying hair and wire-rimmed spectacles. He so bristled with anger at what his son Jack had done that his advice really was punishment. "But you have a responsibility, and I want you to face up to it."

"How can I, Da, when you won't let me see her?"

"It's not just me and your mother that won't let you see her. It's her parents as well. You're both too young to be doing what you did, and everyone in Eureka is talking about us." Desmond sat down at the kitchen table and began to roll a cigarette. "There's that to consider, too, you know."

"But I love Lauren."

"You do not. You're too young...she's too young, to be in love."

Jack knew that Desmond had been thirty-eight years old when he had married his mother, who had been twenty-one. Nothing was expected of you in Ireland until you were at least thirty or so. But now, here he was, Jack Roman, at eighteen about to become a father himself. He wanted to mention his father's two years in prison for providing the caps to bomb a railway bridge in Galway in 1912. At the time, Desmond had been sixteen years old. Sure, he was a romantic hero to some in Ireland because of that. But had he been old enough to be doing such things? Wasn't he just a lad then, like Jack was now? And, Jack thought with some bitterness, wasn't the little baby growing inside Lauren a better alternative to the world's misfortunes than blowing up the bloody railway?

"In fact, I'll tell you now, young man, how I really feel about this," his father continued. He shook tobacco from a packet into the small rectangular paper on the table. "This is a shameful thing, what you've done. It's as though nothing that your mother and I taught you, nothing that you learned at church or in Catechism, none of that made any impression on you at all." Desmond finished rolling the cigarette. But he was suddenly so angry that he could not light it. "You haven't acted in any way that a son of mine would act."

Jack imagined never being forgiven, and he abruptly left Eureka. There was no announcement to his family. No word. He spent his savings on a railroad ticket to New York, and a steamship ticket to Le Havre.

His father's first letter...a short one...was the saddest Jack ever received.

You betrayed the family, and you betrayed that poor little girl, and now you've betrayed us all again by leaving, by not facing your responsibilities. Jack, we are very disappointed in you. I hadn't thought to raise my son as a coward.

The notion that he had so abandoned Lauren stifled him for years thereafter. He attempted defining the idea of leaving someone so alone that her heart would not be able to open itself again to anyone. Could that possibly happen? Or more to the point, could that possibly happen to Lauren?

According to Jack's father, it had. That first letter spelled out the disaster of their relationship with Lauren's family, the end of the friendship, and the recrimination that Jack's parents felt. But Jack himself thought that, if he had just been allowed to see her, the abandonment would never have taken place. But their parents had forbidden any contact. It was they who had let the thing get out of control.

This wasn't the truth, though. He knew it wasn't. In the end he knew that what happened was simply his fault.

So the correspondence faltered. Jack took classes and painted. He knew that a baby had been born, though no one would tell him what finally happened to the child. He met other artists and started learning about his Paris neighborhood, and then the other *arrondisements*, the revolts, 1789, 1848, the artists and the kings.

But he could not rid himself of the wish to know what their child looked like. He dreamt of her, a small girl always in some lost place…in the corner of a room, in a dark cellar barely lit, in darkness itself. She was voiceless. And, of course, she had to be a girl. In his dreams she resembled Lauren. But she disappeared from the dreams, sometimes instantaneously, sometimes fading into shredded, faltering light, deterioration, and silence.

As well, the little girl was usually in pain. Her eyes were closed as though she were concentrating on trying to let her pain go. But the pain, a ghost-like splinter, was always caught in her heart.

—

"You know, Jack," Lauren said a few days after Clara and Mia had stumbled upon her modeling for him, "it would be nice to have some flowers here."

She sat in the kitchen, a cup of black coffee on the table before her. She wore the smock. The crude sunflowers that flourished before the background red silk made Lauren appear morning-disheveled, lacking sleep, yet to Clara quite beautiful. The light across her lap grew obscure in the dark silken folds. Her hair was gathered up in a barrette, and fell down behind her. It hardly appeared gathered at all, floating around her head and neck in unruly strands.

She laid her cheek in the palm of a hand and surveyed the coffee cup. Her skin was almost flawless against the dark red lipstick she had just put on. Indeed, just now Lauren's appearance dazzled Clara. She was barefoot, and her legs were crossed, the smock opened to expose her knees.

"Some flowers that Clara and I can care for."

Lauren had made an almond torte the day before, and she sliced a piece of it and put it on a plate for Clara. Since Clara's discovery of her in the nude, and Mia's embarrassment, Lauren had paid special attention to Clara. She seemed to want Clara to understand that the lying around on the couch and the no clothes and all that made no difference in anything really. That Clara still was the most important thing of all to her mother. Clara took the torte and spooned a bit of cream onto it, from a bowl Lauren had taken from the icebox.

"I'm only sorry Mia isn't here to have some," Lauren said.

Clara played with the whipped cream, though she was disinterested in it. It came up in peaks, and she pushed them aside and crushed them. She figured that her father must have seen her mother without any clothes on. But Lauren always had been dressed when Clara saw her parents together, though the outfit might be just a bra, underpants, and a slip.

She had never reclined on a couch, though. Or at least, Clara thought, never with nothing on. And never in the sunlight where everybody could just look in the window. Clara's heart quivered. *Where just anyone can see you.*

Jack continued cleaning his brushes. The new painting of Lauren was so imprecise that, at this point, it made no sense to either Clara or her mother. As far as Clara could see, it was a bunch of curved lines decorated with a splotch. To indicate, Clara guessed, a mouth...or maybe a mistake, she could not figure which. None of the paintings Jack had done of Lauren actually looked like her. Clara wished he could show how delicate her mother was, instead of laboring so intently over these cloud-light swatches of color and soft affection that somehow now and then had faces.

Jack glanced at the canvas, and then abruptly stood up. He swirled some colors about in a shallow pan, took up some of the resultant gray onto a narrow brush, and touched the canvas with it, leaving a strip. Shaking his head, he wiped it away with a thumb. "What kinds of flowers?" He leaned close to the canvas, studying the still wet smear.

"Iris. And some azaleas over there by the windows. What would you like, Clara?"

"Could we get some peonies for my room?"

Lauren smiled, her eyes quick with the hope that Clara had forgiven her.

Jack nodded and placed another line, quite similar to the first, in the same place. "Okay. It'll be expensive. But we'll go to the flower market tomorrow, on the way back from the cemetery."

He had told Lauren and Clara about Père Lachaise in the same way that he had described the Moulin Rouge, Versailles, and the Jardin de Luxembourg before taking them to those places…with intense, wizened anecdotes and a humorous interest in how memorable they were. Jack's version of things was always a peopled one. He explained who was who. He made the Tuileries, for instance, exciting to Clara because she could actually imagine Marie-Antoinette walking through them, sampling some delicate fresh oysters and sipping champagne from a gold goblet. Jack's verbal tours were often quite long, but for Clara they had substance and humor. Anecdotal news about these famous people furthered her ability to imagine them…especially to imagine them strolling about on lovely days in places like the Tuileries.

Jack's knowledge was almost better than books because he made it into more of a story, and Clara enjoyed how varied the stories were. He described the *sans-culottes* at the Bastille, making so memorable the reducing of the prison to a vast rubble of broken mortar and stone that Clara made him take her the flea market at Bastille, just so she could stand where the prison had stood, and imagine its ruination. She loved the fact that the Île Saint-Louis was the original Paris, but one made up many, many thousands of years ago of rude mud huts. Imagine Parisians being illiterate, she thought, smudged with dirt and tribal. She envisioned Erik Satie strolling up the hill to Sacré-Coeur dreaming of his *Gymnopédies.* "Broke, crazy," Jack described Satie, as he composed the music for René Clair's movie *Entre Acte.* "You know, Clara, think of the whole orchestra in tune with rifle fire and a runaway hearse." Clara longed to see the movie. When Jack described for her how Marie-Antoinette had thought that cake would make the peasants happy, Clara laughed at how snooty the queen must have been. When he told her what ultimately happened to Marie-Antoinette, Clara shook her head once more. The sweet, grand woman, so beautifully coiffed, that Jack had described with her handsome, dying little prince... the guillotine.... It was so terrible a way to die.

The poor, lost queen.

—

They were to go to Père Lachaise the next afternoon, Saturday. But Lauren woke up in the morning with a cold, and when the moment arrived to leave for the cemetery, she had just gone to bed again. Clara figured that's what you get for going around without any clothes on. Actually, she smiled with that thought. Her condemnation of her mother's action was weakening. She nursed Lauren, taking the cup of tea from her and placing it on the table next to the bed. Lauren's nose was red and puffed. She rolled the cloth handkerchief about her fingers and blew into it.

Jack looked on. "You don't think you can go with us?"

It was, for early March, an oddly warm day, and he wore a broad straw hat and a white linen suit, a white shirt, and black tie. To Clara, he looked like a crumpled strawflower. The tie was not secured, and the suit had been taken directly from the armoire and put on, so that it was tracked with wrinkles. An open straw shoulder basket in which there was a sketchpad, a notebook, some cheese, and three apples hung from his shoulder. Disappointment sullied the smile on his face. He had badly wanted Lauren to go to the cemetery, and now sat, very disgruntled, on the edge of the bed.

Clara too sighed with disappointment. She had wanted to visit Père Lachaise ever since Jack had explained that it was filled with the famous dead.

"No, you and Clara go on." Lauren's voice was musty, a kind of gravelly whisper. "I want her to see it, and it's such a beautiful day."

Indeed it was almost as warm as it had been the previous summer. But the air was blue and clear, with none of the dampness that had made Clara's blouses so clammy-feeling the previous July. As Jack and Clara waited at a bus stop, high clouds, very transparent, passed behind the buildings and reappeared in the ragged spaces between, like silken, delicate smoke.

The bus was crowded, and Jack and Clara had to stand on the back platform. There was room for about six people and, as the bus made its way across the river, Clara clung to the railing, watching the buildings pass away behind her. The fact was that the balcony, as she called it to Jack's amusement, was her favorite place to be on the bus because from there she could watch everything. Paris was such a big place, yet the shops and narrow alleys that she spotted from the bus made up myriad small scenes of their own. Each was a separate landscape.

She had written many, many letters to her father since he had left, but had not been able to tell him, the way she wished to tell him, how much she was enjoying the spring in Paris. The sadness that overtook each writing discouraged her from the effort. But Clara wrote on. One letter took a week to write simply because she felt so bad doing it. Despite the now budding leaves on the trees, the bright air, and the almost daily walk down some ornate street filled with old-time dusty shops laden with books, antiques, cheeses, *patés*, or vegetables of every sort, she simply longed to see her father. Her heart felt old when she thought of him, like a deadened rose.

"Clara, I'm worried about these flowers of your mother's." Mottled light passed over Jack's face as the bus passed beneath some trees. "She wants all kinds of them, and I want her to have them." Jack surveyed his own hands. They were smudged with ground-in paint. Where he had chewed at his fingers, the skin showed through in tiny, abrupt shards. His tie lay crumpled down his chest. "But all this costs money. I mean…"

The buildings basked in the brightening sun, celebrating it with the abundant appearance of the new leaves.

Suddenly, Jack smiled. "There was a time I couldn't even afford the pots to put them in."

"You didn't have any?"

Jack laughed. He removed his hat a moment and ran the fingers of one hand through his hair. "I had just one one, actually." He replaced the hat on his head, making sure it was secured at a tilt. His eyes remained on the street. "I bet I've put it in a dozen paintings."

"Did it have flowers in it?"

Jack sighed. "At first, no. The flowers were more expensive than the pots. So, although I had the pot…"

Clara glanced at him.

"I imagined the flowers."

She nodded. Before the fire in Eureka, she herself had had a collection of dried wildflowers in a big book at home, a history of the Civil War. Her favorites were three faded trillium squashed between a couple of photos of Edwin Stanton. The trillium, Stanton, the book…all were now gone.

The bus came to a stop at the corner opposite the entry to Père Lachaise on the Avenue Ménilmontant.

"Come on." Securing the basket to his shoulder, Jack led the way across the street.

When they passed into the cemetery, Clara smiled at the three workmen who stood outside a small entry building. They wore the same blue pants and cotton jacket that almost all the laborers in Paris wore. One of them, a little man with an emaciated face who appeared not to have shaved for several days, frightened Clara, causing her to hold Jack's hand more tightly. The man stared at her, his hands hanging before his jacket like wrinkled bags. The handle of a shovel leaned against his chest. The scoop dripped with mud that formed a puddle at his feet. His eyes were huge, and his nose took up most of his face, like a beak. *A buzzard in a blue coat,* Clara thought.

Jack led her into the graveyard.

Clara had humorously hoped to see the dead walking around lost in their oblivion at Père Lachaise. The way they would be at the end of the world, as Sister Anna Constance had described that event in Catechism class in the fourth grade. The Jaws of Hell would open, and Satan's accursed would stagger once more onto the earth's surface, their skin falling away like underdone bacon. Clara had mused whether such frightening minions would appear everywhere in the world.

It came as a shock to her to find that Père Lachaise indeed was a miniature city, with buildings and neighborhoods everywhere. There were street signs and gardens and sidewalk curbs. Mourners went about with picnic baskets. The place reminded her of San Francisco on a sunny day.

There were hundreds of statues, and Clara decided that they were the ones who lived here and came alive at night, to dance and sit down to infernal ceramic banquets. *Maybe they're alive right now*, she thought, *but just don't want to be caught moving.* Clara grinned to herself, imagining that, as soon as she and Jack rounded a corner to move on, the statues would break once more into motion and do normal things like everybody else…like, look at the sights or have a coffee. Champagne.

She enjoyed especially the statues of angels. There weren't many, but they all stared off into the distance as though there were celestial happiness out there, at which they wanted to look. Indeed they appeared surprised by whatever it was, so that their hands were held out in gestures of wonderment. They wanted to know what had happened. But they were so frozen in their movement that Clara guessed no one had yet told them what was happening. Their wings were spread out. They looked like innocent teenagers, and most of them were covered with bird-do.

Jack pointed out many of the important resting places. They passed by Marcel Proust's, then paused a moment for Jack to prattle over the grave of Eugene Delacroix.

"The greatest of them all, you know," he said finally. Hitching the basket to his shoulder, he shook his head. "The recipe for a man like this is not well understood."

Clara preferred a couple of the graves that had less important people in them, like Croce-Spinelli and Sivel's. This one had two statues on it, of two dead men lying side by side. The feet of one of the men came out from under a sculpted bed sheet. They were very big and ugly feet, and a cobweb, a real one, quivered between them.

"They went up in a balloon." Jack smiled. "And they went up so high that they ran out of air."

Clara wondered how they had ever gotten back down, to get buried here.

Then there was Victor Noir.

"I don't know much about this fellow," Jack said, his hands folded before him.

"But what happened to him?"

Noir was represented on the slab over his grave by a life-size bronze statue sprawled on its back, passed out. He was a young man, fully dressed in a suit with a long coat and vest, a rumpled overcoat, and a wrinkled open-collared shirt. For that matter, everything was wrinkled.

The statue mystified Clara. Most others she had seen—like that of William McKinley in the main square of Arcata back home, the next town over from Eureka—were upright, awake, visionary and well-groomed. This man looked like he had not taken his clothes to the cleaners for months. As well, he looked like he had been run over by a streetcar.

"Somebody shot him," Jack said.

Dried-out flowers filled the sculpted top hat that lay at the statue's side.

"He was a writer."

He was cute, Clara thought, with thick, more or less curly hair, a mustache, and a nice mouth, kind of like a soldier in a cavalry movie. She could see Noir's chest where his shirt was opened. And there was a shiny protuberance at the zipper of his pants, which embarrassed Clara because she realized the only way it could be so shiny was that lots of people had rubbed the lump of metal there. She did not rub it, although she had trouble not looking at it.

They walked around for another half-hour, and stopped finally at a park bench to have some of the camembert and fruit. Jack cut up an apple. Clara did not care much for camembert except when she had it with very sweet apples, and this one was delicious. She bit into a slice, and reached up to replace a strand of hair blowing about in a breeze, balancing the apple in her free hand.

I don't think Père Lachaise is haunted at all, Clara decided. Death, of course, led to heaven, she knew that. At least, she hoped that everyone who had died in her family had gone there. The trouble was that, even when the soul flew away to eternal happiness, it still left behind an old worm-filled body. So there had to be something in all these graves. But Clara had never imagined a place intended for corpses as beautiful as this place, which was filled with trees, birds, and flowers in pots, with visitors and conversation and laughter.

Jack finished his apple and wiped his hands on a cloth napkin. He pushed the hat back and looked up at the trees for a moment. Stretching his legs out and crossing them at the ankles, he folded his arms before him. His suit sparkled in the dappled sunlight.

"Clara, I've wanted to say something to you about your mother and me."

Clara ceased chewing for a moment. The apple and the cheese coagulated in her mouth.

"About what happened the other day, you know, with her modeling for me."

She swallowed a bit of it. "That's okay, I—"

"No, please. I think it's important. I hope you know that I love your mother, and that I've loved her for years."

Clara stopped chewing once more. She could see, from the corner of her eye, that Jack was now watching her. With difficulty she swallowed the rest of the apple and cheese, looking down at Jack's scuffed black shoes.

"And that I'd never ask her to do anything that wasn't right."

Clara's face became quite hot, and she said nothing, hoping that Jack would change the subject.

"It makes me very happy that you decided to stay here with us. Having you and Lauren both takes away a real...well, glumness. An emptiness."

A kind of pleased affection for Jack softened Clara's resistance. Indeed she leaned against him as the trees sighed in slow confusion. But she thought again of her father and the dismay his absence caused her. *What kind of...what did he say? Glumness? What glumness could Jack possibly have? He took my mother away from my father.*

"I'd been writing to your mother all those years."

Clara nodded.

"But I didn't intend to steal her from your Da or anything of the kind. I just…just wanted to—"

"Were they love letters?"

For a moment there was silence, until Jack reached up and removed his hat. He leaned forward onto his knees, turning the hat about with his fingers. "You often ask questions like that, Clara." His voice was soft and slightly raspy, barely discernible in the dying retreat of the wind. Clara felt her face getting even hotter. She played with the apple slice. "I hope you aren't angered by my saying that. It's one of the things Lauren told me about you, and I think it's wonderful."

Clara tightened her lips. She felt exposed. She was hurt that her mother could talk about her behind her back.

"And after a long time she wrote back to me. But Clara…" Jack touched her arm. "She only wrote about you. About your family. Never about…."

Clara stood up, now even more distracted. In her thoughts, she saw her mother pregnant and scared, a girlish phantasm. Clara looked over her shoulder, suddenly afraid that a ghost would jump out at her, the ghost of a tossed away little baby. She threw the apple slice into a receptacle at the end of the bench.

Jack's voice wandered. "No, our letters were very different. Mine were more…." He replaced the hat on his head and leaned once more onto his knees. "More insistent."

Clara turned to watch him, taking advantage of the fact that he was staring at the ground. He reached up to wipe his eyes. His fingers were so thick that they appeared incapable of delicacy.

"I didn't think…for years I didn't think that she'd be able to forgive me. The way I just…ran away."

"The way you treated her, too."

The brim of Jack's hat hid his hand.

"She told me," Clara said.

He looked up at her and caught her staring at him. His eyes were washed over with worry. "But now your mother has saved me from that…from the anguish of that. And soon, you'll see, I plan to, to…."

Jack took a handkerchief from his back pocket. Clara imagined Lauren nude, laughing…but then suddenly in tears. A teenager with her baby in her arms, having to give it away, and giving it to someone she didn't know. One day the baby was just gone. There was nothing left to be said. It just disappeared.

With a silent inhalation, Clara then saw herself abandoned like that, with no one around to see. Vanished. Nothing said. *How could that be?* Her birth, the nestling in her mother's arms, and the suckling affection…. It would just come to an end in a sort of nothing.

—

Jack looked over the damp sheen on his fingertips. He wiped them on his pants legs and joined his hands together, leaning forward and placing his elbows on his knees. Clara remained beside him. Her eyes had fixed on a few flowers across the pathway. She seemed to be waiting for the moment to pass, and waiting for Jack to recover himself.

The way he'd treated her, Clara had said.

His heart knocked about in a hurrying movement. He and Lauren had finally arranged a secret meeting, in Carson Park, a few blocks from Lauren's home. She had entered the park bundled in a scarf with a heavy coat. Her face was mottled with cold. Their greetings were embarrassed. Jack finally came out with the brusque announcement that he was leaving Eureka, and that it was her fault that she was pregnant. She should have done something to prevent it. She should have known what to do.

Her eyes took on a kind of accused wonderment. As he walked away, his hands thrust in his jacket pockets, he turned to look back. Lauren sat on the swing, her hands clasped on her lap, and wept. His pause, his hand resting on the top of the gate, and the wish that he…no, the certainty that he owed her an apology and much more, all of it was fumbled away in his own panic and fear.

In that moment, Jack betrayed Lauren.

His heart had been frozen ever since by what he had done to her and their lost baby. It beat, and blood passed through it, but it felt to Jack like ice, its affections hardened by the gaze of his self-hatred. He felt he had become the worst sort of observer…someone who understands the truth and does nothing about it. For years he did not tell it to anyone else. Nothing else was possible. He was so afraid, although he acknowledged his betrayal of her and loved Lauren, thousands of miles away. But even now that she was here with him in Paris, he could not tell her what it had cost him, because he knew that it had cost her terribly. So much more.

The years he had spent wondering what their life would be like together had been just that, a broken fantasy. Jack had been a coward, and felt that his cowardice had defeated him.

"You do love my mom, don't you?" Clara glanced at him.

"Of course I do."

"And me too?" She smiled, looking away.

"Both of you."

Clara continued smiling, sitting back on the bench.

"Do you think she loves me, Clara?"

Clara lowered her hand to her lap. Her eyes seemed to lose their focus for a moment, and she could not look up at Jack. Resignation fell about her shoulders.

"Yes," she whispered.

———

Her answer was confusing to Clara. She realized suddenly how much she enjoyed the small moment of conversation. But she could barely reply to Jack, because she saw in this moment the possibility of her betraying her father with too clear an answer. The figure of her father obscured the truth, that her mother indeed was crazy about Jack.

"Can I go down there?" She pointed down one of the pathways…it was called the Avenue de la Chappelle…that they had not yet explored. At the bottom was a monument in a circle surrounded by tombs.

"I don't think so. There's not much to see."

"But can't I go anyway?"

"No, Clara, you can't."

Jack's response was suddenly so angry-sounding that Clara stood and headed down the pathway.

"Not without me," he said.

"Fook off," she whispered to herself.

"Clara!"

She looked over her shoulder. Jack resembled a suave skeleton, his white suit a cloud draped over his long bones. The basket lay on the ground, and the handkerchief remained in his hand.

She hurried down to the end of the path, and passed a young woman seated on a bench reading. The woman was startled by Clara's arrival, and closed the book as she hurried by.

Clara paid no attention, so quickly startled was she herself by a statue to her left. It was the figure of a woman dressed in hanging robes that covered her body entirely. She appeared to have been punished, condemned maybe to cover herself forever. The robes were so finely sculpted that they appeared to be made of real silk that fell down the woman's body, folded and draped everywhere. Very little of her could be seen, but Clara could tell she was in anguish. She slumped against the stone wall to her side. She was a grotesque in mourning.

Most remarkable of all was the arm that reached up from the robes, the only part of her skin that was visible. The hand reached for a barred window in the wall above, as though the woman were hoping that someone inside, in the prison, would take it.

The darkness of the weathered green moss on the stone caused Clara's shoulders to tingle. The thought of the stone suffocated her, as though Clara herself were encased in it, searching for the window with her own hand. She felt the stone pressing against her face, the moss making it impossible to breathe.

Grimacing, she turned away and was abruptly enveloped in white. She screamed, pushing herself from Jack, who had come up silently behind her.

"Clara, it's all right."

"Leave me alone!" She hit his chest, and his basket fell to the ground. "Let me go!"

She pushed herself away from him. Her mouth was dry, and her knees seemed barely capable of carrying her. Suddenly the worry that had attended the last months burst from its hiding places. Jack's refusal to let her be on her own, and his grabbing at her like this…with all that, Clara's refusal of Paris, now a complete refusal and an outraged one, raced into her heart. She could not stand being dictated to by him, as though he owned her, and owned her mother.

"Please. Clara." Jack knelt before her to gather up the basket.

She hated him. Jack had stolen her mother away, and had exiled Clara from her father. Her eyes burned. She wished to attack him. "Oh…" She placed a fist against her mouth, shocked.

"I know. It's awful, isn't it?" Jack looked up to survey the dark window above the statue, as though searching for the face of the prisoner. "I've never been able to bear this thing."

He had no idea of the source of Clara's reaction. *The statue!* she thought. Even though, indeed, Clara could not bear the thing either. She struggled for breath, feeling the granite, now quite hot, pressing tightly against her face, into her eyes, and killing her. She knew that the robed woman was trying to get into the prison, not to get someone out. She had committed some terrible sin, and it was the devil himself in there. The woman was striving to speak with him.

Clara turned and ran from Jack, back toward the Avenue de La Chapelle.

As she approached the bench, slowing to a walk, the woman placed the book at her side. She was young, twenty, perhaps twenty-five. Even in her distress, Clara saw that she was unusually lovely, with a delicacy in her skin that made her appear like a fashion model or an actress. An ingenue, a quick smile appearing on her lips. Clara closed her eyes, fighting against the rage she felt and the anguish of discovering how intensely she resented Jack's intrusion on her family.

"Clara?"

Clara stopped up short. Her breathing came from her in quick gasps. It was pained and hurried.

"May I talk with you?" the woman said in English. Her Parisian accent was quite pronounced. She laid a hand on the closed book, and inadvertently re-opened it as Clara tried to figure out who she was.

"Don't run away. Please. I've wanted to meet you."

"Who are you?"

"Me?" The woman looked down at the book, her fingers playing with a page that she turned to the right and left. "My name is Emma."

"Do I know you?"

"No." Emma looked up once more at Clara. "But now I am glad to meet you."

Clara looked over her shoulder. Jack stood with his back to the statue of the shrouded woman, watching the conversation. His face was downcast with a look of aggrieved worry.

"Because I'm your sister, Clara."

17

Clara fingered the saucer that held her cup of hot chocolate. But she did not care about the chocolate or about the *croissant* that the waiter had put before her. Instead she wished just to stare at Emma. To study her, her eyes, and the long fingers that were so much like Lauren's. And the cheekbones that reminded Clara actually of Jack's, except for the finesse they had and the finesse of her mother's profile that brought such arresting authority to Emma's appearance, and demanded Clara's attention.

But Clara's shyness got in the way. She tried not to stare because she did not want to be rude. For one, she knew she had seen Emma before. She was the girl kissing her boyfriend in line at Berthillon, and the girl getting out of the *deux-chevaux* in the Place Vendôme.

Clara studied every movement of Emma's smile anyway, the way she moved her hands through the red silk scarf that hung about her neck, and the manner in which her lashes flickered with such slow darkness as she contemplated an answer to one of Clara's questions.

It was all too much and too detailed for Clara to take in in so little time.

Clara learned that Emma was a student at the Sorbonne, as a pianist. "So my hands, you see," she said, displaying them to Clara. "There's not much that I do with them because they're so...." She had done her nails carefully, crescents of intimate carmine. "Most of the people I work with don't have to worry about such things," she smiled, after Clara complimented her nails. "They're men, most of them." Her eyes remained on Jack's for a moment, and she touched his sleeve with affection.

Clara surveyed the long green dress, narrow down Emma's legs below her knees, and the seamed stockings. "I can hardly wait for you to meet my mother." Already she had a plan for this. Lauren would be so excited, and it would be Clara who would usher that happiness in, hand in hand with her sister. "I mean, *our* mother." She imagined the embrace.

Emma's smile disappeared.

Clara imagined the surprised look on Lauren's face as she faced her foundling child, the new re-opening of Lauren's heart....

Emma glanced at Jack, and then looked away.

"I mean, you know, so you can get to—"

"Clara, I don't...." Emma's eyes lost their fine light.

Jack's hand wandered across the tabletop to his hat. He turned it about. Clara awaited more of a reply. The *espresso* machine whined. Waiters made their way through the café, which was gray with cigarette smoke. The noise of all the other conversations whelmed about the small table at which sat Clara, her father, and sister. Clara realized that no one in the cafe could possibly sense the discomfort she now so suddenly felt, or why there would be such discomfort. But she did not understand the resistance that now made this first meeting—so heart-electrifying a meeting—hardly a meeting any longer.

"I mean, why isn't she here?" Emma's voice descended to a mutter.

Jack shook his head. "Emma, Lauren's—"

"You told me that she'd be coming with you."

"I know, but...." Jack took the hat onto his lap. "She's sick. She's...." Jack, who always talked, was now unable to move the conversation from the disquiet into which it had descended.

Emma glowered. Her eyes now seemed flattened, as though the lovely aqueous fluid that so filled them had partially drained from them or had faded. "She's never wanted to meet me." Her eyes fell to her hands. "She doesn't know who I am, and has never wanted to know."

Her face had paled, and the dark purple ceramic earrings now appeared like metallic stones, their sharp intensity hardly appropriate to the fragility that was so apparent in Emma's eyes. Her short hair, cut so that it swept back directly behind her ears, was one of the first things that had dazzled Clara when she had first encountered her. But now it seemed too shiny and too varnished.

"She's got a cold, Emma," Clara said. "That's all. She's home in bed."

"Clara." Jack's voice caught, and he cleared his throat. "Emma thinks Lauren won't want to meet her."

Emma looked into the street.

"I know that's not so. And you do, of course. I'd been looking for months for a way to introduce them, and that was supposed to happen today. I especially wanted it to happen now, since you'd...read that letter."

Further chagrined, Clara moved to speak.

"No, no. It's all right." Jack was attempting to comfort her. "It's just that I had hoped we could *all* come here today to meet Emma. I mean, that's why I was so worried this morning when Lauren was so ill. And I wanted you to come. Because I figured it would be...well, easier, if you were here, too."

"But can't we just go back to the studio?"

Emma grimaced. *"Non, Papa."*

The appellation—*"Papa"*. So different from the word "Daddy" that Clara used for her own father, the formality of it—startled her.

"But you can meet our mother," Clara said.

"Papa. Non!"

"Why not?"

Emma and Jack were startled by the abruptness of Clara's question, and Clara shut up. She'd gotten out of line. She grumbled at herself for being such a loudmouth. "Sorry," she whispered.

Emma's mouth turned down. She studied her hands again, which joined each other, became intertwined, and turned palms-up. The chocolate-brown cup that held her *grand-creme* formed a rounded tableau for it, the aerated cream, and the dissolved shaved-chocolate in ruins down the inside rim. A cloth napkin lay crumpled to the side as Emma finally spoke. "I tried so often to imagine what she was like."

Clara sat back.

"There was always a future in which we would meet. When I was five...you know, I knew I hadn't been born here. My parents had told me that my mother lived far away, in the United States, and that they didn't know who she was." Emma smiled, wrapping her fingers about the brown cup. "They wanted me to think that she was kind and happy, even though they didn't know anything about her."

Clara thought of the many times Lauren had bandaged a cut on her arm or arranged her hair in a barette, and felt sorry for Emma that she had never experienced that.

"But I couldn't imagine she could be kind and happy, because she had treated me so badly. Thrown me away. And I tried to imagine what it would be like to meet her. I imagined a movie star. She was one of those American ladies we saw in the movies. Sometimes they were glamorous and sinful, you know, like Lauren Bacall. And other times they were the perfect American mother, making pies and smiling and waiting at home for their husbands." Emma gave a brief, pained smile. "*So* American, those movies. But always, my mother was beautiful. And mostly unim…unimpea…." Emma turned toward Jack.

"Unimpeachable."

"Yes. Gold dresses. She wore furs and jewelry. Or she was some kind of sweet slave-girl. Lovely lips." Emma shrugged. "And she was my mother."

She took up the cup of coffee and sipped from it. Holding it in her hands, so that her nails looked like touches of arranged precision, she took in a breath. "There was a secret I had."

"What was it?" Clara said.

"What she must have looked like when I was born. When I got older, I figured she must have been young when she had me, maybe someone as young as me. But then I used to dream that I *was* her, and that I was having the baby." Emma's lips wavered. "That it was my baby coming out from… well, you know."

A hurrying kind of spectral swoon swirled through Clara's feelings.

"With all the blood," Emma said. "Sometimes it was a thrill for me to feel that."

Clara swallowed.

"But then, in my dream, I threw the baby away." Emma took in a breath, and then sighed, waiting for the tension to dissipate. But for Clara it did not dissipate because she could see the little baby floating away in its blood waste, abandoned and dead.

—

Clara walked up the stairs as noisily as possible. She felt the need to alert her mother that something was about to happen. Something, she had hoped only an hour before, that would be quite wonderful.

But given the bus ride back across the river and the nervous trudge up the Rue Mouffetard toward Contrescarpe, Clara was not so sure how successful this meeting was going to be. Jack made small talk with the two girls, grateful to Clara for having asked Emma once more to come to the studio. Clara pleaded with her to do so. Emma and Clara sat together on the seat behind Jack's as the bus progressed toward the Left Bank. But Clara recognized that Jack's enthused, touristic observations about the light passing off the budding leaves or the green, sunny sheen of the Seine were just a fraud. All they did was to expose his worry about what was going to happen between Emma and Lauren. There was a tone in his patter of clipped tiredness, which extended Clara's worries and caused her to study that sheen despite how tiresome and intrusive it really was. Her hands knotted with each other in her lap. She wanted the flutter of the leaves and the increasingly crisp cold of the afternoon to brighten the hope she had had for celebratory surprise. The trouble was that sweat was oozing from beneath her arms, which was all wrong because it was so cold on this drafty, rattling bus. Jack's voice made her as uncomfortable as the sweat did. It sounded out of place and unbearable. Clara pulled about her neck the collar of the sweater she had brought.

For the last half of the bus ride, Emma stared out the bus window in silence.

Both Clara and Jack had keys, but neither made a move to find them when they reached the door to the studio. Emma stood quietly, holding her purse by the strap before her with both hands. Clara, biting her lower lip, wished she could run away. By now she was convinced that she was doing something quite wrong. The opening up of her heart had ceased, constricted by Emma's censure and the story she had told in the cafe. She worried that Emma's feelings were like Jack's had been when he discovered Clara with the doll theater, and that if some secret of hers were revealed, Emma would hurl herself into a rage.

"So...." Jack took the key from his pocket, rattled it a few times in the lock, and opened the door.

—

Rain fell against the cafe window like sharp pebbles. There was thunder, faraway, a casual dark roll of sound that passed even farther into the distance.

Feeling better, Lauren had gotten out of bed to come down to the Place Monge market for some pears, planning to make Clara a dessert. She wished to do something for her, to make up for the past few days in which Clara's behavior had been so badly criticized by Jack, and her own had been perceived as so unnatural by Clara herself. Everything in Clara's life was new, and each day such a scattered one, that she sometimes seemed frenzied by all the things that were happening to her.

Lauren herself was having a similar problem, although she could never have imagined anything more pleasure-giving than simply being in Paris with Jack Roman. But she sympathized with Clara, and hoped that the surprise of a sweet made of pears with some fresh cream would alleviate the rise and fall of confusion brought about simply by stepping out into the street in this city.

Waiting for the bill for her coffee, she recalled the conversation she had with Jack while she was posing for him a few days before.

It was clear to Lauren that Jack was dazzled by her. Her sad complaints to him about money and that she was not accustomed to the strictures that Jack's art sales placed on her wishes...at that moment, when she had been warmed by the sun coming in the windows, and Jack had adjusted the wrap about her legs...those things had not seemed to matter. They were even laughing about it.

"But Jack, I *am* sorry that I seem so angry sometimes. I just...it's so difficult, doing what I did. And sometimes I feel that I've betrayed Clara, dragging her along like this, making her miss her own home." A fresh passage of sunlight passed across her, only slightly salving her heart. "Did I make her lose what I lost?" There was a silence. She adjusted the wrap. She could not get the corner of it to fold properly, and the difficulty compounded her isolation. "You can't imagine what it's like, Jack, to have a family and to...abandon it."

"Don't you think I've felt that?" Jack stood before his canvas, a brush hanging from the fingers of his right hand. The end of his tongue slipped across his lips as he looked at his work. He laid the brush down on the table and wiped his fingers with a corner of the shirt he was wearing, an old shirt multicolored with years of splattered, wiped, and splotched paint. He moved toward the end of the couch and sat down. He was a large man, crumpled, romantic and humorous, nonetheless feeling the self-recrimination that Lauren's remark had brought about in him.

To Lauren, his silence felt sultry and angered. She examined the curvature of her body, and its changes in texture, from her breasts to her stomach and legs. She studied the place in which their baby had been engendered and had grown, before she had been taken away. She remembered for a moment the blood and gelatinous liquids that had surrounded their little girl, the protective nourishment it had given her, and the way that, after a moment, the sea of it had been ejected by Lauren. It had been left for dead after the girl's birth. The entire event had been conceived with childish excitement with the sweet boy Jack, who was now this contemplative man whose heart and sadness she so loved. The two of them had made that little girl, and just months later, Lauren had been grieving for her.

That baby was somewhere in the world even now, Lauren knew, and would likely know what it was like to be so in love as Lauren had been with Jack. Lauren had been so lost in it that she did not care at the time what the consequences were, or could be.

Lauren finished her coffee. She left a few *centimes* for the waiter, and then checked inside the cloth bag on the cafe table for the three pears she had bought. The green-yellow volumes nestled together, like breasts, full

163

stomachs, flesh-filled hips. One was cut slightly, and the white flesh inside oozed a shining silver liquid.

———

There was no light on the stairway, and the darkness intimidated Lauren a moment. Usually she just made her way up the stairs to the studio door. There was no effort to it. But the way she felt now, with her cold, her stomach feeling leaden with the deterioration of her feelings, and the hem of her skirt rubbing against her legs, gave the stairway an additional feverish gloom. She looked up toward the door, where light showed in the crack between the floor and the door itself. The passage felt ruined.

She gripped her purse and held the bag of pears close. Her knees were unsteady, and she held on to the railing as though it were the single connection she had to any kind of calm. The memory of her life in the United States cluttered her mind. Martin's—and Clara's—voices meandered about in unuttered parts of words and cluttered phrases. The stairs felt at an angle, and Lauren held out a hand to steady herself against the wall. Old paint crackled beneath her touch. She kept her eyes on the light beneath the door. Her breath came in short clutches.

When she opened the door, light from the studio flooded her face. Clara sat at the table. The smile on her face, unusually bright as though she were opening a large luxurious present, distracted Lauren. But there was someone else in the studio, a young woman—a girl, really—standing at a window, a handkerchief in her hands. Her hair was cropped short. She wore a long green dress and porcelain earrings. She wrung the handkerchief about her fingers.

"Mom. This is…" Clara paused. Her voice caught with nervousness. The other girl's eyes flickered toward Clara. Then she looked back at Lauren. Jack himself stood aside. "This is Emma," Clara said.

The silence that filled the studio lasted only a moment. But it contained genuine brightness, which was emphasized by Clara's obvious happiness.

"She's…" Clara gripped her hands before her. "She's my sister, Mom."

Lauren's breath seized.

"She's your lost baby." Clara's smile broadened as she beamed toward Emma.

"No. What?"

"Mom, she's yours."

Lauren saw the quick brimming of Emma's tears. "Oh…." She stepped toward her. "Angel." The painfulness of the years in which she had not known what had become of her baby now washed through her. Her worries lay about in her heart like scarred limbs. "You're so…." Her vanished daughter stood before her. She took up Emma's hands, held them a moment, and then embraced her.

—

Emma shivered in Lauren's arms. She was unable to take hold of her mother. Clara's heart felt overtaken by yearning for her happiness. Lauren laid her head on Emma's shoulder, unable to let her daughter go, as though this embrace were intended to make up for all the lost ones, all the dreamed-of embraces, and every moment she had wondered what her daughter looked like and where she had been taken. Each empty moment. Each devastated exhalation of breath.

"Let go of me." Emma pushed herself away. "Get away!" She grabbed her coat from the chair, took up her purse, and walked toward the door. Hatred flickered from her eyes. "I never wanted to meet you. I never even wanted to see you."

She hurried out the door and down the stairs into the dark.

LE CLUB DE
JELLY ROLL

18

Lauren dreamed that night that Emma was unclaimable. She was a baby in the dream, but so elegantly dressed that she seemed hardly an infant at all. Her face was mature, that of a young woman, Emma as she was now, dressed in mourning in a child's deathly swaddling.

When she awoke, Lauren lay in isolation. She felt alone and separated, although she was in Jack's arms. She had sought him out for comfort as she wept. For a moment now, she wished to wrest herself from his embrace. It was he who had caused her to lose her daughter.

But then the disorientation of the dream left her, and she realized that it was Jack who had brought Emma back to her.

In another dream, Lauren was again dismissed by Emma, whom she had once loved similarly to the way she loved Clara. This made Lauren's isolation—in the memory of those few days that she did have little Emma in her arms—almost unbearable.

But unlike with Clara, she had loved Emma so intensely because she had lost her.

—

The barman served two patrons the following Monday afternoon in the Deux Cygnes...Clara and a workman standing at the bar sipping an *espresso*, wearing a dark blue coat. The freezing rain falling over Paris appeared gray and darker gray, spilling from a lowering wall of iron-like clouds. Clara gathered her scarf and pulled it close to her skin. Water coursed down the gutters of the Rue Mouffetard, and the few old cobble-stones showing through the pavement gleamed with it, like loaves of slick, cold bread.

Steam from the *grand creme* rose up toward her face in a brief caress. Her fingers were warmed by the coffee, but she felt they would not stay warmed.

The cafe walls were hung with old mirrors bordered with gold that now, with age, had bubbled and flaked. One of the reasons it was Clara's favorite was that she could look at her reflection…her reflections…and make up stories about all those different girls in the mirrors, about whom they had come to the cafe to meet, and what secrets they held.

Clara now knew the pain that secrets could cause. Jack's trunk, for example, and its mystery. How angering it had been for him to have it discovered, even though the Personal it held was so shortly to come to such remarkable life. Although the treasures in that box were not all smiling and pleasurable, at least at that moment Clara had set them free.

In other pictures that Clara had seen of her mother as a girl, Clara had recognized only Lauren's eyes as suggestive of her own. But in the photo of Jack and Lauren on the dock, Lauren reminded Clara of herself *especially* in the eyes, which had glimmered in the photograph with the moment's gathering of affection. Also, Clara now saw, on herself in the mirror, the smile that Lauren had in the picture.

Clara had never really considered what her mother had been like as a girl. But the photo made it clear that Lauren was once very much like her. Now, though, the secret that there was another girl who was also like them, and was then nowhere to be found, that secret….

The Saturday before, Lauren stood staring at the open doorway, down the black stairs, as Emma escaped to the street. Clara, furious with Emma, sat at the table with her eyes tightly closed, to ward off the sight of her mother's grief.

Jack tried explaining to Lauren, as he had attempted explaining to Clara in the cafe earlier, how this had happened. But Lauren would not listen to him. She walked about the studio, her hand gathered into a fist before her lips. She appeared caught up in a seizure of rage, glaring at Jack from time to time where he sat on the couch.

Jack's large body had given in. His hands were joined between his knees. He followed Lauren with his eyes, but then averted them when she glanced so angrily at him.

"Jack, why didn't you tell me about her?"

He could not reply. When Clara attempted an explanation…that Jack understood that Emma was afraid, that Emma didn't know what it would be like, that Emma…. Lauren shushed her, sweeping aside an empty water glass from the table to the studio floor.

Clara's breathing stopped. She let the shards of glass lie, afraid to move, and her mother picked them up herself, carefully, as though each one was a kind of grave pain. Lauren apologized. For Clara, the sound of her voice was that of someone wandering from a lost mind, unaware that anyone else was in the room.

—

Mia Phelan hurried up the Rue Mouffetard, her umbrella buffeted by a surge of wind. Earlier that afternoon, Clara had been called from the classroom to go to Sister Madeleine's office, where a *pneumatique* had arrived for her. Jack had told her about these things…written messages that people could send from post office to post office through air-driven tubes…and she hoped that someone from somewhere would send her one someday. She even thought of sending one to herself, just so she could see what it would be like to get one. So when Sister Madeleine handed the *pneumatique* to Clara, and watched as she read the note—that Emma wished to see her at the Deux Cygnes that day after school—Clara felt as though she had been elevated to a new level of prestigious influence at the school. When she asked Mia to join her—passing on to her friend some of the guarded mystery of the surprise note—Clara glowed with self-importance.

But actually Clara wished Mia to join her for fear that Emma was going to spill out her obvious pained anger, with Clara the target. She hoped Mia's presence would interfere with the rage, and stem it at least for a moment so that Clara could maintain herself.

Mia lowered her umbrella as she arrived at the door. Making her way between the other tables, she avoided the workman's glance. She held her arms about her in mock freezing. "Bloody cold, isn't it?"

She removed a woolen beret. The barman approached their table, and Mia ordered a *petit creme*. The several inches of hair that had come out from beneath the beret were sprinkled with raindrops, and she took up the cloth napkin that remained unused by Clara, to daub them away.

Clara felt suddenly intruded upon, despite the fact that it was at her insistence that her friend join her.

"Clara, you all right?"

"There's someone else coming."

"This afternoon? Your mother?"

"No, it's not her. It's...."

The door to the cafe clattered open, pushed by the wind, and Emma hurried in, dropping her umbrella into the receptacle just inside the entry. "Clara, thank you for coming," she said in French as she approached. For the moment, she remained standing at the table, not sure that she would be asked to sit down. She glanced at Mia. "I need to talk with you."

Mia glanced back and forth between the two others. Emma continued, this time in English.

"I feel so badly—"

"This is my friend." Clara's reticence—to the point of not even mentioning Mia's name—had unsettled both Emma and Mia. "This is Mia Phelan. Mia, this...." Clara swallowed, and continued. "This is my sister." There was another silence. Mia smiled, but Clara could see her confusion. "My sister Emma."

Emma sat down at the table, struggling to produce a smile. Clara knew—had immediately recognized—that it was an invasion of privacy to blurt out the truth like that to someone Emma did not even know. So intimate a truth and, it seemed, so angering a truth.

But for the moment Clara didn't care. She waited for Emma to settle herself, and then asked the much-rehearsed question. "How could you be so mean to my mother?"

Emma turned away. Her fingers grabbed at the napkin Mia had used previously.

"Just treating her like she was a...criminal or something."

Mia sat back, intertwining her fingers. Clara was in immediate pain, a kind of distracted wish taking her glance from the coffee cup and directing it out the window to the street. She placed her chin on the palm of a hand and leaned forward, taking up the spoon and stirring her coffee. The spoon made an isolated sound, like a nail dropping to a ceramic floor.

"Clara." Emma grimaced.

Clara's back slid against the red leather. The faded gold on the mirrors gave everything in the cafe a look of deterioration and tired age.

"It's because I hated her." Emma leaned forward, taking the napkin again into her hand and bringing it to her eyes.

"You hated my mother?"

The workman finished his *espresso,* paid, and left the cafe. The barman removed the cup and saucer from the counter and took them to the back. Now, except for Clara, Emma and Mia, there was no one in the cafe at all, and the mirrors throughout the room made the cafe look like a theater, an enormous stage-set with tables and windows, chairs, *espresso* machines and *Bar/Tabac* signs everywhere, with three women, identically repeated here and there, in silent separation from each other.

Although, suddenly, one of them, the oldest one, leaned her head down toward the napkin now held in the fingers of both hands.

"Terribly," she said.

Clara's hands lay in her lap. The slim fingers and the gold ring she wore, with a single pearl, reminded her of her mother's hands in the photo of her as a girl on the dock in Eureka. "Do you...do you still hate her?"

Emma lowered the handkerchief to her lap. "Please, Clara. Don't ask such a question." She picked at the nail polish on one of her fingers. "When Jack told me that he'd been in contact with her, and that you and your family were coming here to Paris, I begged him...I asked him not to say anything about me." Emma raised her hands to the table. "Nothing. I couldn't stand the idea that Lauren would know who I was. That she'd know I was alive. Or anything about me."

"Why?"

"Because she hoped I had disappeared."

"She did not."

Surprise bristled in Emma's eyes.

"She did not." Clara took up her spoon again and began stirring her coffee, with clear aggravation. "That's dumb."

"Dumb! What is that, `dumb'? What does that mean."

"Stupid, it means."

Emma glanced at Clara's spoon. Clara looked as though she wished to throw it.

"You just don't get it," she said.

For the first time in the conversation, Mia smiled, still charmed by Clara's American usage.

"I was certain, all those years, that I would never have to meet her." Emma's eyes grew larger. "Ever." She sighed.

Clara's face began to heat up. It felt swollen.

"Or that I would ever even know who she was." Emma lowered her head. "I told you about my dream yesterday?"

"Yes."

"There were others. Once, she was a French woman. There was a farm. A fire. And she died in the fire. She was floating in the darkness up above me. I couldn't see her, really. Couldn't make her out. Except that I felt that somehow she looked like me."

"Than that part of the dream was true."

Emma averted her eyes. "I suppose so. The dream came after the war."

She smiled toward Mia who, listening to the conversation, remained completely silent. Her face had had a look of stricken discomfort as she had observed the harsh words between Clara and Emma. But Emma had just gone ahead and pursued the argument, not caring how Mia might feel about it. This moment was something between her and Clara. Now, though, her demeanor toward Mia softened.

"After Jack saved me," she said to her.

"You were in the war?" Mia said.

Emma shrugged. "So many people suffered, Clara. And my parents…I mean, my parents who adopted me. Their name was Dusel."

The two girls nodded, Mia moving with nervous discomfort in her chair.

"They were both killed. I don't know what I would have done without

Jack. He…." Emma gazed out the window at the scurrying rain. The black buildings across the way appeared sodden, like soaked coal. "He found me."

—

Jack left Riquewihr after midnight on foot. The road was a bare path in the black snow. He walked in the middle, fearful that if he stumbled to either side of the road he would fall away into the darkness. The poster fragments he had stuck in his boots did little to keep the wet out, and soon his feet began sliding about inside the boots. Stones pressed through the paper, jabbing the soles of his feet.

Once he was outside the town, the main road would be too risky for travel. It had been this way all the way from Paris.

It had taken two months just to get out of Paris. When he had received his father's letter, he had gone immediately to the prefecture, to get permission to leave. He applied for papers. But the police…now suddenly patriots again, keeping order for the new French state, even though they appeared to be the same police that had until recently been keeping order for the new German state…the police had told him to go away. Until the Germans were pushed from France completely, it was out of the question to even consider going out to the Vosges.

So finally Jack had decided to risk whatever would happen, and he had walked to Riquewihr.

It took him three weeks. Some American soldiers helped him once, amazed by the presence of an Irish civilian in such chaos. But for the most part, Jack depended on French partisans and the Free French Army. They helped him especially when he explained that he was searching for his daughter. There was such smoke and carnage everywhere that Jack's heart sickened at the thought of what he might find when he got to the Dusels' vineyard. If he could find her at all, he imagined her murdered, like so many of the dead he had seen on his journey to Strasbourg and farther south.

Toward the end, he had stayed off the roads. It was very difficult. Certain that going out during the day would be an impossibility, he traveled at night, despite the cold. But at night, Jack thought, alone and unseen in the black, struggling through the ravaged vineyards…. He imagined himself the victim of the war's general disaster, an exploded body tripped up on a landmine or mistaken for a German by the Americans. There would be a disappearance, a cry as Jack abruptly died. Yet another body, unnoticed by anyone. Even if he did get to the Dusels' vineyards, he expected to find such horror there as well. How could there not be, with warring armies everywhere?

The armies themselves were still just a few miles ahead of him, up and down the Rhine. Jack avoided whatever skirmishes there were, coming across the aftermath of many of them. He had to scurry through destroyed villages still scattered with dead, and often stopped to watch the American black men cleaning up the bodies. There was smoke and rubble, the war moving back toward the river. Then, of course, beyond all that there was encircled Germany. Dead Poland, brimming with dead Russians and dead Germans. The disappeared Jews. Russia itself.

Jack was not sure which soldiers he would run into out here. He expected panicked Germans cut off from the Rhine, the *Maquis*, Jewish partisans, Communists and gypsies, as well as the expected French and American armies, the British…in short, everybody, all of them shooting everywhere. So he stuck to the fields and vineyards for the last several miles. He plodded on in a kind of frozen madness. Everywhere there were gutted and smoldering tanks, ruined buildings, trucks drowned in the mud and snow, and bodies blackened by the cold, now and then dismembered, peacefully frozen and grotesque in crumpled winter gear. Jack's fingers twitched, and he held his coat tightly about his throat. His boots were mud-clogged. He was riveted with cold.

He arrived at the gate to the Dusels' winery at four in the morning. He sat down in a grove of trees to wait for sunup. A few hours later, the gloom of first light appeared, and the horizon of hills was a simple, undulating gray line. The winery was a few hundred yards up the drive on a hill.

Three airplanes came out of the west, American fighters headed for the river. Terrified that he would be seen by the pilots, Jack cowered beneath the trees. He pulled his coat about him. But the aircraft passed away toward the Rhine, and he felt his heart calm, though it hurt just the same, rigid in his chest. He stood and walked into the open, picking mud from the front of his coat.

The blue-black grassy stubble and gnarled vines shivered in the wind. The pebbled muddy drive on which Jack walked was frozen, lacking all life. Clouds settled toward the ground in slabs of wet. The patches of snow through the vineyards lacked the grace that Jack usually associated with such cold. They were simply lumps of dirt and gray-white. They sullied the view, adding nothing to the gray that sprawled across the rest of the fields and into the distance.

At the edge of the winery grounds, he spotted a black mound beside the drive several feet before him. At first he thought it was just a pile of sticks covered over with an old rug or something. He brushed his hands, though the mud remained on them, stuck to them with cold. He hated the need to move on, and he hated the pain in his legs. But he began walking again. The straw-laced mud was gristled with ice, and nothing was growing. The misshapen mound he had seen fell away at an angle.

As he approached, he saw that it was the body of a girl.

Her face, where it lay half-submerged in a frozen puddle, was smeared with mud and what appeared to be vomit, beneath a gathering of filthy hair. The collar of her coat quivered in the wind blowing across the hills from the Rhine, and her left arm lay out from her side, the hand twisted into a kind of malformed fist. Her legs were folded, and she appeared to have been kneeling before she died. There was a sock on one of her feet. The front of her throat and her jaw had been ripped open by the bullet that had killed her. The blood and torn skin were frozen in place.

She lay glittering with frost.

Jack secured the collar of his overcoat about his neck, as though afraid that the contagion of her death would seep in with the cold. The possibility that had so terrified him through the entire journey from Paris now seemed a certainty, congealed in the frozen body before him. A very sudden wire of fear, kris-like, pierced his heart, as he realized that it could be Emma herself.

He knelt down and carefully pushed back the collar of the girl's coat. He grimaced with terror. He brushed aside a clot of hair and stared at the destroyed face.

Placing his hands over his own face, Jack lowered his head to the mud. The corpse was completely still, and though he recoiled from it, he could not leave its side. The jaw was shattered. The upper lip was pulled back in a grimace. Her remaining teeth were soiled with mud. The stillness with which she lay on the ground was betrayed by the flapping of the cloth about her neck. It seemed unnatural. Since she was dead, the cloth shouldn't move either. But it did move, indeed with a kind of insouciance, as though her destruction were something gleeful, to be laughed at.

Jack straightened up, still kneeling at her side. He took in a breath and fought against the gall that rose from his stomach. He reached down to comfort her and adjusted the collar of her coat so that it covered at least some of her wound. But the wound itself was frozen, and the fragments of destroyed skin roughly caressed the backs of Jack's fingers.

He mused that, were he to stay sprawled in the mud next to the decaying body that lay before him, the mud would sear and steam.

He stood and started walking toward the farm.

Only the back half of the farmhouse remained intact. The rubble of the front of the building was blackened by fire, and the few rooms left standing lay exposed to the weather. An old farm lorry was turned over on its side, crumpled. The grounds around the house were strewn with wreckage, and there was a fire in the distance, several buildings on the neighboring vineyard.

There was a gruesome field down the hillside behind the house, on which lay six uniformed bodies, all German. They appeared to have been discarded as junk, and a few of them were almost unrecognizable as human. There was no community to the dead. Each seemed to have been solely abandoned. Jack turned toward the stone winery building.

It had survived, but was riddled with bullet holes. He entered the building through the main door. Another German laid inside, face down, his hand still clutching a rifle. A portion of the smashed door lay over him. Jack skirted the body, and began looking around.

Nothing in the winery had escaped the battle. A crucifix hung over the door, but most of the ceramic angels that had hung to either side of it had fallen in pieces to the floor. The boards on which they had hung still showed their dark imprints.

Some of the larger wine barrels appeared intact, but Jack could smell the decay of spilled wine. Most of them were destroyed, the entire winery smashed. Iron-colored light shined through the door at the far end of the building. There were other odors…of shit, putrid blood, and fire. The sweet odors sickened him so much that he gathered the collars of his coat before his nose.

There was no light. Looking about, Jack found a broken candle on the floor. Wiping it on his coat, he walked to the worktables that were attached to one wall. There was a small box of phosphorous matches in one of the drawers, a remnant from before the war. To his surprise, the first one lit after a few tries, and Jack took the flaming candle with him as he walked the line of barrels. His feet were immersed in the semi-frozen wine that covered the floor.

He heard a scurrying movement, someone moving around. Jack halted and listened for it again. Something scuttled along the floor. There was a whimper, a high voice.

"*Est-ce qu'il y a personne?*" He took a few steps forward. He heard another sound, an intake of breath. "*Qui est là?*"

He walked the length of the winery. A pile of rags and old jute bags lay in a corner at the end of a still-intact barrel. Hay was scattered about as well, brought here for warmth, Jack guessed. His candlelight barely revealed the bags, but he started as he saw that someone was hiding among them.

She had darkened eyes and skin. Her hands hid her face from view. She was maybe twelve, and cowered against the wall. Jack held the candle out, the better to see her, and the girl winced and pulled farther away. Her skin was tight across the bones of her face. She was covered with dirt and scratches. She had no shoes, and shivered in the dank cold.

"Emma?"

The girl held her hands before her mouth, and her eyes widened with anguish.

"I'm Jack. Jack Roman. I'm a friend of your parents." The French came from him with deft authority.

The girl pulled her knees up tightly against her chest.

"Are you all right? Emma?"

She could only tremble in the warren that she had found for protection. Jack got down on his hands and knees and crawled toward her, holding the candle before him. She ground herself against the wall behind her.

Jack reached out to take her hand. She screamed at him to leave her alone.

"I won't hurt you, Emma. I know your parents. I've come to help you." He held the candle near his face, so that she could see him. "I've come to get you, Emma. Please. It's safe." He held the candle out before him. "Your parents wrote to me to come help you. I was there when you were born. Please."

Suddenly, without warning, she pushed herself from the floor. She clutched his coat. Jack held the candle out to the side, afraid it would be extinguished. He took Emma in his free arm and kissed her forehead and her eyes. His heart beat from the freezing cold and with love for the girl who had scurried into his embrace.

———

"Where were you?" Mia said.

"Riquewihr," Emma said. "A town near Colmar, in the east. Do you know it?"

Both girls shook their heads. They had sat in increasingly stunned silence as Emma told the story of her rescue by Jack.

"I was living there with my parents, and the Germans came, and everybody was killed. Everybody. There was a servant girl, some workers...." Emma opened her purse and took out an envelope. Opening it, she removed a photo that showed Jack and Emma, then about twelve years old, sitting on a sunny lawn beneath a tree. "This was taken in Neuilly, at the American hospital there, in the summer after the Germans were defeated. I was still... still sick."

Emma sat on a wooden lawn chair with a light sheet over her legs. Her hair was gathered up in a bun. The sleeveless blouse showed her thin arms, which seemed to have little strength.

"It was so cold when he found me, and he carried me out in his arms."

"Did you know what had happened to your parents?" Clara said.

"No. I barely remember anything from that day. Only that he covered me with his coat and carried me down the drive. He covered my head even. He said it was so cold, and there was nothing to see…everything was on fire."

Clara looked down at the photo again.

"And some American soldiers helped us get back to the main road and away from there."

In the picture, Jack stood behind the lawn chair, his hand on one of Emma's shoulders. He wore a white shirt with the sleeves rolled up high, an old pair of pants, and a belt cinched tight. The shirt was very blousy, too big even for him.

"And I stayed with him for years after that." Emma perused the photograph. "I had a lot of dreams. The war was so awful, so much dirt and noise, and I was running in the snow, the fire, trying to find my mother…in the dreams. My real mother. And she was never there."

Clara's fingers rested on the photo. She bit her lower lip. The notion of this Personal of Emma's dismayed her. It was a secret always searching, until now, for its own explanation. Clara felt cold herself, and she placed her fingers on her lips.

"I imagined lying down with her on a blanket at a picnic. In her arms. A happy little girl. And, you know, the woman in the dreams was always some strange woman, someone whose face I couldn't really see. But I could smell her, the lovely perfume, the way the silk blouse she wore—"

"Did she fix food for you in her dreams?" Clara said.

Emma crossed her legs, turning on her chair and leaning over the table. She actually smiled, although the effort was brief. "Yes, but what she made for me were odd things for a little girl to eat, probably." She folded her hands. "Like artichokes. I always liked those."

"Me, too."

"But it was the smell of her hair, Clara, that made the dreams so wonderful."

"How?"

"I could just allow myself to be lost in it. Cared for by it. Surrounded."

"When did Jack tell you that he was your real father?"

Mia's head turned toward Clara, surprise brimming from her eyes. Emma's eyes softened after a moment, her lips giving way to the first genuine smile Clara had seen from her that morning. She seemed to be acquiescing to Clara's next question, if not inviting it.

"And that my mom was your real mother?"

Mia whispered a groan, caressing her left hand with the fingers of her right. She remained silent.

"Right away. He told me that he had had to live with the knowledge of that for too long, that he couldn't bear carrying it on for the sake of people who had died."

"I...I know about the secret."

"How?"

"I saw the letter from Jack's father."

Emma's lips curved into another soft smile. "I know. Jack told me you'd found it."

Clara turned to Mia and explained what the letter had contained, and how she had sneaked it from the trunk.

"Jack went back to the winery to get that trunk," Emma said. "After the war. I had told him about it. It was in the fire when the house burned."

Clara nodded.

"What did you think about the letter?" Emma said.

Clara hunched her shoulders. "It made me so happy." She still felt considerable anger with Emma. But in the same moment she enjoyed the fact of the information the letter had contained and the warmth that it was bringing to her relationship with Emma now. They were sisters, and this knowledge was the one certain thing they had together. That and the picture that Clara held in her thoughts, of little Emma immersed in her mother's womb. So, just now, Clara could not truly rekindle her conflicted feelings. They sputtered and lurched, but remained quiet.

"But how can you just hate her like you do?" she said nonetheless.

"I always wondered what I had done to her that was wrong, Clara. Why did I get left behind? And then I was alone for days before Jack found me.

Hiding. It was dark. I was so cold. And all that time, I thought about her and what she had done to me. This was what she had done to me. This place. The freezing and the blackness. It was her."

"It was not." Clara lowered her head, and Mia covered Clara's right hand with her left.

Emma reached across the table and took Clara's left hand. Clara contemplated the flaking nail polish on her own fingers, by comparison to the carefully luminous dark red of Emma's nails. She felt a blur of defeat.

Emma caressed her cheek. "Please don't punish me, Clara."

"But will you come to visit her again?" Clara could not control the high waver of her voice.

"No."

The door to the cafe opened, and a damp coldness rushed across their table. "Not now."

Clara looked around to see who was coming in, and was surprised, immediately, by the face of a very handsome man whom she recognized.

Emma broke into a smile. Clara barely had time to look at him a second time before he approached the table and took Emma into his arms. A cigarette burned between the fingers of his right hand.

"Paul." Emma laughed. She feigned pushing him away.

Wearing a white shirt open at the neck and a thick black overcoat and brown slacks, he was unkempt and beautiful, with large lips and brown eyes that had very black lashes.

Indeed Clara *had* seen him before, with Emma at Berthillon. Her breath caught in her throat as Emma kissed him. Emma clutched his wet hair with one hand for a moment, until her fingers fanned out and turned about the back of his head, lowering to his neck. It was a motion Clara had seen only in the movies, performed by someone like Eva Marie Saint when she was kissing Marlon Brando or someone. Sometimes Cary Grant got kissed like that, too. She recalled Montgomery Clift. Clara herself could not imagine doing anything like it.

But suddenly, for a moment, she *did* imagine kissing Paul like that.

"So, this is Clara," Paul said in French, smiling at her. He extended his hand, and Clara, embarrassed, took it.

"I am Paul Michel, and I am the…." He turned toward Emma once more, taking her hand. "How do you say it in English?"

"The 'boyfriend?'"

"Yes, I am the 'boyfriend' of Emma.'" Paul buttoned his coat, then ran a hand through his hair. "Emma has told me about you, and I have an invitation for you, Clara." He pulled a chair from the next table and sat down. "There's a *bal des artistes* in two weeks, the *Club de Jelly Roll*, and I hope you'll come with us."

Mia suddenly interjected in French. "Oh, it'll be fun, Clara. Have you ever been to one of those?"

"No."

"You've got to go."

"Can Mia come, too?" Clara turned toward Emma.

"Your friend?" Paul said. "Of course. But you have to come in costume."

Clara did not understand the phrase, and when Emma translated for her, she blushed with almost pure pleasure. She blushed even more as she surveyed Paul's face. She was crazy for him right away, with his dark skin and the small beard that surrounded his lips. His curly black hair. The kind of sensuous smile that he had, with the triangle of beautiful skin between the unbuttoned collars of his white shirt.

"Oh, I know just what I'm going to wear," Mia said.

"What?"

"I'm not going to tell, Clara. I want to surprise you."

———

Even in Eureka, where the north coast rainfall imbued the gray-blue winter light with a kind of universal seepage that oozed beneath all of her clothing, Clara had not felt the kind of cold she was experiencing now in Paris. At least the rain had stopped. But the black knee-socks she wore barely protected her against the dampness. Her hands were stiff within her wool gloves. She knew her cheeks were splotched red.

So when she arrived at Emma's apartment, with Emma, Mia and Paul in the late-afternoon darkness—Emma hurrying a pot of water onto the stove for tea—Clara sat down on the couch with the happy expectation of warmth.

And now that they had their tea, and Emma had told Clara that her eyes were so beautiful that she hoped she would let her make them up for her, that warmth was assured.

"But you need to be careful with eye-makeup, Clara." Emma laughed. She applied it with the smallest of brushes, and the caress of it against Clara's eyelid tickled her.

The two girls sat on the bench of Emma's grand piano. Paul stood by the side of the piano watching, a glass of wine cradled in his hands. A cigarette burned between the index and third fingers of his right hand, yellowed fingers that gave off a suggestion of romantic ruin. Clara continuously glanced at him, although she didn't want anyone to know how attracted she was to him. What excited her most was the sweet brooding in his eyes, as large as they were, and the way his laughter rang through the apartment when Emma had suggested she do Clara's eyes. Clara felt safe flirting with him a little, because she was being made beautiful and was supposed to be flirtatious. Emma even said so as she was laying out the different rouges, lipsticks, eye shadows, and other liquids and colors on the little black-lacquer table she had placed at one end of the piano bench.

As Emma applied the eye make-up, Mia watched her and Clara with humorous jealousy. She had reminded Clara on the walk down the hill from the Pantheon that she was an only child, and here Clara had a sister, and "so nice a sister, too, Clara. I wish I had someone like Emma." Mia marveled at the care and precision with which Emma applied a second hue of blue to Clara's eyes. She put down a narrow line of it so carefully that Clara could barely feel it.

Clara herself felt caressed by the attention everyone was paying to her. Emma's enjoyment of having found her was obvious in the jokes she made about Clara's eyes and the admiration she had for her pretty skin. The compliments flooded Clara with happiness, and she felt that if she ever had another day like this one, in the company of her new sister and her best friend, with the kind regard and excitement of Paul's beautiful eyes making everything even more special…the black glimmer of the piano in the lamp-lit, dank afternoon, the soft masking of her cheeks and eyes in such rich softness, the blood-like shimmer of the red wine in Paul's glass…all of it lifted Clara to the notion that she would never again be as happy as this.

19

"But what did she say to you when you asked her about me and Jack?" Clara wished to keep the meeting a secret, but as soon as she came home, Lauren noted the makeup. Unable to contain herself, Clara told Lauren about the *pneumatique* and its excitement, and her meeting with Emma.

Clara shrugged her shoulders. She and Lauren were walking up the Rue de Buci, shopping for tomatoes. The buildings were gray in the afternoon light.

"She seemed happy, Mom. I don't know. In love." She appeared to Lauren to be harried by this conversation, and Lauren wondered whether Clara were telling her everything. "And she told me a story." Clara remained standing before the vegetable stand. "A sad one."

They turned up the sidewalk, passing more vegetable carts and cafes. Clara told of Jack's rescue of Emma, the details of the broken crockery angels in the winery building, the cold and the constant noise and smoke of the gunfire that had been so terrifying to the little girl Emma. She described Emma's hunger and, ultimately, the executions by the Germans of her parents.

They stopped at a stand laden with different kinds of vegetables. The carrots were splayed apart like a fan, and the tomatoes were particularly rich, despite it's being so early in the season. Lauren passed her fingers across them, until the woman who owned the stand told her not to do so. They were of every dimension and shape, not simply round and hard as Lauren would have found them in the supermarket in Eureka at this time of year. These tomatoes were imperfect and voluptuous.

Clara's recounting of the story rambled without a plan. She gave one detail here and another there, as she and her mother meandered back and forth across the Rue de Buci, passed through the *carrefour,* and then walked the Rue

Saint-André-des-Arts back toward the river. But as Lauren listened to it, she realized that Clara's telling was affected by the difficult brutality of the tale itself.

—

"But is she going to come see me?"

Clara swallowed. "She said she can't just now." She took off the beret she had worn and hung it over the back of a chair. The beret was silvered with mist.

"She's too busy?"

"No, it's just that…." Clara really wanted to tell her mother about the invitation to the artists' ball. But she realized how inappropriate it would be to bring that up now. "She says she's…well, that she's kind of—"

"What is it, Clara?"

"Angry with you." Clara bit her lower lip. The words had come from her as almost a whisper. She looked away. "She says you left her."

Lauren closed her eyes, sitting down on the couch.

"Mom, I—"

"No, it's not you."

"You're not mad at me?"

"Of course not." Lauren seemed to shrink into the couch, and Clara sat down next to her. Her own hands were quite cold.

"Does she hate me, Clara?"

Emma's insistence, that at best she felt betrayed by her mother, came into Clara's thoughts. But she knew she did not want to be the vehicle for such knowledge. She hoped the moment would pass. Visions of the *Club de Jelly Roll* also remained in her mind. Bright lights flashing in her eyes. The Sailor Girl Clara dancing with The Handsome Sailor Paul.

"I'm sorry. I shouldn't force you to answer that question."

Clara took in a breath. "Mom, do you love Emma?"

The warmth from Lauren's fingers spread across Clara's. "She was my first baby, Clara. And they stole her…just took her away. I couldn't say anything. I thought…you know, I was only fifteen."

Clara swallowed, realizing that she herself would be fifteen in a few years, and capable, even herself, of having a baby like that. *Gosh! A baby.*

"I thought it was impossible to protest, to say to them that I loved my daughter and couldn't bear giving her up." Lauren's voice fell away.

"Who was that?"

"My mother and father."

"They wouldn't let you keep her?"

"No. They didn't want to have anything to do with her. Emma was... well, to my parents, Clara, Emma was a sin. No one was ever supposed to know."

Clara nodded.

"Did Emma say anything else?" Lauren said.

There were footsteps on the stairs. Jack's familiar step came up in a slow ascent.

"Yeah. She wants me to go to a dance."

"A dance?"

"An artists' ball. It's called the *Club de Jelly Roll.*"

The door swung open, and Jack entered the studio.

"She's going where?" he said a moment later.

He was dressed in a dark blue pea coat and black workpants with old black laced shoes. He had two bouquets in his hand, of daisies: one for Lauren, the other for Clara. He removed the coat and tossed it across the chair back, next to Clara's beret.

Clara was barely able to keep herself from shouting the news. "It's an artists' ball. It's—"

"What artists' ball?"

"It's one that Emma's boyfriend—"

"Paul, you mean."

"Yes." Clara detected in Jack's voice the beginnings of the anger that had victimized her once before. Jack's disdain of Paul was quickly obvious, in the simple pronunciation of his name. Clara feared she was doing something bad just because she knew him.

"You shouldn't let her do this," he said to Lauren.

Lauren held the flowers on her lap. Jack turned toward Clara and offered her the second bouquet. Clara wasn't sure that she should accept it.

"What's wrong with him?" Lauren said.

"She's been going out with him for more than a year now. And I just don't trust him, that's all."

"What don't you trust?"

Jack grimaced. "I don't think *she* can trust *him*." His shoulders slumped. "Look, Lauren, these artists' balls are…. I'm just not sure that Clara should go, that's all."

"Why not?"

Jack's eyes appeared to center, motionless, as his jaw tightened. Clara watched his right hand, opening and shutting at his side. The large fingers pressed against the palm, causing his fist to look like it was made of weather-scarred stone. "She's only twelve."

"I'm old enough."

"There's a lot that goes on at these balls that a twelve-year-old shouldn't see."

"Oh, come on, Jack."

"Lauren, I don't like this fellow Paul. He's…" Jack turned about, scratching his head. "I never liked him, and Emma seems to be crazy about him."

"Maybe she loves him because you *don't*," Clara said.

Jack's hand remained on top of his head. But the scratching stopped. He glanced at Lauren.

"Clara," Lauren whispered.

"What'd I say wrong?" Clara sat back on the couch, suddenly hoping it would envelop her and allow her to disappear. Censure radiated from Lauren's eyes, so much so that they appeared darker and smaller, like heated jade.

"Mom—"

"You don't know what you're talking about, Clara." Jack turned about. "But even so, there's nothing I can do. She loves this idiot. I don't know why she loves him, but she does. And there's nothing I can do."

WHEN CLARA WAS TWELVE

In her mind, Clara hurried to a quick defense of her sister's boyfriend. *He must be okay if Emma's in love with him!*

"So you can't go to the *bal*, Clara." Jack said.

The graying evening darkened. It continued raining, and the lights in the apartments across the Place de la Contrescarpe appeared far away, like yellow-grey beacons in the tempest, fading as the rain increased in intensity.

"Can't go?" Lauren said.

"Lauren, it's just—"

"I tell Clara what she can do, Jack…'

"Lauren, Emma's my daughter, and I don't like the fact that she's going out with this Paul."

"…and what she can't do." Lauren took Clara's hand again. "And Clara's going to the *Club de Jelly Roll*."

"Lauren."

"Whether you like Paul or not. Because I want my two daughters to be together, and I won't—"

"Lauren, please."

"I won't let you dictate, again, what I'm supposed to do with any daughter of mine."

20

C lara paid little attention to the poverty in which she and Lauren now found themselves. With the industry they showed cleaning up the studio, painting and decorating it, and decorating Clara's bedroom, they both thought that Jack's lackadaisical atitudes about their income would change. Clara herself was sure of it.

He sometimes stood before his canvas in silence as Lauren explained some new efficiency, some new plan that she had. He acted, at such moments, as though he were being invaded by a lot of sullen instructions. Finally one day he protested that he was sorry he wasn't like Martin, sorry he didn't make more money, sorry he didn't just do whatever Lauren wanted. He walked away from her, his back broad and graceful in the sunlight coming through the studio windows.

Lauren had told Clara that she sometimes lay awake counting, seeing the coins in her purse and the few crumpled bills, one by one, clearly. The contemplation of money was now an angering task. She told Clara how she sometimes imagined them out beneath a bridge by the Seine—a well-dressed mother with her well-dressed daughter, charming as could be, but *clochards* nonetheless—bumming a few *centimes*. The story made Clara laugh. But some version of it became a very direct concern of hers, one that caused her, in the darkness in bed, to moan with repeated anxiety.

Jack did sell his paintings. But while the income from them had been sufficient when he was alone, now the requirements of three people made each month a worrisome undertaking, in which Lauren had to make daily choices of the sort she had never had to make.

There was more to Jack's anger than complaint, and more than just bad manners. Clara sensed that a kind of heated engine was working within him, It was a combustive anguish. It seemed so guarded and tight-lipped to her. Even so, the unleashed insistence upon his feelings, from which she had once suffered—the fury of them when he had caught her with the open trunk—had now been absorbed by her, and she understood it better. She had learned so much about him at Père Lachaise, and from Emma. Indeed, the source of that intensity, and the history of it—the past that Jack and Emma shared—now fascinated Clara.

She loved Jack's eyes when he looked at her mother, and the manner in which his rough hands, so used and battered by the paints and solvents that covered them every day, seemed in their embraces to soften. His curved, formed mouth, his obvious delight in Lauren's love for him, and his caring so for Clara herself moved Clara. She cherished the views out the windows, of the rooftops and the smoke rising from the old chimneys, the dark blue of early Spring Paris just at sundown, the way that that blue remained in the sky for so long after the sun had disappeared, and even the dried-out, brownish smell of the old books on the quays. She owed most of what she felt about those things to Jack, and to the way that *he* so loved them.

But lately when she looked at his paintings, whelmed over by the seething flows of color, her eyes also fell across the wineglass spattered with paint, the pair of canvas shoes in the corner equally spattered, the cigarettes in the ashtrays, and the bills.

Clara worried about them because her mother so clearly did.

"Money comes, Lauren," Jack said. "Money always comes."

But Clara knew that money didn't always come. Since they had been living in Paris, she had seen her mother begin to anguish over the shortfall most months.

There had been a monthly ritual in Eureka, on the first banking day of each month, in which Clara would come home from school to find her mother paying the bills. There were two stacks of paper...the unpaid ones on the left and the ones that had been paid off on the right, with the checkbook between the two piles. Lauren also had a ledger in which she kept records of everything that was coming in and going out. Clara always enjoyed sitting and talking with her mother when she was doing the bills, because there was a feeling of real industry connected with the activity.

At those moments she was part of the workings of the house. It mattered. This was business, and the importance of it all to her mother made Clara feel important herself. Clara knew how much was paid to the gardener Mr. Ladrillo every month, and the same with Winnie Mae, who did the ironing. The same with everybody.

Lauren took on the same duty in Paris, to try to bring some order to Jack's sparse finances. Now, though, the number of unpaid, or put off, bills did not diminish. The curtains she and Clara had sewn, the extra coal they had ordered, a new cover for Jack's old couch, and the paint for Clara's bedroom…all of these had been bought on credit from the Rue Mouffetard merchants, who had opened accounts for Lauren based on how she was dressed, thinking that she was the wife of some wealthy American.

Payments came. But sometimes they were partial payments. Jack passed money on to Lauren, and the money went. Now, though, the shopkeepers were treating Lauren less well than they had in the beginning, even though a few of them had agreed to extend her payments, or re-structure them from monthly amounts. She got more credit. But she confided in Clara that the bills were getting worse.

Clara herself had even been snickered at, on two occasions. Once, Monsieur Malouf, the Algerian from whose shop on the Rue du Pot-de-fer it was her job to get a bottle of wine every other day, had quizzed her about payment. The second time this happened, it came from Monsieur Malouf's wife.

Clara enjoyed going to their shop. Other than the *maitre d'* Sammy at *Les deux palestiniens*, they were the first Arabs she had ever met, and the smells of chicken, onions, sugar, and cous-cous that Madame Malouf and her mother prepared in the kitchen behind the shop, and especially the language the family spoke among themselves, made Clara feel that she was going off on an adventure every time she was sent out for a bottle of wine.

Monsieur Malouf had been happy to meet Lauren, because she represented to him a kind of stability that Jack himself had always had trouble achieving. He had even said so to Lauren once, when she and Clara had been visiting his shop on a Saturday afternoon.

"I have one of Jack's paintings, you know," he said. "This one." A small oil, showing puffy globs of color in blues and greens, hung from the wall behind the table in which Monsieur Malouf kept his cash drawer. It hovered above the Algerian's globe-shaped head like an angled mollusk floating on sun-laden water. "It's a pity that he's poor. But what an artist!" Mr. Malouf grinned. "That fellow…what's his name? Picasso? He was poor once too."

That moment observing Jack's work—the three of them looking up at it, Clara translating Monsieur Malouf's French for her mother while the wood, bottles, and shadows of the wine shop surrounded them like illustrations from one of Grandma Adela's old Charles Dickens novels—had provided for Clara a moment of humorous romance.

But just the other day, Monsieur Malouf had come to Jack's studio to collect a payment, and he had not been so romantic.

Clara was alone, washing a blouse in a bucket in the kitchen. The radio was on, to a recording of some old tango music, a singer named Gardel. When she opened the door to the studio, soapy water dripped from her fingers to the floor.

"Your mother is here?" Monsieur Malouf asked in French. He did not wait for a reply, and pushed his way in.

"No. I don't know—"

"When will she be back?" There was a downturn to his lips, but his eyes nonetheless paused on the painting Jack had now almost finished, of Lauren. Monsieur Malouf's breathing came quickly and sharply. He sounded winded from coming up the stairs, as though each breath had to struggle to release itself from water in his lungs. The music was very slow, and Gardel's voice made its way in and out between the syncopated fire of the guitar-music that accompanied him. Monsieur Malouf was a stout man with thick shoulders and feet, the roll of fat around his waist stretching the cloth of the green shirt he wore, as well as that of his dark blue apron. His hands had the look of large-fingered chops.

"I don't know." Clara knew quite well that her mother would return within a half hour. She feared Monsieur Malouf would want to sit and wait for Lauren. He refolded the piece of paper he held in his hand. It was creased, and smudged on one corner, as though he had spilled gravy on it and then wiped it away.

"He's a very good painter, Jack," he said. "I've told my customers about him."

Clara implored him, silently, to leave.

"Beautiful colors."

"I don't think my mother will be back until dinnertime."

Malouf's eyes were so large that they formed almost a pool of dark brown and black. Clara's fears were eased by his heavy, grandfatherly grace, and by the kindly look he gave her over his shoulder.

"What is your name?"

"Clara."

"Yes, Mademoiselle Clara, I...." Monsieur Malouf shrugged and looked down to his left. He was resigned to unpleasantness. "Your mother is very pretty, very elegant. But I am suffering from a problem."

"What problem?"

"She has been cheating me, *mademoiselle*."

"My mother?"

"Well, 'cheating' is too harsh a term. We like tourists like yourselves to visit us here in France..." His bald head, very brown, with a mustache like a squashed broom, turned back and forth, as though he were watching a slow tennis game. "We prefer tourists who pay their way."

"My mother pays."

"Then will you tell her that I *must* speak with her?" Monsieur Malouf held the paper out before her. "You have to settle this bill."

"Of course I'll tell her."

"She is conscientious, I know she is. But we need larger payments, *mademoiselle*. Even Monsieur Jack never let bills go for so long." Monsieur Malouf let out a breath. He handed Clara the paper. "I'm sorry."

—

Clara could not muster the courage to tell her mother about Monsieur Malouf's visit, even when Lauren asked her the next morning to go down to the shop for a bottle of *bordeaux*. Clara was planning on meeting Emma later that morning, and when she told Lauren so, Lauren became very excited.

"I'm fixing a special *coq au vin* for us tonight, you know, with roasted potatoes and carrots with *fines herbes*. It'll be delicious, Clara. And I have a little cheese tart for dessert." Lauren looked out the windows. "Maybe you could ask her to come."

"Mom, we already have wine."

Lauren nodded. "But it's not good wine, Clara. I want this meal to be special for us."

"But, Mom—"

"Just go get a bottle of the wine, Clara. Don't worry. You can charge it to the account."

"Mom—"

"And ask Emma to come for dinner."

When Clara entered the wine shop, Madame Malouf was sitting behind the counter with her mother, listening to some music on a record player. Normally Madame Malouf sat on a stool in the doorway between the shop and the storeroom in back, where her husband kept his better-quality stored wines. Every day she wore a different black cotton gown and a tight headdress, with jewelry wrapped about her neck, her fingers covered in silver rings, her wrists with numerous bracelets. She was quite corpulent, with lovely black eye makeup, and she barely spoke French at all. She greeted Clara whenever she came into the shop, in a few words of heavily accented French. But the language she spoke to Monsieur Malouf, a staccato Arabic with every sort of aspirated glottal consonant, amazed Clara whenever she heard it. Madame Malouf always sounded like she was arguing with Monsieur Malouf.

Just now neither woman looked at Clara, and the languid soporific of the Arab music that floated through the shop was punctuated by the intensity of the conversation between the women, which rose and fell in spurts, principally when Madame Malouf seemed to be criticizing her mother. The older woman was defenseless against her daughter's gravelly sputter, and it seemed to Clara that she was being forced to glumly agree with everything.

After a few minutes, Madame Malouf stood and addressed Clara in Arabic.

Clara interrupted her. "A bottle of that *bordeaux*, please, and...."

Her French had a similar effect on Madame Malouf as her mother's Arabic. Madame Malouf dismissed it.

Clara pointed into the back of the shop. "I mean, one of the bottles in there."

Again Madame Malouf put her off, shrugging her shoulders in a clear indication that she did not know what Clara was talking about.

"I want to buy some wine."

Madame Malouf walked to the far end of the counter. There was an oak table there, very simply made, and a chair. Monsieur Malouf conducted his business from this table, and his wife pulled an accounts book from the drawer and opened it to a page, at the top of which was hand-written the words "Monsieur Roman." There were columns of numbers, some on the right, some on the left, all in pencil. Madame Malouf began berating Clara, tapping the open book with an index finger. The noise reminded Clara of a scratch on a record, and each tap sounded more disapproving than the previous one, more condemnatory and short.

Very abruptly, so much so that she startled Clara, Madame Malouf blurted out a word in French. But it was only one word. "Pay!"

The darkness of the wine shop, which had seemed so alluring to Clara before, now turned to a sepulchral cold that was not soothed by the rise of the violins on the radio through some sort of syrupy slow Arabic song. A love song, Clara guessed.

Madame Malouf stared at Clara over the tabletop. "*Mademoiselle!*"

Clara fumbled with her shoulder bag, looking for her coin-purse. She had saved just enough for her hot chocolates with Mia for the next week, and she pulled the crumpled bills from her purse. "This is all I have." Clara threw them onto the counter, and they skittered apart. Madame Malouf grabbed for them, her fingernails scraping the counter-top. The many bracelets she wore sounded like chains dragged together across the wood. She then threw Clara out.

—

Emma spotted her walking back up the Rue Mouffetard. Feeling sickened and probably a little pale, Clara told her what had happened, and they walked further up the hill to the Deux Cygnes.

"I love my father," Emma said, after they had sat down at a table. "But he's not a practical man." She handed the menu back to the waiter. "It's lucky for me that my money comes from the vineyard in Riquewihr." She opened her purse. "How much do you owe M. Malouf?" She brought out a billfold.

She handed Clara sufficient bills to satisfy the debt. Clara sat isolated in her chair. She took the bills and folded them up, stuffing them into a pocket. Emma, sensing the girl's embarrassment, seized Clara's right hand and held it in both of hers.

When the waiter brought Clara the chocolate that Emma had ordered for her, Emma sat in silence a moment. "You know, you could come to Paul's with me," she said. "He's a very good artist, too."

"Would he mind?"

"No. I'm going over there now. I model for him. It's—"

"Will you have your clothes on?"

Emma laughed, putting her hand before her mouth. "No. Of course not." Clara frowned. "I don't think I should."

"Clara, it's safe. The studio's a little cold. And Paul can be…sometimes he's a little difficult."

"He is?"

"Sometimes. But you should come. He lives in Montmartre. You'll like it. Please come with me."

As they approached his studio, which was down from Sacré-Coeur church on Rue Bachelet, Clara secretly hoped for the same smile she had seen on Paul's face when she had first met him. She remembered the flash and immediacy of it. He had appeared so happy to meet her. Clara didn't want it to be that she was just Emma's little sister, though, to whom he might feel obligated to smile so affectionately.

He did smile when he opened the door, but only at Emma. He ushered them into the studio, barely looking at Clara. She felt she was overly loud in her greeting, and hated the shrill laugh that burst from her upon seeing him. He walked up the hall, paying little attention.

Paul's dark eyes and statuesque straight nose, so elegantly shaped, and the gruff inelegance of his growth of beard, gave his appearance a desert-like roughness. This extended to his hands. They weren't like Jack's, which were large and lined by all the work they had done for so many years. Paul's hands were refined and very white, a compliment to his sculpted looks.

"You sit there," he told Clara in French. She had just made a joke, also in French, that she was Emma's assistant. Edith Piaf was singing in the background, her song *Non, je ne regrette rien.* Her insistence upon singing the strong-minded lyric in so monotonous a buzz rasped against the back of Clara's neck.

Paul indicated a backless stool against the wall. "Never had a model with an assistant before."

Her joke ruined by his disinterest, Clara sat down on the stool.

He exchanged small talk with Emma. But he was quite preoccupied, and his patter sounded threatened.

"Get ready," he said to Emma. He pointed out a half dozen nails pounded into the wall near the door, where he intended that she hang her clothes. He walked to the back of the studio to put on a smock.

"Did I say something wrong?" Clara whispered.

Emma removed her blouse and folded it over the back of a wooden chair, ignoring the nails. She too remained silent, causing Clara to worry even more. Stepping out of her skirt, Emma laid it on the chair seat. She took a blanket from a shelf and wrapped it about her shoulders, which were already goose-bumped with cold, despite the coal fire in the heater at the far end of the room. She slipped out of her underwear and stepped to the platform. Paul asked her to lean down over a chair, one foot resting on the seat itself. He had done a series of drawings, which rested scattered on a table, of a woman getting out of a bath. The renditions looked pretty rough to Clara, hardly like a woman at all, rather like a gathering of dust-caked bones. The drawings did not look anything at all like Emma, which Clara also found unsettling. *How can he make a painting that shows what she's really like, from those scratches?*

But Paul was well into the painting itself, and as he stood up from the table and approached the easel, he finally smiled at Clara. The stool was so tall that her feet hung down above the floor. She remembered when she was little, sitting in the kitchen watching Lauren prepare dinner. Then, her inability to touch the floor had been fun and had made her feel as though she were floating like a bird. Now, in the studio's cold, she felt immobile and defenseless. She leaned against the wall, gathering her sweater about her. She smiled once at Emma, and then took a copy of *ParisMatch* from the cloth bag she had brought with her.

She thumbed through it. There was an article about Spain that didn't look too interesting, with a lot of photographs of generals. The most important general of them all—Franco was his name—was also the littlest, apparently. A tassel hung from his army cap.

Clara moved on. She read the ads about makeup and jewelry, and then looked at some pictures of Yves Montand in a pair of trunks on a beach somewhere.

Paul's studio was a dark room, very large, with water-stained walls. Its windows looked out and up, to a view of several buildings toward Sacré-Coeur. A great deal of light came in. But the walls, that seemed to have been painted hundreds of times perhaps hundreds of years ago, served only to diminish it, rather than elevating it. So Clara sat quietly and looked back into the magazine. She felt suffocated.

Paul's painting, though, provided a great deal of color, in dark hues carefully made of one color upon another. The woman in the painting surveyed herself as she stepped from the bath, and Paul had been able to give a similar sort of sunny glimmer to her hair that, in the light coming through the windows, Emma's had. The hair had the look of lovely black lacquer. The bath water moved in swaths of liquid marine blue and orange-yellows.

The entire painting contained an effervescent celebration, of which Paul himself just now seemed incapable. It was a cloud of angles and color so finely rendered that Clara, who could not explain why she felt so about it, thought that the painting had feelings, and that it showed that Paul loved Emma. The brushstrokes and the oil caressed the canvas the way the light itself fell across Emma's skin.

On the platform, Emma was immobile. Her skin gave off a light-softened gleam. Her hair hung down toward one shoulder, and in the gloom it appeared wet, as though she had just come from the sea. The darkness of the platform and the curve of Emma's pose drew Clara's eyes to her. She closed the magazine.

"Move your leg, Emma." Paul pointed to the left with his paintbrush.

Emma moved her foot a few inches.

"Not like that. Not flat-footed." He placed his hands on his waist. "Don't you know how to model?"

Paul! Clara thought with unhappiness. *Look at her!* She surveyed the milkiness of the flesh in the small of Emma's back. The airy lime-green of her eyes was so like that in Lauren's, as was the darkness of their lashes. Emma was transformed for Clara, from her newfound sister into a daring marine jewel. The cluttered art against the walls, the cut-out newspaper articles and dog-eared announcements of gallery openings that were tacked up in one corner, the set of shelves that held vases, plates, old pots and books, even Paul, even Clara herself...all seemed just to disappear.

Throughout the session, Paul's eyes rested longer on Emma than they did on the surface of the painting. He gazed at her, his eyes turned from disgruntled obsidian into pools of pleased reflection. His lashes were so pretty, Clara thought, as he pondered her sister. His daubing the canvas was a contemplation of what he had just seen, and he hurried through it in order to get to another glance.

Emma, motionless, gathered all the light to herself.

The cold of the studio touched every part of Clara's face, even though warmth from the coal-heater also fell against her cheeks. She knew that the only way to withstand the cold was to relax and try to think of it as something other than cold. But there was a damp, motionless listlessness in the air that made the temperature impossible to ignore. Movement made it even colder.

She wrapped Emma in the blanket during the break. The tea Paul gave them served to lift Emma's spirits, especially as Clara sat behind her on the stool combing her hair. She was expert at it, and she brushed Emma's hair through many times, making sure that it fell evenly against her fingers.

Emma luxuriated in the moment, asking Clara to comb specific parts of her hair, particularly that swatch of it that came down from her left temple.

Paul placed his empty teacup on the table and approached them.

"It's like there's light in the comb," Emma said.

Paul leaned over to kiss Emma. *"Je t'aime, amour."*

Emma reached up to put her arms around Paul's neck, pulling away from Clara's hands, and they kissed once again.

Clara laid the comb on her lap. The blanket fell away from Emma's left shoulder. Paul's hand caressed her shoulder, and as Emma kissed him a third time, and then once more, her right hand grasped the back of his head. Clara studied Paul's fingers, embarrassed to be doing so, and wondered how they must feel to Emma as they caressed the clear skin of her lower back.

—

An hour later, Clara continued thumbing through the *ParisMatch* while Emma went to the bathroom at the far end of the studio, to dress. Clara had saved the best for last, an article about Jerry Lee Lewis that contained several photos of the rock-and-roller on stage. His white bucks were like little boats up on end. The Killer. She could not imagine how it was possible for a guy to play the piano, hold on to the mike while he was singing so crazily, and get up on his toes like that, all at once.

"Clara?"

She looked up, turning the page. Paul was drying a brush between his fingers, the cloth splotched with oil and color. Clara glanced again at the magazine, at a picture that showed a childhood Jerry Lee and his mother cheek to cheek. It was funny, she thought, how such a dumpy-looking mom could have a son who got to be so gorgeous.

"Would you like to model?"

He stood before her, his brush between his fingers. The blue-tan paint that spattered the front of his smock lined the brush-hairs as well. Water dripped from it to the floor. For a moment Clara could not speak at all. Paul smiled at her, and there was a suggestion of actual kindness in his eyes. She noticed again how stained by tobacco were the pale fingers of his right hand.

Clara looked quickly at the magazine. Jerry Lee's hand rested in his mother's, on her knee.

"I would like you to model for me." Paul cleaned his brush. His voice maintained its grumpy, monosyllabic tone. It was not threatening. Nothing had happened. But Clara imagined herself alone with him, standing on the platform. Her skin blue and bumpy, white-blue, with nothing to protect it from the cold or from the light that would make her look even more naked than she already was. Her heart seemed to stop as she imagined Paul touching her hand and making her hold it against her hip, adjusting her fingers so that his own hand brushed her skin.

"No." The word came out like a whine, and Clara looked away.

"Just a suggestion. You could do it after school."

"No." She folded the magazine and held it close on her lap. "And leave me alone."

Paul pursed his lips, shrugging his shoulders. His eyes surveyed her shoulders and her neck. "As you like. I'd pay you, of course."

"Shut up," Clara said in English.

He returned to the table. The heels of his shoes were worn down at the outside, and his passage across the floor caused the boards to creak below him. He had made Clara feel very soiled. He glanced once more at her, over his shoulder. Clara's breaths shortened. The palms of her hands felt greasy. He was so beautiful.

As though he were feeling some sort of contrition, he smiled, and then turned away.

Clara's knees continued quivering. Her mind rushed with hurt. It was scandalized by images of Paul gazing at her back and the backs of her legs, at the curve of her tummy and...other things.

21

Madame Cleve swirled into the room. For Clara, the room itself was awash with wealth, gold, beautiful objects, and glorious art. She felt right away that Madame Cleve was herself one of those glories.

She wore Chanel, and Clara was pleased with herself to be able to recognize the simple black skirt and white silk, long-sleeved blouse by their simplified, clean style. The black patent leather flats were perfect for the intensity of the outfit, Clara felt. Madame Cleve was about forty, with long curly hair and excessively fine hands. She greeted Jack with both, taking each of his into hers and going up on her toes to kiss his cheek.

"I'm sorry Jean-Claude isn't here, Jack." Madame Cleve spoke English with a schooled British accent. She noticed Clara, and suddenly turned toward her. "You're the American girl." She took Clara's hands in hers. "Jack's told me about you." She held them as she examined Clara's face. "So pretty."

"Thank you."

"And I want you to call me Polly, if I can call you Clara."

"Oh, yes, ma'am."

Madame Cleve looked toward Jack a moment, a glance of delight with this new acquaintance. She turned back to Clara. "Please. Polly."

Clara, embarrassed, hurried to correct herself. "Yes, Polly. Excuse me."

"We'll have pastry and coffee in a moment. But in the meantime, let me show you around."

Getting ready in his studio for their visit, Jack had been buttoning his suit coat and straightening his tie. "This is a special place, Clara," he had said. He told her about the Boulevard de la Tour-Maubourg. "Very exclusive neighborhood. Near the Eiffel Tower. And Madame Cleve and her husband live in a single building, which over there means a very large and luxurious place." He helped Clara with the bouquet of roses she would be taking to Madame Cleve. "You'll like her."

Nervous, straightening the roses and hoping she wouldn't say anything foolish, Clara followed Jack down the stairs to Contrescarpe.

The living room of the apartment looked out from high double windows onto a garden, which was enclosed by a high wall. Clara heard traffic, but the sounds of it were seemingly far away. The garden was large, a single lawn and many tailored plots of flowers and greens. The combinations of flowers seemed little organized, and Jack explained that an English garden was usually much less rigidly put together than a French one. "They let everything express itself," he said, "while the French are in march step."

The living room itself had a similar feel. It was filled with formal, comfortable furniture and, above all, a cacophony of contemporary art. Color was everywhere, and not necessarily very formalized. "There's something going on in New York City," Jack explained. "Like that." He pointed to a small painting in a corner of the living room that was a massed flurry of curved, piled color, and swirls. "He died two years ago," Jack said as he stared at the painting a moment. "Fellow named Pollock. Renowned."

The room and, Clara was to find, the entire building was filled with such modernity, and Jack and Polly gave Clara a meandering and, for Clara, amazing tour of most of it.

"And Jack's piece...." Polly motioned toward a large space just inside the entry to the main bedroom that, Clara surmised, had been cleared to provide a location for a new painting. "I hope you'll hurry it up, Jack," Polly smiled, raising her eyebrows for Clara's gleeful benefit.

Clara especially liked the dining room, which had a long table, curved at each end, that was made of some sort of beautifully varnished, veined hardwood. Just now, it had a single large vase in the middle, filled with peonies pink and white. There were eighteen chairs around the table. Here too the walls were covered with art, large and small paintings, all confusing to Clara, but very beautiful in their seeming lack of organization.

"The table's English, Clara. Sometimes I...." Polly put a hand to her lips. "It always makes me think of Miss Havisham's dining room table."

Jack chuckled, while Clara wondered who this Miss Havisham could be. Was she one of Polly's old teachers or something?

Polly recognized Clara's wonderment, and as they walked from the dining room into the library, she explained the plot of *Great Expectations*, and how she knew that Clara would enjoy the book.

The library too was a large room, but had little of the chaotic color of the other rooms. Here the walls were lined with shelves containing books, floor to ceiling, all of them appearing formal and carefully bound in leather and hardcover. Two tables in different parts of the room were covered with art magazines and newspapers, surrounded by comfortable-appearing, cushioned easy chairs with pillows. Polly led Clara to a varnished wooden ladder that could be moved right or left on wheels, the entire width of the shelves on one wall. "You want to climb up, Clara?" Clara assented, and Polly motioned her to the second level of shelves. "*Great Expectations* is up there. Go on. The second level. You'll find it."

When Clara lowered herself from the ladder, she handed the book to Polly, who began thumbing through it. "There's a scene in here where Miss Havisham tells Pip, who's the main character, that, no matter what, he must remember to care for the young girl that lives with Miss Havisham. It's... it's...." Polly turned the pages, searching. "Here it is. 'Love her, love her, love her!' Miss Havisham says." Polly followed the print with an index finger, showing it to Clara. "'If she favours you, love her. If she wounds you, love her. If she tears your heart to pieces—and as it gets older and stronger, it will tear deeper—love her, love her, love her!'"

For the moment, Clara was stunned.

"She's such a wonderful character, Miss Havisham." Polly handed the book back to Clara. "Would you like to borrow it?"

"Oh. Yes, please."

From behind, Polly looked over Clara's shoulder, and remained silent as Clara ran her hands across the book's surfaces. "Keep it for as long as you wish. And when you're done with it, bring it back in person, so we can talk about it."

She nodded to Jack.

"And let's talk about the paining, Jack? Do you need some money?"

"I do. The painting's on its way."

"But when?"

"Two weeks, I think."

Polly took Clara's free hand and walked with her toward the door leading from the library. "Good. And bring Clara when you deliver it."

Clara, thrilled, tucked the novel beneath her arm and squeezed Polly's hand.

22

Clara stood with her back to the full-length mirror, suffering a stomach ache. The sun was shining in through the windows of Jack's studio, and Lauren knelt behind her, a pincushion strapped to the back of one hand and a few pins sticking out from between her lips. She adjusted the hem of the satin cape she had made for Clara. The *bal des artistes* was that evening.

Clara's heart raced with the wish for her mother to hurry up and finish. She felt sick, but Lauren had offered the explanation that she was probably just excited and nervous with anticipation of the evening. No matter what it was, Clara was not going to miss this. She could be sick enough to die, she thought, but she wouldn't miss the *Club de Jelly Roll*.

Lauren sat back on her haunches, her hands splayed on her thighs, as she observed Clara in the mirror. "Take a look."

Clara turned around, and saw herself as a slim sailor girl in white tights, a sequined white jacket that was close-fitted at the waist, a wide black leather belt, and the white cape. The squared sailor-collar came over the back of the cape, and the blue-sequined borders that Lauren had sewn on it sparkled as brightly as the satin itself. Clara wore a pair of patent-leather flats with ribbon shoelaces, that she now pretended were tap shoes.

Lauren handed her a cap, and Clara put it on her head at a tilt. It was a white beret with a red tassel.

"Do you like it?" Lauren said.

"Perfect."

"I'm glad you gave up that showgirl idea, Clara."

Clara grinned. The fact was, she would never have gone to the party so underdressed. You had to be...*Well, I don't know what*, she thought, to be a showgirl.

They had gone to the flea market at Place de la Bastille the previous Saturday, and found a large panel of white satin. Lauren had gone through the coins in her wallet, trying to figure out whether she could afford the cloth. It was unmarred, perfect for the costume the two of them had in mind. She counted the coins twice, her lips pursed with unhappiness at the necessity to do so. She despised such moments. The trouble was that such moments were now frequent.

At the flea market, other women had been rummaging through the piles of used cloth and remnants on the table in front of Lauren. Some of the women were threadbare, in rough wool coats and caps. A few even had wool gloves with the fingers removed, like the fruit vendors. Lauren's worry appeared ridiculous. She was dressed, as always, elegantly in blue, with a black *cloche*. When she grabbed the satin from one of the other women, who had taken it up to look it over for imperfections, her elegance suddenly appeared cruel-hearted and cheap, and Lauren came away from the flea market stuffing her bag with the satin, anger with herself brimming in her eyes.

Clara turned from the mirror. "Can we put the makeup on now?"

"But, it's so early."

Clara took a few steps toward Lauren and Jack's bedroom, smiling at her mother over her shoulder. "Mom?"

Lauren stood, acquiescent and, as far as Clara could tell, joyous, and followed her.

She sat down before the vanity mirror, and Lauren applied rouge to her cheeks, and then put on lipstick. Clara was glad to be sitting down, though she felt shy admiring herself. Her face, being beautified, masked the queasiness in her stomach, even though her worries were eased when her mother smiled at her in the mirror, pausing simply to admire Clara's new sophistication. The transformation caused Clara's breath to quicken. Her eyes appeared larger, and much lighter green, than they had before, and her lips actually glistened with the pale rose-red carmine of the lipstick. Lauren took out an eyeliner pencil and darkened her eyes. Then she made them up in sky blue and evanescent light purple.

This makeup had the kind of subtlety that Clara had seen and loved in the pages of her mother's American *Vogue* and *Harper's Bazaar*. Staring at herself heatedly in the mirror, she was afraid to touch her face, fearful she would smear it all.

She spent the rest of the afternoon sitting still in the studio. She wished that the earth could turn faster. She wished she felt better.

Clara had never been to a ball before, though she had read about them. She imagined high wigs powdered white, and tight-bodice dresses that, below the waist, resembled bell jars. The balls she had seen in the movies—in *Gone with the Wind*, to be precise, which she had now seen four times—had featured extraordinarily handsome young men with mustaches who looked like they owned the world. She hoped the *Club de Jelly Roll* would have a few of those.

She imagined herself in Paul's arms, his having dressed up just like her as a handsome sailor, svelte and smooth on the dance-floor, reserving his time for Clara alone (except for all those times he'd be dancing with Emma, Clara chided herself.) They would slide across the floor, the spotlight causing Clara's eyes to flash. Paul's lips would be shaped like those of the Greek statues her mother had showed her at the Louvre…although he'd have more clothes on.

She felt considerable excitement thinking about these dances. Paul's face, made up and illumined by the colored lights, would be dreamily sophisticated. She hoped he would be dressed as an American sailor, because she liked the pants the Americans wore, with their tight waists and swirling bellbottoms. His dark eyes would be very dark. His arms would be slim and muscular, and Clara would be swept about in them as Ginger Rogers was swept about by Fred Astaire in the old movies, like a piece of chiffon on a pink breeze.

So it was to Clara's considerable surprise, and, indeed, pleasure when she first saw Paul that evening, that he had dressed up as an urbane *flaneur* in a fitted black tuxedo beneath a severe black overcoat cut with sharp precision, his hair pomaded and glistening black, a svelte black eye mask not only making him look like a an aristocrat, but somehow specifically as a French aristocrat, the kind of man featured in the pages of *ParisMatch* or, this time, French *Vogue*. He even entered the studio the way Clara imagined such men would, unbuttoning his coat with a casual, even indifferent, flourish.

It was a cold evening, threatening rain, and Paul urged Clara to wear her heaviest coat, despite her loud complaint that it wouldn't go with her costume. Jack had not wanted to greet Paul, and had gone down to the Deux Cygnes for a glass of wine. But, as Clara had imagined would be the case, Lauren was very kind to Paul, shaking his hand warmly as Clara introduced her to him.

Paul kissed Lauren once on each cheek. He complimented her, remarking how similar her eyes were to Emma's, which Clara translated for her. Clara was embarrassed, thinking how extraordinary Paul was in his costume. Emma had not been able to accompany him, Paul said. "Not ready yet. Clara and I will go back to get her on our way to Mia's apartment." Both Clara and her mother knew he was lying. But for the moment neither of them cared. His eyes were so intent on Clara's that they fanned her heart, even as she worried about how, with the mask he was wearing and its clarification of Paul's obvious sensuality, they made her feel uncomfortable. A smile came from beneath the mask and gleaming hair, his teeth—for a moment like Montgomery Clift's—disarming Clara and her mother. The touch of the smile spurred Clara's recollection of Clift in *Red River,* which she had seen on television just before they left Eureka. He was playing… *What was his name? Matt Garth?* Paul, like the shy cowboy Matt Garth, only this time dressed up as a French count.

They went to The Dome. There were several artists there, all in costume. Many of them drank red wine to excess, so that their lips were dyed with it. Guttural laughter, phlegm-filled and raucous, came from the women as well as the men. The ashtrays were so filled with cigarette butts that they resembled piles of destroyed jacks, the butts sticking out like spines at every angle.

Clara was intimidated by these people. In Eureka, at parties at her parents' home, the revelers were usually subdued and went home early. Here, there was chaos in all the conversation, and many of the artists performed rather than conversed. The mild chitchat to which Clara had been accustomed in Eureka hardly existed here. Instead there was coughing, shouting, riot, and contention. Everything was loud.

Everything was fun.

She sat in silence nonetheless, worried that Emma was nowhere to be seen. Despite sitting right next to Paul, Clara was too shy to say anything to him, and she wished Emma were here, so that she could more safely flirt with him. But when Emma finally did appear, Clara felt her heart sink, and she suddenly wished that she had already been talking to Paul, or sitting on his lap or something, instead of being such a lump at the end of the table. Because when Emma came through the door of the Le Dôme and removed her coat, her costume made Clara feel like some little twit dressed up for the school play.

She wore white, and her shoulders—which barely held up the toga—appeared to glisten in the yellow-brown light given off by the cafe chandeliers. She wore a feathered mask that swept up above her cheeks...blue and gold feathers attached to a black eye-mask, the whole thing shimmering in the light. Her eyes showed through, made-up the way Clara's were, but in such a way that their beauty was actually enhanced by the mask that surrounded them.

Clara imagined that any Roman emperor would love to have Emma as his slave. She also imagined that few Roman emperors would ever care about some mousy little sailor girl like herself. She sat back in her chair as Paul took Emma's coat and gave it to the waiter. Then, the exquisite Paul gathered the heart-breaking slave girl—the one with her mother's arresting eyes so large that they shined like watery jewels—into his arms.

Everybody except Clara broke into applause as Paul kissed Emma.

———

The last stop was at Mia's apartment on the Rue Soufflot. They had to wait a few moments, Mary Phelan told them, because she had to alter Mia's costume one last time. There was a problem with a hem.

"But wait until you see it, Clara." Mary put a hand on Clara's cheek. "I worried about it a little, you know. But Domnhall said it was all right, and if he says so, I guess it is." She hugged Clara. "Though it's hard to say which of you is the more lovely." She pronounced the word "loovly," as Clara's grandmother always had.

Finally Mia came into the living room. She too was dressed in a heavy overcoat, ready for the cold weather.

"What's your costume?" Clara said.

"I'm not going to tell you." Mia too was smiling as the two girls faced each other. "You'll see."

"Come on, Mia."

"No. You'll see." Mia wore her beret. Clara could see that Mia's mother had helped her with her makeup too. Nonetheless, Mia looked a little dumpy. The coat made her resemble a thick pile of wool, and although Clara noticed with some jealousy that Mia was wearing high heels, she let it go. Neither of them looked their best, and it had begun seriously to rain, so that the heavy coats ruining the beauty of their costumes at least protected them, and kept the girls warm.

They stood next to each other on the Metro, talking about their makeup. Clara wished once more that she hadn't had to wear the coat, because she could see that other passengers on the Metro car were watching her and Mia, enjoying the sight of them so beautifully made up. The subway was very crowded, and in fact Clara had to move into a corner of the car, and to hold her umbrella in front of her coat, to protect herself from a small, mustached man in a suit and a fedora who, she felt, was standing too close. Luckily, he got off after only two stops, and Mia rolled her eyes as he passed from the car, having noticed the man's odor as well as his interest in Clara.

Moments later, Emma's slave girl costume shimmered in the colored lights of the entry to the ballroom, which was in in a warehouse sort of building in Montmartre. Outside, the facade had been made over to announce the *Club de Jelly Roll*, the script written on a large musical staff, to the left of which was an enormous painting of a black man's face, all smile and eyes, with a piano in the background. The building front was sprinkled with white lights.

They waited in line inside. Clara could see little in the ballroom itself. Her view was blocked by the Empire headdresses, clowns' wigs, and cowboy hats of other revelers. A jazz band played a ragged version of "Do you know what it means to miss New Orleans?" and Clara saw a woman standing on a huge platter, held aloft by several slaves dressed in loin-cloths. She was sprayed with light, blue and white, and danced the hula, even though she wore no hula skirt. Or, for that matter, no flower lei. She was herself colored silver, and, as she danced on the shield, her breasts floated as though caressed by soft ocean swells.

There was a second spectacle that featured several Indians. They were Sioux or something. Arapahoes. Clara didn't know. They were performing a sacrifice, and the virgin was carried along on a leather stretcher, high up on the shoulders of the Indians themselves. She writhed about, seeming to reach peaks of rhythmic fear...or something...with each rush of applause from the audience. She had a feather sticking up from the back of her hair. She was dressed in a necklace that was made of a half dozen large animal teeth.

Clara turned around, looking for Mia. She had disappeared, as had Emma and Paul. For the moment, Clara was worried she would be lost in the press of the crowd the whole evening. She spotted a coat checkroom, and removed her coat and beret, keeping some money in a little pocket in the jacket of her sailor costume. She put on the sailor cap, then asked directions to the ladies' room. When she got there, she saw, to her relief in the mirror, that her make-up had survived the Metro ride intact. No smears. No droops. She patted her cheeks, and pouted at herself in the mirror, puckering her lips.

She thought...well, she hoped...that she looked a little like Eva Marie Saint had looked in her slip in *On The Waterfront*, acquiescing to the amazing Marlon Brando.

Clara eased herself back through the crowd, jostled by the revelers. She could not find her way. Cigarette smoke floated in layered clouds throughout the *Club de Jelly Roll*. Lights flashed, and there was a good deal of drinking. A nude woman in angel's wings danced with the singer from the band, a very dark black man in a tuxedo. She wasn't completely naked; rather had on a kind of loincloth covered with silver sequins. At one point, to Clara's wonderment, the woman seemed to crawl up and down the man's leg.

Clara was very surprised by the lack of decorum on this woman's part. But even more so, she was surprised by how little shocked she herself was.

The nudity…. She liked it, actually, although she kept her eyes averted. She worried that her mother might sneak up behind her and catch her staring at this writhing seraph. Then Clara recalled her mother's own nudity. Her almost *complete* nudity.

She could not find Emma or Mia. She crept along a wall until she reached a fake tree, made of wood and canvas. The leaves resembled a cartoon fire. Pausing next to it, she turned to look out at the dance floor. Emma, her costume swirling about her like silver water, was dancing with Paul at the edge of the floor, her left hand resting against the back of his neck. Paul's profile was backlit by a spotlight, and Clara groaned with pleasure as she studied the precision of his neckline disappearing in a glimmer into his shirt. She sighed to herself.

Sneaking around the tree, she came upon a couple embraced against the wall. This woman too wore a loincloth. Her head rested on the shoulder of the man who stood before her, facing her, and her arms were wrapped about his neck. He did not have much on either. The couple feverishly caressed each other. The woman's hands quivered on the man's shoulders. Her face, eyes closed, quivered as well, where it appeared over his left shoulder. She seemed to be in a fever of some sort, and reminded Clara of the Pont Sully and the high school girl in the park.

—

A half-hour later, she felt a pain in her stomach, deep down, as though there were a stone lodged in her gut. She touched her abdomen, and then kneaded it with the fingers of her left hand. She leaned against a cement pillar, and the music—a cacophony of brittle jazz trumpets, drums and saxophones—began to rattle her. She wished there was a little rock 'n roll. Frankie Lymon and The Juniors. Elvis. Or something soft…how does it go?…"Only you…can make this world seem right". Clara loved The Platters, and owned that 45.

Blue and red lights splashed her sailor costume. They made her sick. She turned her back to the pillar and looked again onto the dance floor at the couples dancing past, wrapped about in one another, dancing to the music's clatter.

"Clara?"

Emma had come up next to her. Clara placed a hand against her stomach. She winced as another shard of pain laced her gut.

"Are you all right?" Emma placed a hand on Clara's cheek. Her palm was very cool, and felt so comforting to Clara that she leaned against Emma.

"I don't know. I just...."

But Emma had turned her attention to the dance floor. A couple danced across the center of the floor, alone, watched by almost everyone. It was Paul, dressed as a now sweat-sodden sophisticated French count, holding his partner close and propelling her across the floor in some sort of *apache*-like step, a tango or something. His hair shined. His right arm pressed firmly against his partner's back. His hand held her below the shoulder blade. The woman's right hand fit into his left, splayed at an angle. She wore black mesh stockings and a red silk showgirl suit that cut high above her hips, an effect that lengthened her already long legs. The suit was so heavily sequined red and black that she appeared bejeweled by dark stars. There was a blood-red chiffon trail that floated down behind her from the small of her back, almost as long as her legs themselves. Her breasts, small, hardly noticeable, yet just right for the slimness of her body, lay annealed to Paul's chest. Her head lay against Paul's shoulder, and her blonde curls, so luxuriant by comparison to the severe black eye-mask she wore, passed beneath the lights, blue to red, shades of grey-blonde, smoke-laden curls reddened and darkened.

"Oh, Clara. That's...."

The couple danced away.

Clara kneaded her stomach. She worried she was going to faint. "Mia," she said. She groaned as she closed her eyes.

"Clara, are you all right?"

Emma took Clara's hand and led her toward the ladies' room. Clara's stomach felt filled with water, bloated and thick. The music bashed about behind them. Her gut hurt even more...or at least the part of it just below her stomach, and she suddenly felt a kind of slickness, like thick sweat, between her legs. She stopped a moment, waiting for it to go away. It felt like warm oil. When they got to the ladies' room, she realized that she was indeed sweating very heavily, her forehead and cheeks blotched with perspiration.

"Clara!" Emma said. The sadness that had been on her face as they had watched Mia dance away with Paul suddenly changed to a look of humorous consternation.

Clara held the front of her sailor suit, trying to press the pain out of her stomach with her hand. She looked down and saw a stain on her pants, where her legs met, a blotch of red.

"Oh."

She clutched her stomach.

23

Emma sat on the couch grumbling about Paul. About men.
Clara, who felt like she was floating about on a slowly roiling sea of oil, her eyes swollen and her legs feeling filled with fat or grease or something.... Clara wished Emma would shut up.

Clara too sat on the couch, or rather lay on the couch in her robe, propped up on several pillows. It was not even eleven o'clock yet, and Emma had accompanied Clara home in a taxi, after a chilly-sounding explanation to Paul and Mia about where she was going. Mia had begged to come along, realizing that Emma was angered by her dancing with Paul. She had gone to get Clara's coat, and now sat at a studio table. She was still made up. Parts of her showgirl costume showed from her open coat.

"How does it feel, Clara?" she said.

"Weird." Clara had hated Mia's costume. It had made her own costume appear rustic to her. She felt like a hick. So maybe it was good, she thought, that her sailor pants—that had been washed and now hung over a kitchen chair before a heater—had been ruined.

Even if the blood did come out of the pants someday, Clara knew she'd never wear the costume again. It was now obvious to her that, for a party in Paris, you *should* dress up like a showgirl. Even though you were only almost thirteen. Except, of course, she grumbled to herself, Mia *is* thirteen. But it didn't matter how old either of them was. Nobody...not even the prettiest girl in all of France...would look good in a sailor suit.

"Have you..." Clara said to Mia. "Has this—"

"Me? No, not yet." Mia looked to the floor. "It kind of scares me."

Clara folded her arms, diverting her eyes toward the pants once more, and then looking out the window into the darkness. She took in a breath, and then rather grumpily let it out. *I guess I win something, though!* She was thinking about herself and Mia. *Even when I didn't get to dance with anybody. Even when it was Mia who got to dance with Paul instead of me.* She glanced down toward her waist. *At least I've got this!*

"Did *you* get to dance with Paul again, Emma?"

Emma grumped. "Me? No. Paul was angry with me."

"About what?"

"He's always angry." Emma took Clara's feet into her hands and began to rub them.

"Why?" Mia said.

"I don't know. He's…." She folded her hands and laid them on Clara's leg. Emma's mouth formed a tight pout.

Clara laid her hands in her lap, the fingers entwined. They reminded her of the fingers on one of the statues by Canova that Jack had showed her at the Jeu de Paume, one of those white marble naked ladies lying on her side the way Lauren had been lying on the couch when she was modeling, like a range of soft hills awaiting a kiss.

"Men feel they can do that, Clara. Get angry whenever they want."

—

Jack's hand grasped Lauren's as they walked through the Place de la Contrescarpe. When she had gone out to meet him at La Hachette—a workingman's cafe they went to sometimes for dinner—she had turned all the lights out. So now, noting the light coming from the studio windows, she worried that something had gone wrong.

They hurried up the stairs and, when Jack opened the door to the studio, Lauren pushed past him.

"Hi, Mom."

The light from the table lamp illumined the faces of the three women awaiting them. Mia Phelan, looking like a vamp in her twenties, in what appeared to be a chorus-line dancer's outfit, waved to her.

"Hullo, Mrs. Foy."

"Hello, Mia. How are you?"

"I'm okay, thanks."

Clara, still lying on the couch, appeared shy and pale, as though someone had been speaking very harshly to her. Lauren walked straight across the room, sitting down on the couch with her and taking her hand. There had been some accident or something. She placed a hand against Clara's forehead. "Are you all right?"

"Yeah. I'm…."

"Hello, Emma."

Clara lowered her eyes toward her lap. Emma sat in silence at the opposite end of the couch, staring at Lauren. She was of a dazzling beauty, barely clad in white. She sighed and surveyed her own fingers in curt silence. She was impatient and disapproving, and Lauren suddenly felt that she did not deserve this. She was being told, with that sigh and the distracted perusal by Emma of her hands, that she was of little importance to her.

But in the shock of seeing her again, she longed for Emma's affection. "What happened?" Lauren wished that she could just kiss Emma, without risking the explosion that would surely come with such a display. Even now, restrained by the disgruntlement that filled the room, and the air of insult, she felt the desire to put all that aside and simply offer to Emma the caresses that she had wished to give her all these years.

Those imaginary caresses, so many proffered in darkness, in the middle of the night, to a baby who, as far as Lauren had known, existed only in the air…with the hope that maybe she would arrive the next morning in Lauren's kitchen, at the table where Lauren sat every day for a moment over coffee looking out at the garden. She would arrive wanting to see her mother, perfect with need for her mother.

There had been many such wishful moments….one warm August afternoon, for instance, at their summer home in the redwoods playing with Clara, when Clara had been only two years old. The little girl had just been put down on a blanket on the grass in front of the ranch house, her already long hair curly and unkempt on the pillow Lauren had provided for her nap. A breeze coming up from the river caused Clara's loose little dress to flutter. Clara. Mortal. Defenseless. The blood running through her veins could easily spill, and she'd be gone, Lauren thought. Gone.

In that moment, Lauren had thought of her first baby, a little girl just like Clara, who would have fallen asleep just as affectionately in the shadow beneath the apple trees. A pink bare foot coming from beneath her cotton skirt. Smiling in a dream. Watching Clara asleep that summer day, Lauren saw that her daughter's body, even then, contained everything she would need to provide for a child of her own someday, with all of the longing that such an event brings, including the possibility of loss, of anger, and the danger of abandonment. Lauren sat silently in the shade. She was suddenly mired in grief for that other daughter, now twelve years old somewhere, whose name she did not even know. Her body would be awaiting the arrival of its own flow, and maybe the first murmurings of the kind of temptation that could change that flow, the beginnings of desire for someone.

The Douglas fir trees on the hillsides across the valley formed a pulsating green blur.

Clara had gone on to become so direct a little girl that she was very unlike what Lauren imagined her first child to be. Her first was acquiescent, affectionate, and accepting of all things. Surely that was how she was, Lauren had hoped.

But now it seemed that the opposite was true. Clara lay on the couch, seemingly ill somehow and violable, while angry Emma merely frowned. It was Emma who had become Lauren's spiteful daughter.

She worried that her imaginings that day ten years before, and all the others in the years between then and now, constituted a betrayal of both girls. Of Clara, because Clara had been with her always, was demonstrable, was here, and could easily be taken for granted. And a betrayal of her discarded daughter Emma because she had been given up so immediately for lost, and, so, *was* lost.

"We got to the *bal des artistes*," Clara said, not looking at her mother, "and I...I...."

"What is it?"

"Mom, I...." Clara frowned at Jack, who had moved to the table. He stood leaning over it, his fingers splayed open, awaiting her answer.

"Oh...." Clara put her fingers to her lips.

Jack straightened up, and Emma smiled at him, shrugging her shoulders.

He leaned over and kissed her. "I'll go for a walk." Turning toward the door, he re-buttoned his coat. His shoes made a trudging sound against the floorboards. He closed the door behind him and his footsteps receded, in dark rumblings, down the stairway to the front door, and out into the square.

"It's just that I started to bleed." Clara receded even further into the couch cushions, her shoulders held forward as though some uncomfortable secret had been revealed against her will, by which she was mortified. Her face was pale, and the effort of telling Lauren what had happened seemed instantly to fatigue her even more.

"Bleed?" Lauren let Clara's hand lie in hers. She felt a wash of relief and even of happiness.

"Yeah, you know, it was my...my...."

Lauren leaned forward, and Clara acquiesced to her mother's arms. Lauren caressed her back with her right hand. She wished to dispel Clara's embarrassment with murmurs of congratulation.

Emma looked on. There was a condemning glare in her eyes, as though their lightness was to be used for dark purposes. She tossed aside the shawl, stood up and began putting on her coat. She grimaced. It was a rude dismissal and an attempt to gather some attention to herself.

"What's wrong, Emma?" Lauren said.

Emma buttoned her coat.

"Why are you being so mean?"

Emma stopped, her eyes searching the front of the coat. "What does *that* mean? That word."

There was a silence. The question weighted the room with even more unhappiness.

"Emma, 'mean' means stupid," Clara said.

Emma inhaled. She looked at Clara as though she had exposed some secret of Emma's to public view, as though she had betrayed a trust.

"Wait, Clara," Lauren said.

"Of course you care more for Clara," Emma said. "Clara's your real daughter. I'm just—"

"Stop it." Clara struggled to hold back her anger. But she could not, and it surged through her in grit-filled sputters, as though the anger were invading her blood stream itself. Each word coming from Emma's mouth had scoured Clara's nerves like an electric charge. "Don't treat my mother like this."

But Emma's accusations continued—that Clara had been nice to her, but it was all just a manipulation to make her, Emma, forget the betrayal she'd suffered when *she* was a twelve year-old, when *she* had had her first—

"No," Lauren whispered.

Clara was being used just so that Lauren could feel better about the way she had just walked away....

"Stop it!" Clara said.

Emma moved toward the door, past Mia, whose face had grown pale with embarrassment.

"The way you just forgot me...." Emma stopped and turned to face Lauren and Clara. "So that you could go on and have other children like Clara."

"Stop!"

"And not feel offended by me. You did that so you wouldn't have to remember me." Emma pulled the door open. "So you wouldn't have to suffer anything at all, Mother, because of me."

———

Lauren thumbed through Clara's copy of *Gone With The Wind*. She recalled how Clara had so often read parts of her Nancy Drew novels to her when she had been nine and ten years old, so excited by the mystery Nancy was trying to solve. But now, Lauren predicted, Nancy Drew had been passed beyond. For Clara, she was just a childhood heroine, to be cherished in memory.

Lauren put the book aside. She feared she was a scoundrel. Emma's unhappiness was justified. *I* did *leave her behind.*

Clara had gone to bed, exhausted by the evening. Jack had come back home and was now in bed as well, having learned the source of Clara's discomfort.

Lauren laid her head against the couch back. She felt she *could* have done more to take Emma home to Eureka after she had been born, to face up to the condemnation that would have been the result. She could have.

She then recalled that the baby had never been hers to bring, really. The baby had vanished. She had been stolen.

Lauren thought about what it would be like were Clara to become pregnant. Clara reading her *Gone With The Wind* on the couch, five months along and having troubles with spotting and pain in her legs. Morning sickness. Self-recrimination. *What would that be like? What would I do now, the mother of a little girl who was having a baby?* The condemnation in Eureka would be the same. Lots of movies were still condemned by The Church. The Church ruled that divorce was an impossible sin. And Lauren knew that she would never allow even the suggestion of an abortion.

How can Emma hold me so responsible? Lauren recalled the pleasure she had felt when she had held the baby so closely in those first few days, suckling her. *I was just a little girl.*

———

Clara dreamed that blood was running from her. A baby fell down her bloodstream as though down a river.

She awoke in a start. Pulling the blanket up beneath her chin, she looked over her shoulder at the blade of light that came beneath the door to her room from the studio. Her mother was still awake. She thought for a moment about getting up and joining Lauren. But the feeling of the baby remained in her. She couldn't bear the worry of whether the little girl would survive.

24

C lara sat at the table in the studio a week later looking at the pile of bills, which were held down by a glass paperweight. Her period had gone away. There were many bills, and some of the merchants had two and three of them in the pile still unpaid. She had just arrived home from school, and had not yet removed her coat. In all the times she had sat with her mother in Eureka, talking with her while Lauren paid those bills, Clara had never seen so many separate pieces of paper. She saw in the wrinkled, folded, printed and hand-written leaves—some small, some large, all gathered in this wretched pile, all of them seeming to clap for attention—an assurance of her mother's shamed exasperation.

—

Monsieur Malouf especially would not leave Lauren alone. He now would come to the stuio, and the payments that Lauren was able to make, always smaller than he expected, caused her to fear his arrivals. His expectation of her, that he simply be paid in full, was more than she could bear. She wished to pay, and would. But she also owed money to Monsieur Steinberg the florist, Dolores Alain the greengrocer, Monsieur Fornel the butcher… and others.

Money was clearly not Jack's strong suit. He was by no means thoughtless or frivolous. Polly Cleve had full intention to pay, which would give Jack enough money for a year. But Jack was behind on the painting, and insistant on what he was doing with it artistically, so that the money would just have to wait. "I'm not an illustrator, Lauren. I'm not like your Yank, Norman Rockwell." Indeed he had told Lauren a few days before that when he had been on his own he was always able to find ways to buy the things he needed. When Lauren then accused him of hardly caring about her and Clara—"Don't you realize that we've got a kind of family here that you've got to help support?"—he hung his head and apologized, which made Lauren feel like a harridan.

Embarrassed, she went out for the rest of the afternoon, leaving Jack and Clara in the studio. Jack had dallied with his painting the next few hours, looking out the window at Contrescarpe below. Clara told Lauren later, when she found her sitting on a bench in the cold dusk sunlight of the Place Monge down the hill, that Jack had been sitting on the couch awaiting Lauren's return home.

"Mom, he's sorry," Clara said, sitting next to her mother on the bench.

Just in the last weeks, Clara's attitude toward Jack had changed. She knew that he knew what the stakes were, and what he was supposed to do. He was now more avid in his search for gallery representation and possible buyers than he had been since the end of the war. But his art was inviolable and, despite the money worries, Clara knew that Lauren respected that. Even more, Clara herself loved it.

She had always cared for him, from the day he had given them their first tour of Paris. But it had been clear to Lauren that Clara had never really approved of the relationship that *she* had with Jack. Clara's purpose in staying in Paris had been to keep the family together. An irony, given the distance that separated Lauren and Clara from Martin.

But now Clara had her own relationship with Jack, and Lauren could see that the girl's feelings were no longer so clear to her. Part of that was due to Jack, of course. He wasn't just the kind-hearted usurper of her mother's love. He was now also Emma's father, to whom Emma owed her life. Also, despite what had happened a few nights before after the *bal des artistes*, and Emma's anger that evening, Clara still loved Emma, and had so from the moment she had first appeared. So Lauren suspected that it was Emma who had really brought about Clara's change of heart toward Jack.

"I want you to come with me," Lauren said to Clara one afternoon, after she had explained that she did not want to go to the wine shop on her own.

"To see Monsieur Malouf?"

Lauren stood up from the kitchen table and sighed as she slipped a half dozen bills into an empty cigar box. "Yes, I've got money for him, but I know he'll want more."

"Do I have to?"

"Clara, I need your help." Lauren buttoned her coat with an unhappy flourish.

Clara had just come home from school, and had not even had time to remove her own coat. She leaned her umbrella into a corner, where it left an immediate puddle. It was raining so brusquely that the Rue Moufftard had become a wash. Runoff made its way off the roofs and down the curbs in rivulets everywhere.

"I've got to talk with him." Lauren fussed with her purse. She took up a flat cardboard carton from the table and moved toward the door.

"What's that?"

"It's something I'm going to give him."

"A present?" Clara took up her umbrella.

"No, I'm going to pay him. And I'm paying him with this."

The shop-front was made up of wood painted brown and, on the door, kelly green, with two large framed windows on the ground floor of a three-story building. The entry was to the left. A gray canvas awning hung out over the windows, slightly lighter in color than the soot-smeared stone building-facade itself. Lauren had always enjoyed the interior of the shop because of its ancient wood floor, age-cracked oak wood walls and the smell of red wines, an odor that she guessed had been in the place for centuries. The Bacchic cheer of the shop conveyed for her a kind of manly, graceful excess. There were six small coopered oak barrels on their sides against the back wall, tapped, from which Monsieur Malouf and his wife decanted various red and white table wines, all from Algeria. In the backroom, he had an inventory of bottled French wines. They were much more expensive than those in the barrels, and Jack had almost never bought one. Lauren, though, preferred them.

At first when they entered the shop, Clara remained near the doorway, as though she really had no reason to be there. Monsieur Malouf was in the rear of the shop, and his wife told Lauren and Clara in her broken French that he would be several minutes.

Madame Malouf appeared never to have left Algeria. This day she was wearing a cotton smock with voluminous sleeves, a woven cloth belt tied around her waist and a blue and green wool vest. She always wore a wrap of some sort around her head, so that Lauren had never seen the color of her hair. The leather pointed-toe slippers she now wore, turned up at the very tip in front, scraped along the floor. They were scuffed. She wore a pair of dark-blue wool socks. She was several inches shorter than Monsieur Malouf, and spoke in a rough-hewn, snarling way that made Lauren believe that Madame Malouf had more say in running the shop than anyone. Perhaps the *only* say.

Madame Malouf busied herself while Lauren and Clara waited. She had not called for her husband. Lauren knew that she was quite aware of the arrears in their account and the payment schedule that her husband had arranged. But even on those occasions that Lauren's account was paid up, Madame Malouf treated her the same, with abrasive downturns of voice in every utterance. It was Clara who had pointed out to Lauren that she treated even her own husband that way, even her own mother, who was a tiny elderly woman dressed much like Madame Malouf herself.

After five minutes, Monsieur Malouf came into the shop carrying bottles of wine in a straw basket. "Ah, Madame Foy." He turned and asked his wife a question as he placed the basket on the counter. Madame Malouf waved her hand at him, dismissing him as she uttered some sort of reply. "I'm sorry. I didn't know you were here." He glanced toward Clara, who translated for her mother.

"That's all right," Lauren said, seeking a translation from Clara to French. "It's just that I've come to pay you what we owe you."

Clara moved toward the counter, speaking rapidly as her mother placed the cardboard carton before Monsieur Malouf.

Monsieur Malouf rubbed his hands together, a quick smile on his face. "Thank you. I've been worried."

"And to ask for some money."

Clara hesitated before giving him the translation. Monsieur Malouf looked toward the girl. His eyebrows rose with expectant kindliness.

Lauren gestured to Clara to carry on. Clara muttered the translation, looking down at the floor.

"What do you propose?"

Lauren placed the box on the table and pulled the top from it. In the gloom of the shop, the bright red wool jacket that she took up in her hands offered a suggestion of festivity and elegant fun.

"Mom?"

Lauren lay the garment down unfolded on the box.

Clara leaned against the counter staring down at the jacket. "You're giving him the Coco Chanel?" She laid a hand on the cloth.

"Yes, Clara."

"But it's too beautiful to give away."

"I'm not giving it to him. We owe him—"

"I know that." Clara leaned over the jacket. "But, Mom, this is too...."

Monsieur Malouf realized there was a dispute of some kind, and kept his eyes on the two women instead of on the cardboard box and its contents. He spoke no English, but his eyes gave away his interest in knowing what Clara and Lauren were talking about.

"Clara, don't argue with me."

"But, Mom. I love this suit."

"I do, too."

"Mother."

Madame Malouf stood up from her stool and approached the table. Brushing Clara's hand aside, she took a corner of the suit jacket between the fingers of her right hand, to examine it. She did not speak, but her perusal of the cloth included snippy disregard of its luster and the softness of its touch.

Clara was offended. She waited for Madame Malouf to let go of the jacket. But when she did, she merely dropped it, crumpled, on top of the carton. Clara ran her fingers over the cloth, then took it up and folded the jacket properly, laying it back into the carton on top of the skirt.

She recalled the day they had arrived in Paris and their walk up the railroad quay with their luggage, her father leading the way to the street. The station had literally boomed with the hurried confusion of passengers scurrying up the quays beneath the curve of the old building's ceiling. The metal girders were like magisterial toothpicks at all angles from each other, sheltering the foods and coffees offered up from carts and the laughter and noise as passengers crowded through the gates into the gallery lobby. For Clara, all this had had her mother as its center, as she looked up at the light coming through the girders, in graceful progress in her Coco Chanel through the bright clamor of the Gare du Nord.

That the Chanel could be reduced to a remnant—like those at the flea market at Bastille—hurt Clara's heart.

"But these are just clothes," Monsieur Malouf said.

"It is very valuable," Lauren said. "And I'll sell it to you."

"For how much?"

There was silence. Clara's fingers ground into the palm of her right hand.

"Yasmín." Monsieur Malouf turned to his wife and spoke a few minutes, in Arabic, explaining the situation. Then he began speaking French once more. "How much?"

Lauren shrugged her shoulders. "Thirty-five thousand *francs*," she said in English.

"Mom, that's not enough." Clara felt mortified interrupting her mother and disputing her in public. But this wasn't Sears Roebuck. This was Coco Chanel. Lauren was asking Monsieur Malouf to settle her account, and then to give her an amount about the same as what she owed. The suit had to have much more worth than that. It was worth a great deal more than a bunch of bottles of wine.

"*Mademoiselle*, please. What are you saying to your mother?"

"She wants seventy thousand *francs* for this."

"Is that what she said?"

"*Monsieur*. Seventy thousand."

Madame Malouf, apparently understanding the conversation, waved a hand before her and turned away, walking into the back of the shop. Monsieur Malouf was embarrassed and, shrugging his shoulders for Lauren's benefit, followed his wife through the doorway to the back.

"What'd you say to him?" Lauren said.

"I said you wanted more money than what you told me to say."

"You did?" Lauren's eyes widened. "Clara."

Her surprise was interrupted by an argument erupting at the back of Monsieur Malouf's shop. Although it was in Arabic, Clara knew exactly what it was about. Madame Malouf's voice rose to a gritty clatter. She was berating her husband, and Clara well imagined what she was saying. The very sound of Madame Malouf's Arabic added an acerbic clip to whatever she was saying.

Clara kept her eyes averted. The Chanel suit folded so neatly into the carton made her feel like a thief. It was a thing of beauty that her mother was shamefully bartering away.

"What right do you have to change things like that, Clara?"

Clara could barely mask the disappointment she felt in her mother.

"I brought you along to help me, not to ruin things."

"Mom, it's not fair."

"Fair! We owe him money, and I don't know where it's going to come from."

"But can't Jack—"

"Jack's an artist."

"So what?"

"He told me just the other day that, yes, he *does* have a job. That he's an artist."

"But aren't you supposed to make money when you have a job?"

"Of course you are, Clara."

Clara turned away, her eyes feeling weighted down by her mother's stricture.

Monsieur Malouf came back into the shop wringing his hands. "The suit is very beautiful, Madame." He motioned toward Clara to translate. "I'm sure it's worth a great deal of money."

He was trying to put conciliatory warmth into his voice. Clara was hurt, and kept her eyes diverted to the countertop.

"I'm glad you see that, *monsieur*." Lauren began placing the top back on the carton. "It's a wonderful design."

She sounded to Clara like a saleswoman in a shop.

"But I want money, *madame*."

Clara translated.

"I told you," Lauren said. "This is better than just money."

The Algerian pointed to the label inside the jacket. "If you can buy a Chanel suit, you can pay for my few poor bottles of wine." He held his hands out from his sides, his fingers splayed like the arms of a starfish.

"Monsieur...." Lauren's voice quivered. She leaned over the counter, one hand resting on the other. Her shoulders appeared to shrink. "Please."

Clara would not translate the word. But Monsieur Malouf understood it.

"I am sorry," he whispered.

To Clara the carton resembled a rain-deteriorated gravestone, for someone of no importance. It contained something truly lovely that had no value for this wine-merchant, and Clara anguished, wishing to get out of the shop. Not just out of the shop or out of Jack's studio with the antique black roofs and the view of the Pantheon and the lovely black river in the evening surging past Notre Dame. Clara wanted to go home to Eureka, to her own bedroom and her own pillow, and to a safe evening of quiet dreams. *With* the suit.

She took up the carton and ran from the shop.

Lauren turned to follow her. "Clara!"

———

She lay in the darkness in her mother's arms.

"Can I be with you for a couple minutes, Clara?" Lauren had asked, standing in the doorway to Clara's room. Clara was awake anyway, and she invited her mother in. Lauren got into bed with her and, after a moment's silence, apologized for what had happened that afternoon.

"I don't know what to do."

Lauren's arms were wrapped about her, and Clara lay with her back to her mother. This was the first time that Lauren had ever come to join Clara in Clara's bed. It had always been the other way around. She placed her hands over her mother's, which were grasped together before Clara's stomach. Lauren's perfume meandered through the folds of the sheets gathered below Clara's chin.

"Did I make a mistake?"

Clara did not answer, hoping to hide herself in the gloom of the late night. She could hear Jack's sleep-filled breathing in the next room. She pressed her feet against the tops of Lauren's toes, which were cold from her transit across the wooden studio floor to Clara's room.

Clara fell away into the dark night. There were just the two of them, she and her mother. She had hated having to translate for Monsieur Malouf such embarrassment as her mother had felt. It was not that she had had trouble finding the words for it. It had just been difficult for her to conjure up the strength for such pained admissions to a shopkeeper. She had been mortified...badly so...by Lauren's plight and her anger. Monsieur Malouf's calming murmurs at the end of the conversation just before she escaped with the Chanel, that they could talk about it next week, and that perhaps the conversation was a little too difficult just now.... As grumpily as Clara had reacted to his kindness, she had been grateful to him for offering the idea, because in the end he had not forced Lauren to pay.

But Clara knew that Monsieur Malouf's wife had no intention of letting Lauren off the hook. So she lay sheltered within her mother's embrace, wondering what she could do.

25

The door was made of thick wood, hand-hewn in panels held together by pieces of black-tarnished iron. It was so heavy that Clara's knocks seemed to have no effect. The sound of her rapping was hardly a sound at all.

The cobblestones in the courtyard had dampened with the river fog. They were aged black-brown, and the two old bicycles that leaned against the building formed a tableau of chipped paint and rust in the cold light. Wooden shutters covered each of the two windows that looked out on the courtyard from either side of the door. These also had the look of deteriorated age, held by iron latches secured to the stone facade.

She knocked again, and heard the approach of footsteps from inside. Her chest felt like it was pulling apart. She breathed quickly, unable to take in more than the most minor of inhalations. She wet her lips. The footsteps got louder, and then stopped for a moment. She heard a cough and the scraping of shoes against the stone floor inside.

Paul stepped away from the door, allowing Clara to enter the hallway.

"Can I—"

"Emma's not with you?"

"No, I came by myself."

He walked up the hall toward the door to his studio. The passageway was airless to Clara, a long dim chamber. The studio, in which she hoped to find more light, offered little.

"What do you want?"

Clara laid the schoolbag on the chair and sat down. She didn't want to give away her nervousness, but felt it grow even as she tried quelling it. Her saliva felt thick with mucous, as though it were resisting being swallowed.

"I...." A kind of oiliness invaded Clara's skin. She felt dirty, as though she were part of some lewd, sullen drama. She clasped her hands on the table. She thought a moment about how it was going to feel to take off her clothes, how nervous…how skinny she was, what a silly dork she was. What a sin it would be.

"I'd like to model."

"Good."

Paul pointed into the studio. For a moment, Clara thought he had not heard her. His reply was so abrupt that she moved to speak again.

"Go over there and get ready."

"You mean, right now?" Clara did not move. She wasn't ready to get ready. She just wanted to talk about it. She wanted to see more kindness from Paul, some sort of smile. She wanted at least an encouraging offer of a cup of tea.

He sat down at the table and, then, he did smile, with such sweet-seeming commiseration with her that she was startled by his gentility. "Are you nervous?" His friendliness made her feel even more uncomfortable.

"No."

"You haven't done this before, have you?"

"No."

"But you want to work for me."

"Yes." Clara groaned. She felt trapped.

"Then get ready."

Grumbling, she took up the book bag and walked to the chair on which Emma had draped her clothing weeks before. With a rehearsed air of none-theless mortified indifference, she dropped the bag to the floor. "I'm sup-posed to take my clothes off?" She could not look at Paul. She pulled off her coat and hung it, with her wool scarf, from one of the nails in the wall. She began removing her shoes, placing the toe of her right shoe against the heel of her left, and pulling the left foot out. The shoes made a clatter as she removed them. She took off her socks. Her toes reminded her of pale garden slugs. The nails were polished red like little, insouciant coins.

She did not want to make a sound. As long as she *had* to do this, she planned at least on removing every article of clothing in complete silence, so that no one would ever know what she was doing. No one would ever hear the sound of the skirt zipper as, just now, she lowered it, or that of the navy-blue pleated school uniform skirt swishing around her legs as she stepped out of it, or the intakes of breath as, silent, she unbuttoned her school blouse.

She looked down at her chest, at the small new puffiness beneath her undershirt, there noticeably only during the last few weeks, and still a secret from everyone. She pulled the shirt up over her head.

Her back was turned to Paul. She hoped he wasn't looking. But when she turned her head to glance at him, he was intently watching her. He held a cup of tea in the fingers of one hand. Clara lowered her eyes. Paul's eyes were glimmering with light as he surveyed her back.

She placed the undershirt on the chair.

Taking the blanket from the shelf, she wrapped it about herself. Then she removed her underpants. "Where?" Grasping the blanket tightly, she walked past Paul toward the platform.

—

"Don't be so worried." Paul had asked Clara to sit on a turned-around chair, so that she was partially hidden by the three wooden dowels that ran vertically up the middle of the curved chair back. He wanted her to lean her head on her hands, which were folded together on the upper rim of the chair. She kept the blanket over her shoulders.

Paul stepped up onto the platform and quite gently removed the blanket. Clara touched her lips to her fingers, feeling the soft white wool's caressing of her neck as it fell away. She was too ashamed to grab it back from him.

Sin enveloped her. She was immersed in it, and her heart beat with crazy irregularity, her knees shaking with a combination of cold and the shame she felt. She reeled for a moment, worried about the condemnation that she knew would come if anyone ever found out about this. Her soul darkened. It was soiled. She almost began crying. But she pushed the weeping back.

"You *are* going to pay me, aren't you?"

Paul folded the blanket and tossed it onto the couch. He faced her, and his eyes moved from her face to her stomach and legs. She covered herself quickly with her hands.

"Of course. Three hundred-fifty francs an hour." He pointed to her hands. "And don't worry."

Clara's fingers moved about, one hand on top of the other. A dollar an hour.

"Put your hands back up on the chair. I won't touch you."

She closed her eyes. For a moment she felt that she could not possibly move. Her hands seemed frozen in place, until finally she lifted one and placed it on the chair back. The wooden dowels resembled slim bars. Her fingers grasped the rounded top of the chair. She laid her cheek against them and, draped in condemnation, lifted her left hand and allowed it to join the right, just beneath her chin.

—

She wasn't doing it right. Paul had told her a number of times that things were wrong, but then he couldn't figure out why that was so. His suggestions to Clara were quietly made, not at all like the ones he had given Emma.

"Do you think you could turn your head to the left? Just a little. Like that?"

Clara's confidence had resurfaced, but only enough to keep her on the platform and to follow Paul's orders. She saw that, indeed, he wasn't going to do her any harm. But the way he looked at her as he drew, his pencil scratching the easeled paper, his eyes softening so that she felt caressed by their gaze, caused her to blush. She turned her head as he had wanted her to, and Paul leaned back against the wall, the pencil cradled in the palm of his right hand.

He cocked his head to the side and looked at Clara, at every part of her, for a couple of minutes.

As long as he was drawing, she felt at least a little comfortable. But his staring at her like this, with no effort to put what he saw on the paper, made her feel that she should not be here at all. Instead of disappearing, as she wished to do, she was being subjected to brazen light, too much attention, and lascivious interest. She did not know what to do. She wanted to ask him not to look.

He took a step toward the platform. "It's the hair."

The hair?

"I thought it was the shoulders at first. Or the chest, the way it's turned away from the chair."

Clara exhaled, insulted by his use of the word "the" to describe her. She felt like a thing. *The* thing.

"It *is* the hair." Paul stepped up onto the platform and stood before Clara. The front of his white shirt and the three buttons that held it together over his slim stomach...the dried, cracked leather belt around his waist, rolled over itself and tucked in like a piece of rope...the pants pocket that had a stain on it from some morsel of spilled food...all this was less than a foot from Clara's fingers as Paul reached down and began to adjust her hair.

He took a length of it between his hands and brushed it with his fingers. He tried placing it in a different way across her shoulder, and the backs of his fingers caressed the base of her neck. He took another length of hair and pushed it back behind her neck, leaning over so that his eyes were directly in front of hers. He placed his free hand on her shoulder. He looked up, trying to see whether her hair could be further adjusted.

His eyes were the blackest, the most beautiful, that Clara had ever seen.

"Clara, what would *you* do with your hair?"

"What do you want it to do?" She took in a quick breath, biting the inside of her lower lip.

"I want it to go up behind...." Paul stood up, his fingers resting against Clara's right temple. "Give me your hand. The right one. I'll show you."

Clara did not move. She did not want to give Paul her hand.

"Like this." He lowered his hand toward her mouth, the fingers lightly brushing her cheek.

The door to the studio opened and Emma came in, a wrapped package in her left hand. Paul snatched his hand away and turned quickly, leaving Clara by herself. Clara's skin suddenly felt transparent. Everything inside her and the cold tension in her skin was revealed entirely. She had no time to react.

"What are you doing?" Emma held the package by the string bow that the store had tied for it.

Clara groaned to herself.

"Paul. What is this?"

Clara had been caught shivering in the cold.

—

Clara's dream that night, as she anguished again and again over what had happened at Paul's studio, awakened her once more. Emma had screamed at her to get out of the studio, and the tearful argument with Paul who, as Clara hurriedly dressed, had berated Emma for her jealousy and—as Mia had instructed Clara were the words in French—her goddamned fucking jealousy...Clara now dreamed that she, Clara, had been consigned to Hell. She lay in bed, in and out of sleep. Her skin bubbled. Her hair dried out and fell away. Satan bent over her, charred, his breath smelling like the ruins of her parents' destroyed house in Eureka. In the remnants of her dream, Clara lay naked beneath Emma's angry gaze.

"What do you *think* she's doing?" Paul had replied as Emma dropped the package onto the studio table. "She's modeling."

Clara scurried from the platform and grasped the blanket around her shoulders. Dressing, the blanket hanging down from her toward the floor, she kept her back to the couple.

"Can't I trust you with anyone, Paul?"

"Be quiet."

"She's my sister!"

"She's not your sister. A few months ago, you didn't even know she existed."

Emma slapped him. "I always knew about her."

"Emma, goddamn you."

Just as quickly, he hit her. She banged against the table, sending it scraping toward the wall, and fell headlong to the floor. Clara brought her hands to her lips. The fingers were cold.

Emma's skirt had come up about her thighs. She got up on her knees and put her hands to the cheek that had taken the blow. Clara's shoes, the left one still on its side where she had removed it, remained on the floor next to Emma. A sock lay crumpled beneath her knee. Paul looked back at Clara. A look of vengeful contrition appeared on his face.

Recalling this in the night, Clara sat up and turned on the lamp next to her bed. Her mother had sensed that something was wrong when Clara had come home. Questioning her after dinner, she had finally caused Clara to break down and tell her what had happened. She left out the part about the modeling.

"He was mean, Mom. He said such bad things to Emma. And he wasn't nice to me at all."

When Lauren quizzed her farther, Clara shut up. She couldn't reveal the modeling. She'd been caught at it by Emma, and Emma's own trouble with Paul served now to deflect any attention Lauren might pay to what Clara had done. Clara did want to avoid that attention. But she mostly wanted Lauren to understand how cruel a man Paul was.

Reaching for her bag beneath the bed, she took out a sheet of paper and a pencil. She glanced toward the wall, where her shadow—a hunched-over silhouette cast up on the wall by the lamplight almost to the ceiling—hung over her. She pulled on a sweater and began writing. But she didn't know to whom to write. She started a letter to her father. But she couldn't write to him. She couldn't be sure that he would even read the letter. She wrote anyway.

Dear Daddy,
I miss you so much. Mom is very mad at me. We don't have much money, and I'm afraid you'll be mad at me too, because of what I did. I wish you were here. Can't you come, please? I miss you. I love you. Please help me.
Love,
Clara

26

"I didn't know you live with Jack Roman." Mary Phelan examined the Coco Chanel. She had just poured tea for Mia and Clara. "I've seen his work here and there." She poured a cup for herself. "He's good."

"There's a lady named Polly Cleve who likes his stuff."

"Polly Cleve!"

"You know her?"

"No, sweetheart. But I know who she is. She's in the upper atmosphere, you know."

She pushed the small plate of madeleines across her work table toward the two girls. "And you say Jack works with her?"

Clara took up a cookie. "Yes, he's just finishing a painting for her." She took a bite. "A big one."

Mary studied Clara. "A big one," she whispered. She took up an edge of the Coco Chanel itself. "It's just lovely, this work, isn't it, Mia?"

Mia sampled one of the cookies.

"Stitch for stitch."

When Clara had told Mary about the failed meeting with Monsieur Malouf, she had immediately congratulated Clara for interfering. "Pretty tough, countering your mum, eh?" She had asked to see the suit, and Clara secreted the carton out of the studio and brought it over to the Phelans' apartment.

"But sure your mum might not like it, your spreadin' this story around," Mary said.

"No, she won't. But I don't know what to do."

Mary refolded the suit, smoothed it, and replaced it in the carton. Once she replaced the carton lid, she took up her cup of tea and surveyed the two girls. Finally, she looked directly at Clara.

"I'd like to see more of Jack's work. Would you ask him to invite me over to his studio?"

—

"Banned?" Jack broke into laughter. "You've been banned?"

Domnhall laughed as well. He was signing a copy of one of his novels, and shook his head. "I have. Not easy to achieve, you know."

"What do you have to do."

Domnhall handed the book to Jack. "In Ireland? Write well. And that's *always* difficult, of course." He replaced the pen in his jacket chest pocket. "Although it's been done, hasn't it? Liam O'Flaherty. Saint John Gogarty. Frank O'Connor." He grinned. "Joyce himself would have been banned too, of course, had they ever allowed him to import the thing to Ireland."

Jack had brought out a half dozen paintings to show to the Phelans.

"Almost as difficult as it is to paint well, right, mate?" Domnhall gestured toward them, and turned to Mary. "Which is what we have here, don't you think, love?"

"I do." Mary stood and walked past the paintings once more, where they were leaned up against a wall. "And this Madame Cleve?"

"I'll be ready to give the painting to her next week."

"Can I speak with her, Jack?"

"I can ask. Why?"

"Well…." Mary took the smallest of the paintings into her hands, and turned it side to side, to take advantage of the light. "I can ask her if I can refer to that commission when I'm trying to peddle…." She turned to Jack, and the smile she gave him cheered Clara's heart. "You don't mind the term, I hope."

"As long as you do peddle 'em," Jack smiled, "you can use whatever words you like."

27

The next morning, Lauren went out into the Place de La Contrescarpe. "For a walk," she told Clara and Jack in an abrupt mutter. She headed up the hill past the Lycée Henri IV, in the cold shadow cast by the Church of Saint-Étienne-du-Mont, then down toward the river and the Boulevard Saint-Germain. She stopped for coffee, but it was an impatient libation that she did not enjoy much. It was just to warm her up. She was on her way to see Emma.

She arrived at one end of Rue de l' Éperon, which was two blocks long, and walked slowly down its length, looking for number 10. Clara had told her about the building, that it had three stories and was a very old place with an entry court and a circular stairway inside. There were four apartments, and Emma's was on the second floor, a large studio with a balcony, with plenty of room for her grand piano. Clara had also told her that Emma's landlords—Monsieur and Madame Sevigny—were very kind about the pi-ano, and didn't mind that Emma practiced sometimes at home in the after-noon. They were artists—printmakers and painters—and enjoyed Emma's caring so much for her music. Madame Sevigny was an American and had befriended Clara, occasionally asking her and Emma to have coffee with her and her husband Dominique in their apartment on the second floor.

Lauren stopped inside the courtyard, suddenly anxious at the prospect of appearing without warning at Emma's door. A small, dark-haired woman carrying a baby came out of the doorway of the building, and asked Lauren in French if she could help her.

"I'm here to see Emma Dusel," Lauren replied, halting in her French, "but I don't know—"

"You're an American," the woman said, in English.

"Well, yes, I—"

"Me too. My name is Sandra Sevigny. Emma lives upstairs."

"Oh, thank you, I—"

"You look like you're related to her."

"Yes, I'm her...." Lauren stopped herself.

"I'm sure you know that her mother died in the war." Sandra turned toward the gate out to the street.

"Yes, I—"

"But she's got Jack, at least." Sandra pointed toward the door to the building. "Go on up. She's there."

Lauren entered the building and turned up the stairway.

The stairs went in a slowly rising circle along the inner wall of the building. There was a landing on the second level, off each end of which was a door to an apartment. Lauren paused, wishing that her footsteps would not sound so heavily against the black-painted wood of the stairs. When she looked up into the vortex of the light well, a misshapen quadrant of sunlight glared on the wall opposite a window facing to the east. The wood that, in the window, separated the four panes of glass formed, on the wall across the way, a parabolic shadow swerve. Just to the left of the splash of light, the door to Emma's apartment made a dark rectangle, inset to an alcove off the stairway. Sighing as though she had to drag her weight up the stairs, Lauren set out on the last several steps toward her daughter's home.

———

"It's you who are abandoning me," Lauren said.

Emma's hands entwined themselves. Resting against her skirt, they appeared like elongated anemones caressing each other. "I am not."

"You think you're the only one suffering from what happened between us. As though *you* are the only one who was...destroyed by what happened."

"Mother—"

"Ruined."

"Mother, you weren't ruined."

There was a silence.

"You have Clara. You've always had Clara. You made a family. You left me, and went on to a new family."

"Emma. Please."

"You weren't left behind. You weren't—"

"Emma."

"You were not destroyed." Emma stood by the window. As she spoke, she held a hand out to her side in a gesture of such disdain and anger that her fingers appeared to age. "Nothing happened to you. You just went on. You got married to Clara's father and had your family and got rich and traveled to Paris…and I…." Emma placed the hand on her piano, the fingernails poised on the lacquered surface of the wood.

"I did not do that," Lauren said, looking away.

"You left me there in that…that place…wherever it was that I was born."

"The convent of the Little Sisters of Mercy."

Emma looked away, unable to meet Lauren's gaze.

"I was like Clara, Emma. How can you—"

"Mother." Emma leaned against the piano. She gathered her hand into a fist pressed against her lips. She and Lauren had broken into argument so immediately after she answered the knock at her door that Lauren hardly had time to consider what was happening. She did not want to be so angry or so vilified. She wanted to embrace Emma, but the vitriol of their conversation made it impossible to do so.

"I didn't even know what being pregnant meant."

"Pregnant? Everyone knows what being pregnant means." Emma moved from the piano and took up Lauren's long overcoat, which had been hanging over one arm of the couch. The belt trailed from the last loop and dragged along the floor like a tendril of flesh. "Good-bye, Mother."

"Good-bye!"

"I can't…" Emma dropped the coat to the floor, slumping her shoulders as she brought the fist to her lips once more. "Mother, please. Get out."

28

When the *pneumatique* came the next afternoon, Clara and Lauren were making dinner...a beef roast, roast vegetables, and potatoes that Clara herself was preparing with olive oil, garlic and rosemary. The courier accepted Lauren's tip and hurried back out to his bicycle in the Place de la Contrescarpe. Coming up the stairs, Lauren paused as she tried reading the message. Clara walked out onto the landing. She held a paring knife in one hand and a scarred, voluminous potato in the other.

"What is it, Mom?"

"It's from Emma."

The potato formed a lumpish oval in Clara's hand. "What does she say?"

Lauren handed her the slip of paper. Clara leaned against the wall, reading, until suddenly she took in a breath. Her hand fell to her side. The note rustled against her skirt.

"It says 'Help me.' Oh, Mom. She says 'Please help me'"

Lauren took the note from Clara's hand. "Put on a coat."

Clara put a hand against her stomach. "Mom, she doesn't say...."

"I know."

"Oh, Mom—"

Lauren pushed the girl back into the studio "Get your coat, Clara"

—

Lauren wrote a note for Jack, and left it on the kitchen table.

By the time the taxi set out for the Latin Quarter, the rain had ceased, but the air remained very cold. For the first time in weeks there was a clearing sky, even though high clouds remained, swollen and slow in the blue expanse. They seemed filled, pear-like in great volumes of white.

The sharp clarity of her worry about Emma did little to alleviate Clara's impatience with her mother. She adjusted the wool scarf she was wearing, turning it about so that the damp ends of it, also quite cold, did not fall against her neck. She knew that Lauren had gone to Emma's apartment the day before, and she was upset that her mother had been so close-lipped about the visit and so unwilling to tell her what had happened. Lauren seemed too calm about everything, as though little really had ever happened. It hadn't occurred to Clara that this reticence had been brought about by the need for self-preservation. She assumed that this lack of interest in passing on information came from Lauren's general lack of interest in Emma. Indeed Lauren jut now seemed to Clara so selfish with respect to Emma that Clara suspected her mother really *didn't* love her, as Emma so feared.

Until the other night, Clara's passion for her older sister, and her wish that Emma simply be treated with kindness by everyone, had seemed a quite easy task, at least for Clara herself. But Clara often felt that only she and Jack really wished that for her.

Certainly Paul didn't. Paul was the one real villain that Clara had ever met, and his cruel treatment of Emma and herself made Clara's heart feel quite demeaned. Although at this moment Clara still recalled—in a memory that gave her brief, but self-condemning rage—how she too had been the recipient of his sweet-seeming smile. But this thought only made things worse, as did the memory of Paul's voice, which was so clear-sounding as he bragged to his friends that evening at Le Dôme about Emma's beauty.

Maybe Mom is on his side.

Clara could barely articulate such a cruel idea. But for a moment she imagined her mother as someone whose indifference came to life in an attitude of disdain, in which she abused Emma simply by paying no attention to her.

Was Emma right? Had she just been forgotten about by her mother the day she was born?

"I hope she's okay." Clara clutched the *pneumatique* message in her hand. In it, Emma's written French had seemed panicked, as though she were scurrying for help.

"*My apartment,*" it had read. "*Hurry.*"

Lauren did not speak with Clara, and as Notre-Dame came into view down the hill—its rain-soaked black towers like two dark barriers rising up in the cold afternoon sun—Clara leaned against the taxi window, disgruntled by her mother's silence. "Do *you* think she's okay, Mom?"

"I hope so."

Lauren folded a portion of her neck scarf in her right hand, and brought it to her lips. She was watching the traffic out the window, and Clara studied the movement of her fingers and their crabbed, nervous clutches at the scarf, as though the scarf were a scratchy rag. Lauren's jaw tightened. Her fingers wished to arrange the scarf, and they could not. Her eyes were taken by the view of cars passing by, ticking back and forth with each one. Her lips were too dry, wetted by her tongue, yet remaining dry. Each quick intake of breath gave way to an obvious, silent sigh.

"Mom?"

Lauren turned from the window.

"What if Paul hit her again?"

Lauren took Clara's hand, but still did not speak.

"What if he tries to hurt her?"

Lauren pulled Clara close. Clara laid her head against Lauren's coat, and listened to her breathing. It came and went, in quick successions. Clara pressed her cheek closer, trying to isolate each breath, to take some comfort from her mother's embrace. Each flutter of air taken in, each exhalation, felt to Clara as though it were filled with terror.

—

Clara pushed the iron gate open into the courtyard of 10 Rue de l'Éperon. The facade of the building was still wet with rain, and the sooty variations in its colors—black to black-gray, like soiled curtains—darkened the courtyard itself. The inside curve of the wall gave Clara some comfort, despite the darkness of the building. It formed a safe, enclosed space that was warm-seeming in the cold. Sandra's few small evergreens, which were lined up along one end of the semi-circle bordered by the wall, gave off a suggestion of verdant summer and heat. Clara led her mother through the main door of the building to the stairway.

"This way, Mother."

The air in the entry did not move, and it was filled with damp. Despite the fresh black paint on the stairway, the wood seemed sodden, as though the rain had found a way to enter the building and infuse itself into the stairs themselves. When Clara put out a hand to steady herself, the chalky surface of the wall to her left was so cold that she brought her fingers away. She put her hand in her coat pocket.

There was an overhead electric light in the stairwell. The switch that was supposed to keep the light on for one minute before turning off automatically sometimes worked and sometimes did not. Emma had told Clara that at night she sometimes ascended the stairs in complete darkness, her hand falling against the the wall, and that she used the lamplight coming from the crack at the bottom of her apartment door as a kind of beacon, as though she were a small boat oddly ascending some dark falls toward a spit of land up above.

She described it as an unsettling ascent, even using the English word "askew."

Clara knocked on the door to Emma's apartment, which, inexplicably, opened on its own. The apartment was as Clara had last seen it, though it too was now cold. With Lauren, she took a step inside.

"Emma?"

Paul sat at the table, his chin resting on his folded hands. There was only silence. He appeared overcome by a kind of stunned paralysis from which he could bring neither movement nor sympathy. He looked across the room at Lauren and Clara, and stared at them through a leaden glisten. Smoke rose up from the cigarette between his fingers in a sodden wisp.

"What happened?" Lauren said.

He remained immobile. He was very pale, and Clara's fear for Emma did little to lessen how suddenly angry she became with Paul. All his pleasing looks and kisses and rugged behavior...his manly, romantic-seeming laughter only a few weeks before...finally treating Emma and even Clara herself badly, terrorizing them...it all now seemed like nothing. She didn't need any of that to refresh her thoughts. She simply hated him, and needed no further justification for that hatred.

Emma's voice came from the bedroom. "Clara."

She lay on her side in bed, almost hidden beneath a comforter. Her skin had a yellow-gray, pallid looseness, where it was not badly bruised. He had beaten her. Her eyes were very large, starved-appearing, and dark. A purple-blue mark covered a lower cheek. She was cut at the top of her throat, a wound about an inch long, the blood already drying just below her right ear.

Clara brought a hand to her lips.

Lauren sat down at Emma's side. Emma could not focus her eyes. Her left hand extended from beneath the comforter, the fingers making a fist, and then opening so that they were splayed across the sheet.

"Please."

"Emma, don't worry." Lauren took the hand into hers. "You're—"

"Please, Mother." A ragged groan of pain came from Emma.

"What happened?" Lauren laid the back of one hand on Emma's forehead.

Clara sat down on the opposite side of the bed, frightened by the pallor of her sister's skin.

"I don't know," Emma whispered. "I don't know why he—"

"Angel, what happened?"

"Why he...."

Lauren turned back the comforter. The sheet that covered Emma was also stained, and when Lauren pulled it back as well, Clara cried out. Emma's shoulder was badly wrenched and disfigured, her right arm quite scraped in places and bleeding.

"I can't...." Emma whispered.

Shaking with panic, Clara remained staring at the sheet.

"Do you think you can walk?" Lauren said.

Emma nodded. Her lips were so tightly pressed together that Clara, terrorized by her wounds, worried that Emma could not possibly describe to her and Lauren how this had happened.

"He wants an abortion."

Clara took in a breath. She glanced toward her mother. "You mean you're…?" Clara could not control herself. Her shoulders hunched forward, and she was unable to move at all. "You're going to have a…."

"I've been so sick, Clara," Emma said.

Such an ugly word. To abort. So violent-sounding and final.

Emma sobbed once. Her lips were so dry that Lauren reached for a corner of the sheet, which she dipped into the glass of water on the bed stand. She brought the wet cloth to Emma's lips.

Clara had learned of abortions at a church retreat that she had attended, at Saint Joseph's. The two nuns running the retreat had explained the procedure, and the girls in the meeting had turned their noses up at the very idea. Letting a boy even touch you was a mortal sin. Getting pregnant was an extra-mortal mortal sin, and an abortion was, as one of the nuns had explained, a profanation in the eyes of God.

"We've got to get her out of here." Lauren pointed into the living room. "Clara. Get Paul to call a taxi."

Clara hurried from the bedroom. But when she saw Paul, she realized he would do nothing. He glanced up from his folded hands. There was a look of actual panicked supplication in his eyes and the wish for forgiveness, which made Clara loathe him even more.

"Get a taxi."

He did not move. He simply stared at her in so guilt-ridden a way that Clara wished to attack him.

She recalled his standing over Emma, after she had discovered Clara's modeling, and how he had struck her. Clara shivered. Emma was pregnant with *his* baby then, probably trying to protect it as he hit her, the little baby now…well, protected, but in danger of being erased from this world, attacked by intrusive metal and lost in a carnal sea.

Stabbed to death in Emma's womb.

"Paul, we've got to get her to a hospital," Clara said in French.

"A hospital!" Paul stood up, turning his head toward the bedroom. "You can't take her to a hospital."

"What do you mean?"

"You want to get me arrested?" Paul raised a hand to his head, looking down at the floor. Cigarette smoke flew about.

Lauren and Emma appeared in the bedroom doorway. Lauren's arm secured Emma's back. She was barely capable of walking.

"You're not going anywhere." Paul stepped toward the two women. Lauren glanced toward Clara.

"He says he won't let you take her to the doctor," Clara said in English.

There were footfalls, heavy on the stairs in a slow progression. They came up from below with insistence, and sounded like slow breathing.

"What do you mean?" Lauren's voice took on a tone of immediate menace. If anything, it carried the possibility of violence.

Cigarette smoke rose from Paul's fingers and meandered up the sleeve of his shirt. "She's not leaving."

Lauren placed a hand on Emma's arm. "Get out of the way."

The footsteps recalled to Clara the darkness of the stairs themselves.

"Emma's all right," Paul said. "She'll be all right. She'll—"

"Get out of our way!"

The footfalls frightened Clara.

"Bitch." Paul put the cigarette in his mouth and took Lauren by the shoulders.

There was a frozen pounding at the door. Paul looked back. The ember of his cigarette was like a twitching jewel. Clara stepped to the door and pulled it open.

Jack waited in the darkness, his face yellowed by the light. He appeared ghostly, a brute's face, its skin rough with disgust, and unshaven.

Clara's heart knocked within her as she embraced him. "Help us, Jack. Please."

He wore the same overcoat he had been wearing that afternoon when he had gone out. Clara nestled her eyes against his dark blue, wool scarf. He held an old wool fedora by the brim in one hand, and an umbrella, which clattered to the floor with Clara's embrace. Jack's right hand grasped the small of her back.

"What are you doing here?" Paul said.

Jack released Clara. Still in Lauren's arms, Emma wore a bathrobe, slippers, and a large cotton sweater wrapped about her shoulders. When Jack saw her, so sickly, weakened, and bruised, he seemed for the moment to diminish and even to falter.

But he turned and hit Paul in the chest with both hands, back against the table. Paul caught himself on one of the chairs. Jack forced him down onto a chair, his hands gripping the lapels of Paul's shirt. He appeared suddenly huge in his rage. He stood above Paul. His back was like a dark, muscled boulder. Clara was struck by the enormity of his hands that, as he released Paul and leaned over the table, placing them palms down on the tabletop, resembled crumpled ridges of sand.

"You did this to my daughter?"

The hands appeared to Clara almost to cover the table with their stained coarseness. In the few seconds that it took Lauren to reach the door and help Emma out onto the landing, Clara worried that Jack was going to kill Paul.

"My girl?"

Paul winced and pulled away from him. Jack grabbed him and pummeled him against the wall.

"Ya feckin' frog!"

The sound banged through the room. Jack turned Paul to the side and shoved him face first to the wall.

"To my daughter?"

"Clara!" Lauren shouted. She stood with Emma on the landing. Clara ran out the door.

—

"Get her into the taxi." The Citroen had pulled up on the street outside. Lauren turned back toward the building just as Jack came out onto the street.

"Let's go," he said.

Clara helped Emma into the backseat of the cab. Emma slumped down against her shoulder.

"Where to?" Lauren said.

"Neuilly. The American hospital."

Lauren sat down on the other side of Emma and put her arm around her, very careful to avoid hurting her even worse. Jack got into the front seat. He hurried some instructions to the driver.

Emma went into a seizure. Her twitching face had the pallor of fresh ashes. Her mouth quivered, and the gush of saliva that came from it dribbled down onto the sleeve of Clara's coat.

"Emma!" Lauren grabbed a handkerchief from her purse and swabbed Emma's mouth and chin. "Hold on to her, Clara."

When they got to the hospital, the taxi raced up the drive to the emergency entrance. Lauren pushed the door open. "Don't leave her." She hurried toward the lobby.

The taxi driver was an old man with white hair and yellow teeth. He had smoked throughout the drive to the hospital. He looked into the back, and then exchanged some words with Jack. He pointed toward the doorway to the emergency entrance. "It's there, Monsieur. Come on, I can help you." His eyes were carbon black, displaying a kind of extravagance that the rest of his face did not possess, which in the dark of the late afternoon was wrinkled and yellowed like the old parchment missal in a church.

Emma went into a second seizure, worse than the first, which began with a watery outcry, a gagging sound, and an intake of breath.

"Oh Jesus!" Jack reached for her.

Emma's head crashed against the window.

"Clara!" He and the driver got out of the car, Jack taking Emma into his arms and carrying her toward the hospital. Clara scurried along behind with the driver, fumbling with the purses and scarves that she had gathered from the taxi, one of the purses dropping to the ground. She picked it up, swearing to herself. Nothing seemed to work. Everything in her arms had an intention of its own. She hurried, stumbling, toward the emergency entrance.

The surgeon, a Frenchman with the ironic name of Doctor Debussy, told Lauren that Emma's shoulder could be repaired. Everything could be…but that this kind of terrible beating could have serious effects on

Emma's mind. "Her thoughts for herself," he said, as Clara translated for her mother. "And you're sure she's pregnant?"

Lauren did not know. For the moment, no one knew except, Clara was certain, for Emma. Surely she knows. Her periods...Her sickness....

—

A week after the shoulder surgery and the repair of Emma's cheekbone, Doctor Debussy scratched his head and sighed. The warming spring sunlight illumined Emma's room, making it into a brightened refuge. He was a thin man with blonde hair and a kind of quiet English-seeming reserve. "No, she's in danger, *madame*. It's as though she doesn't want to come out of it, and I want you and Monsieur Roman and the young girl to understand that."

In a dream that night, Lauren lay in the black hospital room. She could hear Emma choking. The breathing stopped. She threw her arms around Emma who, after several seconds, began breathing again. But she was so ill that she cried out in a whimper, which was a wordless downturn of sound.

Then, in the dream, Emma rose up against Lauren, trying to push her away.

"Emma. Stop."

Emma ascended through a panicked, convulsive rising.

"Help me!" Lauren shouted.

The smell of Emma's death wrapped itself about both women.

"Help!" Emma's body melted away. But Lauren heard her voice clearly even as she disappeared. "Clara, help me!"

—

The next morning, the clear liquid that spurted from Emma's mouth spilled across Clara's hands. She dropped the pan, and it fell over on its side on Emma's stomach. Clara swallowed, and then sat down in the chair next to the bed.

The light coming through the window fouled the room.

"Are you all right?" Lauren was standing on the opposite side of the bed, wringing out a hand towel that she had been soaking in cold water.

The idea seized Clara that she would arrive at the hospital one day soon, to be told by her mother that Emma's breathing had stopped, that the last liquid had come from her, and that there would be no more. Clara was unable to verbalize it. She simply fell into dejection as Lauren took up the pan herself and ministered to Emma's vomiting.

Clara grabbed a towel from the end of the bed and scrubbed her hands with it, trying to rid them of the terrible odor and the smears of color that had laced the vomit. She lowered her head. An intake of breath was simply involuntary, and the exhalation was imbued with saliva that now fell from her own mouth. Her hair hung down around her face. She could see only her own hands entwined with the towel, and the colorless liquid dropping from her lips to her skirt. She put a hand to her mouth, to wipe the saliva away, but her hand quivered so badly that she had to take hold of the towel again and clutch it with both fists.

Lauren came around the end of the bed and stroked the back of Clara's neck, who fell further into immobility. She kissed Clara's forehead. "Love, you're doing everything."

Clara held her breath. She was *not* doing everything she could. But she was so tired that she could do nothing else but put her arms around her mother's waist and press her swollen eyes against the creamy silk of Lauren's blouse.

—

Lauren spent the week in Emma's room, sleeping on a cot and caring for her. She heard every move and every interrupted breath that Emma took. Spelled from time to time by Jack and Clara, she was reluctant to leave, so that when she did go for a walk, she remained on the hospital grounds. She had no interest in going anywhere else. A proper meal struck her as diversionary threat to her worry for her daughter. Lauren was intent upon witnessing whatever happened, and trying to affect it. She would not be responsible, again, for letting her daughter go.

Clara convinced her, though, finally, to join her for a walk through the surrounding Neuilly neighborhood. Clara had always enjoyed cold weather and bundling herself up for a stroll. So to Lauren, an opportunity like this, to spend an hour with her on just such a day, was in the end welcome.

Jack kissed them good-bye, and sat down with his newspaper in a chair opposite Emma's bed. He had spent the night with Clara at home, but neither of them had slept well. Now, seated near the window, he was haggard and bulky, his face dusted with a growth of gray beard, his eyes tinged red. He sighed, and the smile he gave Clara over the top of his newspaper conveyed the worry with which, distracted, he would nonetheless peruse its stories.

There were abundant trees lining the streets, now in new full leaf, and the large Neuilly homes appeared settled and careful with their tended gardens and wealth. Lauren longed to be living in one of them. Their home in Eureka had contained the same feeling of accepted wellbeing as these, as unlike life in Jack's studio as Lauren could ever have imagined. She and Clara paused to look at one of the houses. The iron fence that bordered the sidewalk kept her and Clara out, so that they could only stand and admire the large garden that came down the slope from the house. The rose bushes, still empty of flowers, yet maintained a kind of new-leaf gnarled gracefulness, as though they were aged hands healthy with dark, blood-filled veins.

Clara was several steps ahead, and when she turned from her contemplation of the house and its warmth, she too was pushing back a strand of hair, in a gesture quite the same as Lauren's. Clara would soon be thirteen, and there was still to come the shyness and anguish that would accompany her teenage years, with their gangly clumsiness and self-doubt. But there was also, since Emma's troubles, a kind of intense, new contemplativeness in Clara's conversation. She was no longer a little girl. Lauren needed Clara to help her understand Emma's rages, and to help Jack, who now was feeling that he had abandoned Emma yet again.

The tree branches formed a patterned canopy through which the sky appeared like a crinkled ocean, an orb of smooth water mottled with yellow-white lace. The brilliance from it gathered around Clara, who walked back toward Lauren. Their eyes met in the light.

They found a cafe, and Clara ordered a *sandwich de fromage* and a mineral water, while Lauren asked for a *grand creme*. When the waiter brought the order, Lauren unbuttoned her coat. She laid her scarf aside, and then leaned forward to put her hands around the cup before her.

A ring of white glaze topped the darker brown glaze of the cup. The aerated milk over the coffee eased Lauren's fears a moment. She found in it a suggestion of affection, a light kiss, and even whimsy. And then, in the powdered chocolate disintegrating into the milk—a darkening circle—she saw the pulsing, the blood, and the suggestion of musculature and soft bone of Emma's little fetus.

Her granddaughter?

BRILLIANT TEARS

29

A nurse escorted Clara to a solarium on the second floor of the hospital, at the far end of a hallway, ushering her in to the surprisingly bright room. Passersby on the sidewalk below, a parade of adults and children in conversation and play, strolled through the warm spring. At the far end of the solarium, Emma napped on a deck chair made of wood, with thin cushions. Her legs were extended before her. Nestled on the chair in the light, she wore a robe and slippers. Outside, sunshine enlivened the motionless trees.

Clara sat down on the deck chair next to Emma's. Emma herself was pale, her hair disheveled within a blue scarf that she had tied around it. Clara was happy to see, though, that she had put on some lipstick, the first in the three weeks she had been at the hospital.

Clara took the book she was reading from her school bag. *Little Women.* Opening it—a letter she had just received served as a bookmark—she leaned back and brought her legs up at an angle. She began reading, listening all the while to Emma's breathing.

Lauren had finally gone home to the Place de La Contrscarpe a week earlier. The hospital had acquiesced to her wish to nurse Emma, although there were regulations, Doctor Debussy had said, regulations against this sort of thing. Clara, translating the negotiations for her mother that first day, had come to see that Lauren would not give in, although at first the hospital bureaucracy appeared quite formidable. Clara had to learn to translate not only the words her mother was speaking, but also the tone of stern insistence that Lauren was bringing to all the conversations. Clara had to rehearse, in silence and with unpracticed intensity, how to be difficult.

Emma stirred, her right hand rising to her wounded cheek as she awoke. She glanced toward Clara.

263

"I brought you these." Clara removed the paper wrapping from a half dozen spring roses she had bought at the flower market on Île de la Cité. The white petals matched the paint on the solarium walls, so that Emma's white robe and slippers, the white covers on the cushions and the luminescence from outside gave everything in the room the look of pristine English china. Emma put the flowers to her nose and closed her eyes as she took in their aroma. Lowering them to her lap, she laid the fingers of one hand across the stems. The fingers too were crooked and white.

"Mother will be here in a few minutes," Clara said.

There seemed not to be a shadow anywhere in the room.

"They're so pretty." Emma had still not been able to gather herself. The fatigue that had accompanied her recovery would not leave her. Clara had listened to Lauren's questions of the doctors, to the conversations Jack and Lauren had in the hospital hallway, and to their worried wishes that Emma simply give in to Lauren and let Lauren nurse her. Would she not allow herself some way to love her mother? Clara listened, observed her mother's own guilt, and remained silent.

Clara had realized from the moment they had discovered Emma so badly wounded in her apartment that Emma was in a kind of mourning. When Clara took her hand or placed her head on her shoulder, Emma would acquiesce. But the embrace she gave in return was delicate and nervous-seeming. Emma did not feel that she deserved any kindness at all.

Clara understood what this was. It was a Personal that Emma had not admitted to. It was clear to Clara that, after the attack, Emma had wished little else for herself. So badly beaten and terrorized, she had been defeated.

Clara recognized her own guilt. She still suffered for having been caught with Paul. But Emma's feelings now made up a darkness unlike any Clara had ever attempted to hide within herself, and she did not want to betray her sister's painful privacy. Clara felt too that she was betraying her own mother by not taking part in the conversations Lauren was having with Jack about Emma. But the fact was that Clara was on her sister's side now, and although she hoped that Emma would give in to her mother at some time, she still would not allow herself to betray anything of Emma's personal grief.

"I have a surprise." Clara took the roses back into her hands.

Emma smiled. "What is it?"

"I'm going home for—"

"To California?"

Clara nodded. She took the envelope from her book. She gazed a moment at Emma's face, hoping for an approving response.

Emma dropped the roses to the floor. "You're going away?"

"I.... Well, I'm—"

"Clara. You're going away?"

Lauren came into the solarium, carrying an armful of lilies and green leaves, followed by Jack. They bustled up the length of the room, and the answer Clara had hoped to give was lost in the nervousness of their arrival. But Emma wanted the answer. Her eyes looked down with exhaustion. She laid her fingers on her lap, now empty of flowers.

"How are you feeling?" Lauren asked, sitting down on the edge of Emma's chair. She laid the greens across Emma's legs.

Emma shook her head. The silence that ensued darkened the room. Jack remained standing in his coat, the broad smile with which he had approached them now turning to a look of gray worry.

"What's wrong?" Lauren said.

"Why are you taking Clara away from me?"

Clara crumpled the envelope between her fingers. "She's not taking me away."

The light in the room was empty. Hemmed in as she was by the luxury of the greens and lilies, Emma appeared deadened. Her face was untouchable, as though it were shaped from sleet.

"You're lying. You're—"

"Emma." Lauren leaned forward.

"Lying!"

"Emma! Stop!" Lauren's abrupt order silenced everyone. "I'm going to tell you something that you may hate me for." Lauren's voice calmed as she spoke, as though she had arrived at some sort of dismayed finality. "You *have* been abandoned."

Emma raised her eyes toward her mother.

"And it would be awful to leave you again. Clara isn't going to do that. She—"

"Stop it." Emma pulled her legs up, sweeping the lilies to the floor. "Stop lying to me."

Lauren took in a breath. "She's not going to leave you, Emma, and I—"

"Get out!"

Lauren shook her head. Her mouth turned down. A look of disgraced sympathy flowed onto on her face.

Startled, Clara suddenly imagined what her mother must have felt when they had taken Emma away from her. Her arms emptied of the heart of her baby, a baby despised by her grandparents and left only with the love of her defenseless mother, who now was being absented from her baby against her will. Lauren had been left alone without Emma.

"Get out of here."

"Emma!" Clara's fingers gathered themselves on her lap. "Leave Mother alone." Her eyes widened as she imagined herself as Emma, had she been torn from her mother's womb. She winced, terrified by the vision of it. But the downward turn of her lips was not a gesture of resignation. There was anger in it, as though it were an indication of some kind of re-volt. "You don't know what she's been doing for you."

When Clara looked up at Jack, he gave her a brief smile. Lauren low-ered her head, studying her hands.

"She held the pan for you when you'd…when you'd…." Images flashed through Clara's mind, of dark rags, seared blood left to smell of rot, and of gasoline. It was a vision of war, the Dusels, and the end of everything. "We washed you." Clara recalled the glimmer of the water as it had flowed through Lauren's hands so many times. "And she read to you when you couldn't talk. We held your hands. *She* did."

Clara ceased speaking as she imagined a lacerated fetus covered over with frost.

"Every night."

Her thoughts whelmed in her so intensely that, despite the conflict of them and their competition for her attention one after the other, they gathered into a single clarity in which Clara herself saw, for the first time, how much her mother did love Emma.

"Don't treat her like this."

She hadn't realized it, and now she was distressed by having suspected anything different of Lauren. But she felt that she may be the only person besides Lauren who understood it and the depth of pain that had come to Lauren that day she had first met Emma in the studio. The pain had continued in Emma's subsequent refusal to acknowledge Lauren's shame.

Clara dropped her hands to her lap. "This is just hatred, Emma, what you're doing."

"I'm sorry," Lauren murmured. She looked away.

"Cruelty." Clara fingered the letter, until the silence was broken by the movement of Lauren's hands as she reached for Emma. Clara watched the movement closely, because she was certain Emma would not allow Lauren to touch her.

But Emma did allow Lauren's caress.

"Emma, I know that I left you," Lauren said.

Clara felt a dazzling pain in her heart.

"I'll always know that. And I want to ask you to please forgive me." The light in the solarium revealed each hidden alcove, in every corner of the room. "Forgiveness. Please."

—

February 20, 1959

> *Dear Daddy,*
> *Thank you for your letter. I can't come home now. It's just not possible. But I will after Emma's baby is born. In the summer. And I'll be bringing the surprise I told you about, too.*

In the weeks since Emma had left the hospital, she and Lauren had been planning the trip Emma would take, with Clara, to the United States. Emma wanted to see where Clara was from, where she had lived, and to meet Clara's father, and Clara had taken it upon herself to try to convince Martin that she be allowed to give the second set of tickets to Emma. Although Clara had seen from his letters how disappointed her father had been that Lauren was not coming with her, he finally consented.

Clara completed the letter she was writing now, and left it off at the post office.

When the money order had come to Clara, enough money for the tickets, with a letter from Martin, Clara's heart seemed to swell within her. It was a year and a half since her father had left Paris. Clara felt as though many more years had passed. She couldn't wait for the day she was to leave.

But when, on the Monday afternoon in June that she went to the railroad station with Jack, Lauren, Emma, and Mia, Jack expressed unhappiness that "his two girls" were leaving. Clara walked with him into the Gare du Nord from the taxi. Mia was smiling broadly, certain that Clara would be back within a month or so.

"I'll miss you." Jack glanced at Clara, very worried. "Clara, I love you."

She leaned against the side of his coat like damp flowers.

Their leave-taking was a tangle of muttered phrases, sideways glances, and interrupted silences. Jack wished to continue protesting despite Clara's pained efforts to reassure him of her intentions to return to Paris as soon as possible. Clara held to her embrace with Lauren, taking Jack's hand.

"Don't forget these, Clara." Jack thrust a passport and a separate envelope containing the American Express travelers' checks Martin had also sent.

Clara threw her arms around her mother. She was careful not to hold too tightly to Lauren, who was carrying little Yvette in her arms. The baby gurgled, darling in the white cotton blanket wrapped about her.

Mia wished to see the inside of the railroad compartment, and the two girls turned toward the train. But Clara paused for a moment as she heard Emma's voice.

"We'll be back, Papa," Emma said. She took Jack's hand in silence, looking down at the fingers entwined with each other. The phrase, "We'll be back", in English, was offered with considerable joy. Then Emma turned toward Lauren. "We won't leave you." She kissed Lauren's cheek. "Mother." After a moment, she took Yvette in her arms and turned toward the train herself, to join Clara and Mia at the lowered compartment window.

When the announcement came that the train was to leave, Mia descended to the quay. The train lurched once, and then began to pull away, leaving Jack, Lauren, and Mia in the noisy air of the old station.

Lauren's eyes were bright with a kind of troubled clairvoyance, and even as she waved, Clara realized that she did not want to leave her mother behind. Lauren's eyes betrayed a secret as the train pulled away, a dismaying Personal. She knew that Emma and her baby Yvette would return to Paris. But she feared that Clara might never come back.

30

Clara was reading. The plane would arrive in Eureka in fifteen minutes. She ran her fingers over the leather book cover, enjoying the mottled design of the logotype on the front, a stylized rendition of the letters "CD." There was a note inside, that Clara was using to hold her place in the novel, from Polly Cleve. "Bon voyage, Clara. We'll be here when you get back."

Jaggers was speaking. "Put the case, Pip, that the child grew up, and was married for money. That the mother was still living. That the father was still living." *What's going to happen?* Clara wondered. *Poor Pip!* Putting the book aside, she looked out the window over Emma's shoulder as the DC-3 approached the airport. She recognized the tree-crusted coastline south of Eureka, the sawmill in Samoa, and finally the waterfront buildings along First Street in Eureka itself, far below. Emma rested her cheek against Clara's as they looked out the small window together.

"What am I going to say to Martin, Clara?"

"I don't know. 'I love you' or something."

"But, Clara, I…how can I, when…" She nodded toward the baby in her arms. "When we're going back to Paris in just a few weeks?"

Clara remained silent. She herself wanted her sister to just throw herself into her father's arms. *Just kiss him, that's all.* But she was confused all the same. Because she, too, had thought of Jack and Lauren, worried as they must be about Emma and Yvette, and missing them. For a moment the reunion Clara had so sought with her father—even though it was a reunion without her mother—seemed less happy than she had imagined it would be.

She looked down again at the coastline. "I'm going back too, you know."

"Yes."

"I'd never leave my mother behind."